OXFORD WORLD'S CLASSICS

THE OXFORD SHAKESPEARE

General Editor · Stanley Wells

The Oxford Shakespeare offers new and authoritative editions of Shakespeare's plays in which the early printings have been scrupulously re-examined and interpreted. An introductory essay provides all relevant background information together with an appraisal of critical views and of the play's effects in performance. The detailed commentaries pay particular attention to language and staging. Reprints of sources, music for songs, genealogical tables, maps, etc. are included where necessary; many of the volumes are illustrated, and all contain an index.

EUGENE M. WAITH, the editor of *Titus Andronicus* in the Oxford Shakespeare, is Douglas Tracy Smith Professor of English Literature Emeritus, Yale University. Author of *The Herculean Hero*, he has edited *Macbeth* for the Yale Shakespeare and *Bartholomew Fair* for the Yale Ben Jonson as well as *The Two Noble Kinsmen* for the Oxford Shakespeare.

THE OXFORD SHAKESPEARE

Currently available in paperback

The rest of the plays are forthcoming

OXFORD WORLD'S CLASSICS

WILLIAM SHAKESPEARE

Titus Andronicus

Edited by
EUGENE M. WAITH

OXFORD
UNIVERSITY PRESS

OXFORD
UNIVERSITY PRESS

Great Clarendon Street, Oxford OX2 6DP

Oxford University Press is a department of the University of Oxford.
It furthers the University's objective of excellence in research, scholarship,
and education by publishing worldwide in

Oxford New York

Athens Auckland Bangkok Bogotá Buenos Aires Calcutta
Cape Town Chennai Dar es Salaam Delhi Florence Hong Kong Istanbul
Karachi Kuala Lumpur Madrid Melbourne Mexico City Mumbai
Nairobi Paris São Paulo Singapore Taipei Tokyo Toronto Warsaw

with associated companies in Berlin Ibadan

First published by the Clarendon Press 1984
First published as a World's Classics paperback 1994
Reissued as an Oxford World's Classics paperback 1998

British Library Cataloguing in Publication Data

Data available

Library of Congress Cataloging in Publication Data

Shakespeare, William, 1564–1616.
Titus Andronicus.
(Oxford World's classics)
Bibliography: p.
Includes index.
I. Waith, Eugene M. II. Title. III. Series:
Shakespeare, William, 1564–1616. Works. 1982.
[PR2835.A2W34 1984] 822.3'3 83–19390

ISBN 0–19–812902–5 (hbk.)
ISBN 0–19–283610–2 (pbk.)

7

Printed in Great Britain by
Clays Ltd, St Ives plc

PREFACE

T HE debts incurred by an editor of Shakespeare are so numerous that they can never be fully acknowledged. My largest debts are to the General Editor, Stanley Wells, and the Associate Editor, Gary Taylor, whose attention to every detail of this edition as it went from foul papers to fair copy has been exemplary. I have benefited repeatedly from discussions with my colleague, George K. Hunter, who generously shared with me the results of his own work on the play, and read a draft of one section of my introduction. Many scholars have earned my gratitude by their helpful answers to queries: Philip Brockbank, Peter Croft, Giles Dawson, Cora E. Lutz, Clarence Miller, and Alan R. Young. My work has been greatly facilitated by the staffs of the libraries where I have worked, and in particular by Marjorie Wynne of the Beinecke Rare Book and Manuscript Library, Stephen R. Parks, who made available some of the W. W. Greg papers in the Osborn Collection at the Beinecke, O. B. Hardison of the Folger Shakespeare Library, Daniel H. Woodward of the Huntington Library, Jane Fowles of the Marquis of Bath's library at Longleat House, Sir Harry Hookway of the British Library, Molly Barratt of the Bodleian Library, R. L. Smallwood, who arranged my visit to the Shakespeare Centre Library in Stratford-upon-Avon, and Georgianna Ziegler of the Furness Shakespeare Library. For information about performances of *Titus Andronicus* I am indebted to my friends Morris Tyler and James W. Cooper, to Jeanne Newlin of the Harvard Theatre Collection, and to Pamela Jordan of the Yale Drama Library. For a Senior Faculty Fellowship in 1979–80 which enabled me to begin my work on this edition I am grateful to Yale University.

EUGENE M. WAITH

CONTENTS

LIST OF ILLUSTRATIONS

INTRODUCTION

IN the Induction to *Bartholomew Fair* (1614), where Ben Jonson is making fun of the popular taste of his day, one of the players says, 'He that will swear *Jeronimo* or *Andronicus* are the best plays yet, shall pass unexcepted at here as a man whose judgment shows it is constant, and hath stood still these five and twenty, or thirty years.'[1] The popularity of Kyd's *The Spanish Tragedy* and of old Hieronymo, the revenger-hero, are clearly shown by contemporary allusions and by the number of early editions. By putting *Titus Andronicus* in the same category Jonson is saying that it was one of the most popular plays of its time, and also that it is now, in 1614, very old-fashioned. Whether it was, in fact, twenty-five or thirty years old will require detailed discussion.

Much later in the century Edward Ravenscroft made an equally famous comment on the play in the address 'To the Reader' prefixed to his *Titus Andronicus, or the Rape of Lavinia ... Alter'd from Mr Shakespears Works* (1687): 'I have been told by some anciently conversant with the stage that it was not originally his, but brought by a private author to be acted, and he only gave some master-touches to one or two of the principal parts or characters; this I am apt to believe, because 'tis the most incorrect and indigested piece in all his works. It seems rather a heap of rubbish than a structure.' This devastating judgement, illogically combined with the decision to revive the play (in which he left a great deal unaltered), went far beyond Jonson's light-hearted scoff, while the story of the 'private author' cast doubt on Shakespeare's authorship, which Jonson did not mention. Thus Jonson and Ravenscroft initiated a process of denigration which continued for many years, and often led to the conviction that the play as we have it could not have been written by Shakespeare. Recognition of its merits and of its close ties with other works by Shakespeare was slow to come. It has been more characteristic of the twentieth than of preceding centuries.

The questions of date and authorship raised by the comments of Jonson and Ravenscroft are intimately related to several others: those concerning early performances of the play, its early

[1] Ed. Eugene M. Waith (New Haven and London, 1963), p. 31.

publication history, the relationship between the texts which have come down to us, the revisions they seem to imply, and the sources of the plot. About each of these matters there is uncertainty, and they are so interconnected that an attempt to answer one question inevitably depends on assumptions about the answers to others. It will be best to begin by stating what we know about the play up to 1623, when it was included by Shakespeare's fellow players and shareholders, John Heminges and Henry Condell, in the First Folio (F1) edition of his plays.

What We Know up to 1623

On 23 January 1594 Philip Henslowe recorded a performance by the Earl of Sussex's Men of 'titus & ondronicus', marking the play as 'ne' (i.e. new).[1] It was repeated on 28 January and 6 February. On that same day in February the printer John Danter entered for his copy in the Stationers' Register 'a booke intituled a Noble Roman Historye of Tytus Andronicus' and also 'the ballad thereof'.[2] Sometime in 1594 the First Quarto (Q1) was published with the title-page shown in Fig. 1.[3] On 5 and 12 June of this year Henslowe recorded two further performances by the combined Admiral's and Chamberlain's Men at the Newington Butts theatre.

In the library of the Marquis of Bath at Longleat is a drawing of what appears to be a scene from the play (Fig. 4, p. 21). Under the drawing are lines taken from the first and fifth acts, and in the margin is the signature, 'Henricus Peacham', and a date, usually interpreted as 1594 or 1595. Apparently, then, Henry Peacham, the author of *The Complete Gentleman* (1622) and of several books of emblems, saw *Titus Andronicus* in these years and made a sketch of what he had seen. The nature and significance of the drawing will be discussed below.

On 1 January 1596 *Titus Andronicus* was performed by a troupe of actors from London during the Christmas festivities at Burley-on-the-Hill, the Rutland manor of Sir John Harington of Exton,

---

[1] *Henslowe's Diary*, ed. R. A. Foakes and R. T. Rickert (Cambridge, 1961), p. 21.

[2] For a photocopy of the first entry see S. Schoenbaum, *William Shakespeare: A Documentary Life* (Oxford, 1975), p. 124; for transcripts of both entries see W. W. Greg, *A Bibliography of the English Printed Drama to the Restoration*, 4 vols., vol. i (1939), p. 10.

[3] The one known copy of this edition, now in the Folger Shakespeare Library, was discovered in 1904 in Sweden.

Fig. 1. Q1

cousin of the translator of Ariosto.[1] The performance was briefly noted in a letter from Jacques Petit, a Gascon servant whom Anthony Bacon had lent to Harington as a French teacher for his young son. Petit found the spectacle ('*la monstre*') to be the best part of it: 'on a aussi joué la tragédie de Titus Andronicus mais la monstre a plus valu que le sujet' (Ungerer, p. 102). This is the last performance of which we have a record before the Restoration.

In *Palladis Tamia. Wit's Treasury* (1598) Francis Meres listed *Titus Andronicus* among Shakespeare's tragedies, and two years later appeared the Second Quarto (Q2; see Fig. 2).[2] On 19 April 1602 the copyright for 'Titus and Andronicus' was transferred from Thomas Millington to Thomas Pavier, a transaction discussed with the other transfers of rights in Appendix F on 'Copyright'. An allusion in Thomas Middleton's *The Ant and the Nightingale, or Father Hubburd's Tales* (1604) testifies to the play's continuing

[1] See Gustav Ungerer, 'An Unrecorded Elizabethan Performance of *Titus Andronicus*', *Shakespeare Survey 14* (Cambridge, 1961), 102–9.

[2] Of this edition the two known copies are at the Edinburgh University Library and the Huntington Library.

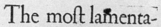

The moſt lamenta-
ble Romaine Tragedie of *Titus
Andronicus*.

As it hath ſundry times beene playde by the
Right Honourable the Earle of Pembrooke, the
Earle of Darbie, the Earle of Suſſex, and the
Lorde Chamberlaine theyr
Seruants.

AT LONDON,
Printed by I. R. for Edward White
and are to bee ſolde at his ſhoppe, at the little
North doore of Paules, at the ſigne of
the Gun. 1600.

THE
MOST LAMEN-
TABLE TRAGEDIE
of *Titus Andronicus*.

*AS IT HATH SVNDRY
times beene plaide by the Kings*
Maieſties Seruants.

LONDON,
Printed for Eedward White, and are to be ſolde
at his ſhoppe, nere the little North dore of
Pauls, at the ſigne of the
Gun. 1611.

Fig. 2. Q2   Fig. 3. Q3

popularity (see note on 5.2.18). The Third Quarto (Q3) was
published in 1611, with the wording of the title-page slightly
altered once more (see Fig. 3).[1] In 1614 Jonson referred to the play
in *Bartholomew Fair*, as we have noted, and in 1623 it was
published in the First Folio with the addition of one scene (3.2)
which had not previously been printed. The earliest surviving version of the ballad, 'Titus Andronicus' Complaint', was published by
Richard Johnson in his *Golden Garland of Princely Pleasures and
Delicate Delights* in 1620.

Date

Although it is generally agreed that the 'five and twenty or thirty
years' of Jonson's quip in *Bartholomew Fair* need not be taken
literally to mean that *Titus Andronicus* was being performed between 1584 and 1589, there is good reason to think it was on the

[1] As G. Harold Metz has shown, seventeen copies of this edition have been
identified. He lists them with their locations in 'How Many Copies of *Titus Andronicus*
Q3 are Extant?', *The Library*, VI, 3 (1981), 336–40.

4

stage before the performance by Sussex's Men on 23 January 1594 recorded by Henslowe. The title-page of Q1, published not long after that performance, gives the most important evidence in its claim that the play has been performed by two other companies – those of the Earls of Derby and Pembroke. It is natural to suppose that these performances preceded those by Sussex's Men, even though Henslowe records the play as a new one. Various links between the play and other dramatic and non-dramatic works of the time have been interpreted as evidence for the earlier or the later dating. Some of this evidence must be examined next.

In a play called *A Knack to Know a Knave*, first performed by the company of Lord Strange (later the Earl of Derby) on 10 June 1592,[1] occur some lines which seem to refer to *Titus Andronicus*:

> as welcome shall you be . . .
> As Titus was unto the Roman senators,
> When he had made a conquest on the Goths,
> That in requital of his service done,
> Did offer him the imperial diadem . . .[2]

Even though it is not the senators but the Roman people who offer Titus the crown, the reference is remarkably exact. More ambiguous is the evidence offered by lines appearing in plays performed before 1594 and closely resembling lines in *Titus Andronicus*. In his edition of the play J. C. Maxwell, for example, points to *The Troublesome Reign of King John* (1591), where the King says:

> How, what, when, and where, have I bestow'd a day
> That tended not to some notorious ill?[3]

Aaron says:

> Even now I curse the day – and yet I think
> Few come within the compass of my curse –
> Wherein I did not some notorious ill . . .
>
> (5.1.125–7)

---

[1] *Henslowe's Diary*, p. 19.

[2] *A Knack to Know a Knave* (1594; Malone Society reprint, 1963), sig. F2ᵛ. Paul Bennett believes that the reference is to a lost play, *Titus and Vespasian*, discussed below; see his 'An Apparent Allusion to *Titus Andronicus*', *N. & Q.*, 200 (1955), 422–4; and 'The Word "Goths" in "A Knack to Know a Knave"', *ibid.*, 462–3.

[3] Part II, ll. 1060–1 in *Narrative and Dramatic Sources of Shakespeare*, ed. Geoffrey Bullough, 8 vols. (1964–75), iv. 147.

If one agrees with Maxwell that the lines are more appropriate for Aaron and hence are likely to have been borrowed by the author of *The Troublesome Reign*,[1] then *Titus Andronicus* must have been in existence by 1591. In such cases, however, it is impossible to prove who was the borrower. A somewhat different situation is found in the texts of *The First Part of the Contention* and *The True Tragedy of Richard Duke of York*, published in 1594 and 1595 respectively, but performed before 1592 by Pembroke's Men. These are now usually taken to be memorially reconstructed texts of the plays later published in F1 as 2 and 3 *Henry VI*, and they contain lines apparently recalled from other plays.[2] In appendices to his Arden editions of the two Henry VI plays (1957 and 1964) Andrew Cairncross shows how lines from *Titus Andronicus* seem to have affected the earlier 'bad quarto' texts of these plays.

Arguments that at least some passages in the play were written no earlier than the latter part of 1593 have been based on a few close connections with Thomas Nashe's *The Unfortunate Traveller*, completed 27 June 1593, and George Peele's *The Honour of the Garter*, written for the installation of the Earl of Northumberland as a Knight of the Garter in June of that year and probably published shortly thereafter. In *The Unfortunate Traveller* the story is told of a bandit who raped a woman after killing her husband, whose 'dead body he made a pillow to his abomination'.[3] Chiron suggests to his brother that they make the 'dead trunk' of Bassianus 'pillow to our lust' when they rape Lavinia (2.3.130). R. A. L. Burnet notes that seven lines after the passage in Nashe's story occur the words, 'Let not your sorrow die', the exact words used by Aaron later in the play (5.1.140).[4] For Shakespeare to have been influenced by Nashe's story before the performance of *Titus Andronicus* by Sussex's Men he would have had to see it in manuscript, since it was not published until 1594. He may have done so, but it is also quite possible that Nashe remembered lines of this successful play from earlier performances. Similarly, one cannot be certain who was the borrower in the case of certain

[1] Introduction to the Arden edition (1953), p. xxvi.

[2] See Peter Alexander, *Shakespeare's Life and Art* (1939; repr. New York, 1961), pp. 77–80.

[3] *The Works of Thomas Nashe*, ed. R. B. McKerrow, revised by F. P. Wilson, 5 vols. (Oxford, 1958), ii. 292.9; J. D. Ebbs pointed out the resemblance in *Modern Language Notes*, 66 (1951), 480–1.

[4] 'Nashe and *Titus Andronicus*', *English Language Notes*, 18 (1980–1), 98–9.

resemblances between the play and Peele's poem, which will be discussed below in connection with the problem of authorship. Neither of these cases of borrowing is conclusive.

A tantalizing glimpse of what might be part of the early stage history of the play is provided by the German *Tragoedia von Tito Andronico* published in 1620 in a collection of plays called *Englische Comedien und Tragedien*,[1] which had been performed by English players travelling in Germany. Although in its plot this play is remarkably like the English *Titus Andronicus*, it differs in the names of all the characters except the hero, in the absence of several episodes, and in several details. It seems more likely to derive from some other version of the story than from the English play as we have it.[2] The German play also differs significantly from the Dutch *Aran en Titus* (1641), which seems to owe something to the *Titus Andronicus* of 1594. It is impossible to be certain when the German tragedy was first performed, since various English players were in Germany from the 1580s into the seventeenth century. We do know that during the plague years of 1592–4 a company organized by Robert Browne was active on the Continent,[3] and Browne, along with a fellow actor, Richard Jones, may have acted earlier in one of the companies which certainly performed *Titus Andronicus* in England. If a version of the play similar to that published in German in 1620 was being acted on the Continent in the years 1592–4, then it would be a virtual certainty not only that a Titus play was being performed in England before 1594, but also that it was a somewhat different play from the one printed in that year. The German play, however, remains a puzzle. Since it may not have been written down until shortly before its publication, and may even have been revised by the editor of the collection,[4] it cannot be taken as proof of the date or nature of an old Titus play in England.

We return, then, to the performance history implied by the Q1

---

[1] A translation of this *Titus Andronicus* by Henry Brennecke is in *Shakespeare in Germany 1590–1700* (Chicago, 1964), pp. 18–51.

[2] See W. Braekman, 'The Relationship of Shakespeare's *Titus Andronicus* to the German Play of 1620 and to Jan Vos's *Aran en Titus*', *Studia Germanica Gandensia*, 9 (1967), 9–117, and 10 (1968), 9–65.

[3] E. K. Chambers, *The Elizabethan Stage*, 4 vols. (Oxford, 1923), ii. 273 ff.; Brennecke, pp. 3–4; Willem Schrickx, 'English Actors at the Courts of Wolfenbüttel, Brussels and Graz during the Lifetime of Shakespeare', *Shakespeare Survey 33* (Cambridge, 1980), 153–68.

[4] Braekman, *Studia*, 9, pp. 25–31.

title-page. The first company said to have performed the play is that of the Earl of Derby. Lord Strange's Men (as they were first called) were an active and important company from before 1590 to 1594, performing for Henslowe such plays as *The Spanish Tragedy*, *The Jew of Malta*, and the play which seems to allude to *Titus Andronicus*, *A Knack to Know a Knave* (Chambers, *Stage*, ii. 122–3). They also had in their repertory the lost play *Titus and Vespasian*, performed in 1592, which some scholars have taken to be an early version of Shakespeare's tragedy, though it is much more likely to have been about the two Roman emperors, who were the subjects of a romance with that name. During much of this period Strange's Men combined with the Admiral's Men, among whom were not only the famous actor, Edward Alleyn, but probably also Browne and Jones, who might in this way have become acquainted with *Titus Andronicus* before they went to the Continent.

The second company mentioned on the title-page is Pembroke's Men, who had a rather brief career, acting mainly in the provinces between 1592 and 1594. Chambers conjectures that the origin of the company was 'due to a division for travelling purposes of the large London company formed by the amalgamation of Strange's and the Admiral's' (Chambers, *Stage*, ii. 129).[1] During the difficult plague years of 1592–4 they may in this way have acquired from Strange's Men *Titus Andronicus*. They are also known to have performed *The First Part of the Contention* and *The True Tragedy of Richard Duke of York*, in which the seeming reminiscences of *Titus Andronicus* occur. By the summer of 1593 they were apparently bankrupt, and disposed of some of their plays to Sussex's Men, the third company listed on the Q1 title-page, and the one which acted *Titus Andronicus* for Henslowe on 23 January 1594.

David George offers a very different interpretation of the puzzling relationships between the acting companies in these years,[2] and, with regard to *Titus Andronicus*, concludes that the three companies mentioned on the title-page 'acted the play in combination' (p. 317). According to him, some of Strange's Men became Pembroke's Men, and after their financial reverses, combined with Sussex's Men. At this time Shakespeare wrote *Titus Andronicus* for the combined Strange–Pembroke–Sussex company. George

---

[1] Also see Schoenbaum, p. 126.

[2] 'Shakespeare and Pembroke's Men', *Shakespeare Quarterly*, 32 (1981), 305–23.

believes that the play was entirely new in 1594, and bases his belief in large part on the articles in which Paul Bennett argues that the allusion to Titus in *A Knack to Know a Knave* is to *Titus and Vespasian*, and that the word 'Goths' in that passage should be 'Jews' (see p. 5, n. 2). Bennett believes that the text of *A Knack to Know a Knave*, published in 1594, was memorially reconstructed by actors who had recently seen *Titus Andronicus* and confused the two plays in the lines about Titus. He suggests that the actors in question were Strange's Men who, in order to help Sussex's Men, were prevailed on to attempt to reconstruct from memory the play which they had acted with success seven times in 1592 and 1593 (Bennett, p. 463). According to George, however, the text was so bad that Sussex's Men never acted it. George admits that 'It is doubtful . . . that those Strange's Men who seem to have been involved in *Titus Andronicus* in January and February 1594 would have risked patching together *A Knack*; someone else, who had no doubt been in Strange's at one time, reconstructed the play' (p. 321). It is equally doubtful, I believe, that the Goths in these lines were meant to be Jews and that Titus was the Roman emperor. Nor does it seem likely that Henslowe would have referred to the company performing for him as 'the earle of susex his men'[1] if it was in fact a combination of three companies. The older theory that the play was acted successively by three companies over a period of at least two years is more convincing.

After their season with Henslowe Sussex's Men disappear from the records. They presumably sold their plays, for by June of 1594 *Titus Andronicus* was in the hands of a newly-organized company which was to become the most distinguished of them all – the Chamberlain's Men (later the King's Men), among whom was Shakespeare as shareholder, playwright, and actor. Some of the other actors had formerly been with Strange's Men, the original owners of the play. It was this new company, temporarily combined with the Admiral's Men, which performed *Titus Andronicus* twice for Henslowe at Newington Butts, and it was probably the Chamberlain's Men who performed it privately at Burley-on-the-Hill on New Year's Day, 1596.[2]

It has been mentioned that Henslowe's notation of the play as

---

[1] *Henslowe's Diary*, p. 20.
[2] See Chambers, ii. 95–6, 126, 131; Ungerer, pp. 106–7; *Henslowe's Diary*, pp. 21–2.

new in 1594 appears to contradict the evidence of the Q1 title-page and of contemporary works that *Titus Andronicus* was being performed by 1592 or earlier, but he makes this notation for several plays which were not new in the usual sense of the word. Foakes and Rickert make the plausible suggestion that 'ne' refers to the securing of a licence, which would be required both for new plays and for those substantially altered (*Henslowe's Diary*, pp. xxx–xxxi). If this suggestion is accepted the evidence so far presented supports a date preceding 1592 for the original composition of the play with a revision in late 1593.

Another sort of evidence that has frequently been brought to bear on the question of dating is metrical analysis of the verse, mainly of the percentage of feminine endings. The assumption here is that Shakespeare's use of feminine endings increased with such regularity that a certain percentage of them characterized each stage of his career. MacDonald P. Jackson describes some of the chief efforts to establish a chronology by this means in his *Studies in Attribution: Middleton and Shakespeare*,[1] citing in particular Karl Wentersdorf's chronology, in which *Titus Andronicus* is the earliest play. Jackson finds that plays grouped together by this test of chronology are usually also linked by instances of words which Shakespeare used only two or three times (pp. 148–9), and that a test for such rare words confirms an early date, though not the earliest, for *Titus Andronicus*. He uses metrical analysis, his vocabulary test, and several other tests in search of evidence that parts of the play were written later than others. The results of these tests convince him 'that there are two strata' (p. 153) – an early one, consisting of three scenes, which he calls Part A (1.1, 2.1, and 4.1), and a later one, Part B, comprising the rest of the play. His conclusions are challenged by Gary Taylor, who has applied other tests to the play. A chronology test based on the frequency of contractions and colloquialisms in verse places the composition of all of *Titus Andronicus* as printed in Q1 at about the time of *2* and *3 Henry VI* (conservatively, 1590–1), but the composition of 3.2, the scene added in F1, closer to *Romeo and Juliet*, and thus possibly in late 1593. Taylor's metrical test and a rare-word test using a larger vocabulary sample than Jackson's test both confirm a date closer to *2* and *3 Henry VI* for the play as printed in Q1 and a later

---

[1] Salzburg Studies in English Literature (Salzburg, 1979), pp. 148–51.

date for 3.2.[1] Here stylistic tests correspond closely to bibliographical evidence to suggest that 3.2 was added when the play
was being prepared for performance by Sussex's Men. If this was
the case, it would have constituted a substantial revision, requiring
Henslowe to obtain a new licence, and justifying his designation of
this version as 'ne'. We shall have to return to the subject of stylistic
tests and to the question of revision in the next section, since both
are intimately related to the problem of authorship.

Authorship

The few facts we have about *Titus Andronicus* include the two
strongest pieces of external evidence of Shakespeare's authorship:
Meres's inclusion of the play in his list of Shakespeare's tragedies
and its appearance in the First Folio. Those who have doubted
Shakespeare's authorship of part or all of the play have done so
chiefly because the material or the poetic style or both seemed to
them unworthy of him. Ravenscroft, the first doubter, set the style
when he said that he was more apt to believe the story about 'a
private author' because the play was so 'incorrect' and 'indigested'
– 'rather a heap of rubbish than a structure', though his sincerity
was called into question by Gerard Langbaine, who reminded him
that a very different estimate of Shakespeare's work was implied by
the prologue spoken at the first performance of Ravenscroft's
adaptation, where it was described as a revival of a play by Shakespeare, to whose 'sacred laurels' the author looked for protection
against unfriendly critics.[2] His later opinion was the one that was
remembered, however, and his story was often accepted as external evidence by succeeding doubters. Of the critical war between
them and the believers in Shakespeare's authorship John Dover
Wilson gives a good brief account in his New Shakespeare edition
(Cambridge, 1948, pp. viii–xix). The long story need not be retold
here,[3] but its outlines will help to establish the main issues.

[1] Letter to the editor, 23 October 1981. Fuller details of the vocabulary evidence
are given in Appendix II of Taylor's '*King Lear*: The Date and Authorship of the Folio
Text', in *The Division of the Kingdoms: Shakespeare's Two Versions of 'King Lear'*, ed.
Gary Taylor and Michael Warren (Oxford, 1983).

[2] *An Account of the English Dramatic Poets* (1691; facsimile reprint, Los Angeles,
1971), p. 465.

[3] For a good sampling of opinion consult the various volumes of *Shakespeare: The
Critical Heritage*, ed. Brian Vickers, 6 vols. (London and Boston, 1974–81), covering
the period from 1623 to 1801.

By the end of the eighteenth century the negative view had gained so many adherents that Thomas Percy, after mentioning *Titus Andronicus* in the fourth edition of his *Reliques of Ancient English Poetry* (1794), had the confidence to say, 'Shakespeare's memory has been fully vindicated from the charge of writing the above play by the best critics' (p. 238). A hundred years later the main effort of the doubters was to show, largely by means of verbal parallels, which of Shakespeare's contemporaries wrote parts or all of the play. The chief of the 'disintegrators' was J. M. Robertson with his *Did Shakespeare Write Titus Andronicus?* (1905), later expanded in *An Introduction to the Study of the Shakespeare Canon* (1924), where he arrived at the conclusion that 'much of the play is written by Peele; and it is hardly less certain that much of the rest was written by Greene and Kyd, with some by Marlowe' (p. 479). Peele eventually emerged as the favourite of critics in search of an author other than Shakespeare. Dover Wilson decided that Peele was responsible for an initial version of the play, the last four acts of which Shakespeare revised (pp. xxxiv–vii), and T. W. Baldwin advanced a more complicated theory of successive revisions, the last of which were made by Peele and Shakespeare as co-workers.[1] The tide of disintegration was already ebbing, however, when these opinions were printed. When J. C. Maxwell published his Arden edition in 1953 he found it 'tempting to assert roundly that the whole play is by Shakespeare' (p. xxxiii), but in reading Act 1 was so often reminded of Peele that he resisted the temptation. Although he considered the style of the last four acts and the structure of the entire work to be Shakespearian, he saw the hand of Peele as a reviser in the first act, and came to believe that the case for Peele was strengthened by Baldwin's work.[2] More recent editors have been divided between those who accept Shakespeare's sole authorship and those who incline to some theory of a Shakespearian revision of Peele.

The great importance of evaluative judgement in the questioning of Shakespeare's authorship is obvious, for, as Sylvan Barnet says in the introduction to his Signet edition (New York and

---

[1] *On the Literary Genetics of Shakespeare's Plays* (Urbana, 1959), especially pp. 420–6. Albert Feuillerat's unconvincing theory of successive revisions by Shakespeare of the work of two unnamed writers was largely ignored; see *The Composition of Shakespeare's Plays* (New Haven and London, 1953), pp. 142–84.

[2] Revised Arden edition (1961), p. xliii.

London, 1963), 'However displeased we may be by part or all of *Titus*, there is no evidence that it is not his' (p. xxi) – none, that is, unless the evidence of revision is so interpreted. The crucial consideration, then, would be the nature of the revision. The superficial revision suggested by Ravenscroft and by some later disintegrationists is totally unlike what Shakespeare did when he made his own *King Lear*, based in part on *The True Chronicle History of King Leir*. If *Titus Andronicus* was rewritten in this way, there is no telling what the old play was like, and the play we have could be called new in every sense of the word. The text of Q1 contains evidence, which will be discussed in a later section, that certain episodes were added to a previous scheme, but, taken by itself, this evidence shows only that Shakespeare had second thoughts while composing the 1594 text. At most, it may suggest that these episodes were not in the old play. Another possibility cannot be overlooked: that Shakespeare wrote the old play.

In the absence of any external evidence of the involvement of another playwright, the burden of proof rests with those who see in *Titus Andronicus* the work of another hand. If there is no inherent improbability in Shakespeare's rewriting only certain parts of the play (as he may later have done in *Pericles*) or collaborating with a fellow playwright (as he apparently did in *The Two Noble Kinsmen*), the argument that either of these things happened in the writing of *Titus Andronicus* depends entirely on a convincing case that certain sections or passages or individual lines are un-Shakespearian. The long history of sceptical opinion about the play reveals two sorts of evidence to support such a case: (1) parts of the play are unworthy of Shakespeare either in conception (as in the sheer brutality of both the rape and the revenge) or in execution (as in what is seen as the stylistic inferiority of certain passages); (2) parts of the play resemble the work of other playwrights (mainly in poetic style or vocabulary).

The assertion that in conception or style *Titus Andronicus* falls below the Shakespearian standard rests on the assumption that all of a poet's work, including the earliest, is of a piece, never departing from a certain range of excellence. To put the matter as baldly as this is to see the fragility of any such argument. The opposite assumption – that a poet will in time improve over his first efforts – is more appealing, even though not always correct. That Shakespeare had a grander tragic vision or wrote finer dramatic poetry in other plays is no argument that he did not write this one. The inferiority of the Henry VI plays to the later history plays once raised doubts about Shakespeare's authorship and prompted disintegrationist theories very like those for *Titus Andronicus*. The general acceptance of the early cycle into the canon is due not only to greater interest in history plays but also to recognition that these were Shakespeare's first efforts in the genre.

The assumption of uniform excellence is further weakened by recognition of the variety of generic patterns to which Shakespeare responded. One of the most conspicuous facts about his early career is his experimentation with different kinds of drama, in each of which the excellence to be aimed at is peculiar to itself. What seem to some critics of *Titus Andronicus* to be extraordinary lapses of taste may be seen as valid means of realizing the revenge play, different as they are from the means Shakespeare chooses in plays of other kinds, or even in *Hamlet*, his later revenge play. The further one pursues this line of thought the more difficult it becomes to assert with confidence that *Titus Andronicus* is not good enough to be by Shakespeare.

The alleged resemblances to the work of specific contemporaries of Shakespeare comprise stronger evidence. The force of this kind of argument can fairly be tested by discussing the case for Peele, the strongest contender. The claim has been that not only do many lines in the play sound like lines in Peele's plays and poems, but also many words and phrases are characteristic of him. A great deal of weight has been given to the curious fact that the neologism 'palliament' (1.1.182), possibly derived from two Latin words for a robe, *pallium* and *paludamentum*, is known to occur in only one other place – Peele's poem, *The Honour of the Garter* (1593). In itself, however, this is no proof that Peele wrote the passage in *Titus Andronicus*. Hereward Price argued persuasively that the different sense in which the word was used in the play made borrowing by Shakespeare much more likely than repetition by Peele.[1] Furthermore, this argument does not rule out the possibility that Peele borrowed the word after hearing it at an early performance of *Titus Andronicus*.[2] To show that other words occurring in *Titus*

---

[1] 'The Language of *Titus Andronicus*', *Papers of the Michigan Academy of Science, Arts, and Letters*, 21 (1935), 501–7.

[2] Both Maxwell (p. xxxii) and Dover Wilson (p. xlvi) believe that the play preceded the poem.

Andronicus are especially favoured by Peele is, of course, exceedingly difficult, since it must be shown that such words are *not* commonly used by other contemporaries.[1] No such proof has ever been offered, and without it little use can be made of the fact, for example, that the work 'architect' occurs in no play of Shakespeare's other than *Titus Andronicus*, but is used by Peele four times (Robertson, *Canon*, 191-3). Even 'palliament' may have been used by some other contemporary, though modern lexicographers have not recorded it. Similarly, the existence of passages in *Titus Andronicus* which parallel passages in Peele's dramatic and non-dramatic verse, though never exactly (see Dover Wilson, pp. xxix-xxxi), can readily be attributed to either influence or coincidence. The vaguer claim that certain passages sound like Peele can be accepted without agreeing that he wrote them. No one can doubt that the dramatists of the eighties and early nineties responded to each other's work. The occasional echo of a 'mighty line' is to be found in many a non-Marlovian play, and playwrights with less distinctive characteristics evolved a style which often seems to belong more to the period than to any one author. Hence the number of anonymous plays which have never been certainly attached to a playwright, even though they contain passages very like Greene or Peele or Shakespeare. We should not be surprised, then, if certain passages in *Titus Andronicus* resemble the work of Peele, or if Aaron occasionally sounds rather like Marlowe's Barabas, but these overtones do not establish Peele or Marlowe as part-authors. We should also remember that all these authors could write in more than one style. On the basis of such different plays as *Richard III, The Two Gentlemen of Verona, The Comedy of Errors*, and *Romeo and Juliet* it would be difficult to define Shakespeare's characteristic style.

The dangerous game of parallel passages has also been played in order to show Shakespeare's hand in the play. Building on the work of T. M. Parrott and others, Dover Wilson (pp. xvii–xxv) amassed a large number of parallels between *Titus Andronicus* and the acknowledged work of Shakespeare, including *Venus and Adonis* (1593) and *Lucrece* (1594). Although this kind of evidence cannot be said to prove Shakespeare's authorship, any more than it proves Peele's in the cases described above, the parallels with the two narrative poems, some of which are indicated in the notes to

[1] The point was made forcefully by Muriel St. Clare Byrne in 'Bibliographical Clues in Collaborate Plays', *The Library*, IV, 13 (1932–3), 21–48.

this edition, fall in a special category, since the Ovidian influence, so conspicuous in both the subject-matter and the style of *Titus Andronicus*, dominates both poems.[1] The close connections between *Venus and Adonis* and 2.3.19 or 2.4.36–7, and those between *Lucrece* and 3.2.17, where verbal similarity is matched by similarity of thought and subject-matter, present us with the overwhelming probability that Shakespeare wrote them all. Influence or borrowing, which may explain many parallel passages, are inadequate explanations here.

Analysis of metre and vocabulary have been used not only to establish chronology but also to give greater precision to stylistic comparisons, and hence to form a more solid basis for attribution. The results have been dismayingly varied. A study of feminine endings in *Titus Andronicus* persuaded Robertson that it could not have been written by Shakespeare (*Canon*, p. 416), while Parrott, working with the same evidence, concluded that Shakespeare revised the work of another playwright (pp. 26 ff.). A grammatical construction unusually common in Peele and in the first act of *Titus Andronicus* kept Maxwell from believing in Shakespeare's authorship of that part of the play.[2] The tests which led Jackson to consider 'Part A' much earlier than the rest of the play (see above, p. 10) did not rule out the possibility that Peele was the author of this part (p. 153), but again Taylor has come to a different conclusion. He used a 'function word' test based on the relative frequency of an author's use of certain very common words. A similar test has proved useful in distinguishing between Alexander Hamilton and James Madison as authors of *The Federal-*

---

[1] See T. M. Parrott, 'Shakespeare's Revision of "Titus Andronicus"', *Modern Language Review*, 14 (1919), 16–37, and M. C. Bradbrook, *Shakespeare and Elizabethan Poetry* (1951; repr. Cambridge, 1979), Chaps. IV and VII.

[2] 'Peele and Shakespeare: A Stylometric Test', *Journal of English and Germanic Philology*, 49 (1950), 557–61. The term 'stylometrics' has more recently been used of a form of computer analysis, the aim of which is to discover an author's use of 'certain words in preferred positions in the sentence' (Louis Marder, 'Stylometrics: The New Authorship Weapon', *Shakespeare Newsletter*, 29 (1979), 42). Applied to *Titus Andronicus*, this analysis has led to the claim that it is statistically almost impossible that Peele was the author of any part of *Titus Andronicus* (G. Harold Metz, 'A Stylometric Comparison of Shakespeare's *Titus Andronicus*, *Pericles*, and *Julius Caesar*', *Shakespeare Newsletter*, 29 (1979), 42), but since the same kind of tests have also led to the unlikely conclusion that Shakespeare was the sole author of *Sir Thomas More* (*New York Times*, 10 July 1980), a play to which it is usually supposed that he contributed only one scene, and since many other objections have been made to stylometrics, these results cannot be considered significant.

ist Papers (1787–8). When this test was applied to Shakespeare, 'the two portions of *Titus Andronicus* delineated by Jackson (i.e. separating 1.1, 2.1, and 4.1 from the rest of the play) both fall very comfortably within the Shakespearian range'. He points out that the three scenes comprising Jackson's 'Part A' 'are linked by no narrative or formal logic, and that dramatic collaboration almost always involved a division of the plot along some obvious logical lines'.[1] While it cannot be said that the evidence of any stylistic tests is absolutely conclusive, the results of Taylor's tests are impressive in that they confirm a great deal of other evidence about both date and authorship.

The date and authorship of the added scene, 3.2, constitute a separate problem and have been the subjects of considerable controversy. Some (e.g. E. K. Chambers[2]) have thought the scene was added considerably later than 1594 and by another playwright. Others have thought it was part of Shakespeare's revision of a play by another playwright (see, e.g., Parrott, pp. 26 ff.). Hereward Price, who argued vigorously and well for Shakespeare's authorship, thought it was part of the original play, but, being marked to be cut in performance, was omitted by the printer.[3] Evidence that it was, in fact, added, is presented by W. W. Greg:[4] in the opening stage direction Titus is called 'Andronicus', as in 'no similar direction', and is given the speech prefix '*An.*'; Tamora is called 'Tamira'. Joseph E. Kramer makes the point that if the scene had been included from the first there would have been no reason to identify the 'Boy' in the opening stage direction of the following scene as '*young Lucius*' when his identity had been made clear in 3.2. Contrary to what one might expect, it is the opening direction of the earlier scene which takes him for granted as '*the Boy*'.[5] As Kramer and others have shown, the addition is somewhat similar in function to the additions to *The Spanish Tragedy*, elaborating upon a situation presented in other

[1] Letter to the editor, 24 November 1981. Taylor hopes to provide fuller accounts of the tests mentioned here in an article provisionally entitled 'The Shakespeare Canon: New Evidence for Chronology and Authorship'.

[2] *William Shakespeare*, 2 vols. (Oxford, 1930), i. 321.

[3] 'Mirror-Scenes in Shakespeare', in *J. Q. Adams Memorial Studies*, ed. J. G. McManaway, Giles E. Dawson, and Edwin E. Willoughby (Washington, D.C., 1948), 101–13.

[4] *The Shakespeare First Folio* (Oxford, 1955), p. 204.

[5] '*Titus Andronicus*: The "Fly-Killing" Incident', *Shakespeare Studies*, 5 (1969), 9–19.

scenes. Its relation to the succeeding scene is also anomalous (though not unique) in that some characters exit at the end, only to return immediately at the opening of 4.1. Largely on the basis of what he considers to be inferior craftsmanship Kramer considers the scene a late, non-Shakespearian addition, but once again, the criteria for this judgement are highly subjective. Those who have argued for Shakespearian authorship seem to me to have made the stronger case, and one which is reinforced by Taylor's function-word test. The many indications that *Titus Andronicus* was substantially revised in late 1593 make it probable that this was when the new scene was added.[1]

One of the most convincing arguments against Peele's authorship of part or all of *Titus Andronicus* was made by A. M. Sampley, who was sceptical of the cases built on parallel passages, typical words and phrases, or vocabulary tests, and proposed instead the test of plot-structure.[2] His analysis of the four plays generally accepted as Peele's – *The Arraignment of Paris*, *Edward I*, *The Old Wife's Tale*, and *David and Bathsheba* – brought out several shared characteristics: a large number of plots, a good deal of extraneous material, a failure to combine plots effectively, and, above all, a fundamental lack of unity (p. 699). These are not the characteristics of *Titus Andronicus*. The first act, the main target of recent disintegrationists, is conspicuous for the way in which it prepares for the plots against Titus in the very process of presenting his triumphal return to Rome. His humiliation of Tamora provides the motive for revenge, while his naïve misjudgement of Saturninus leads directly to her elevation to power. There is some awkwardness in the late introduction of Aaron, the chief engineer of the revenge, whose fiendish energy and invention partly obscure the Queen of the Goths in the central part of the play.[3] Yet, however great his ambition and his personal animus, his actions serve the Queen's cause, as she acknowledges (4.4.37–8). At the end she re-emerges to take charge of her revenge in a way that ironically puts her once more in Titus' power. The symmetry of the whole struc-

[1] On the whole matter of added scenes in Elizabethan drama see John Kerrigan, 'Revision, Adaptation, and the Fool in *King Lear*', Taylor and Warren, 195–245.

[2] 'Plot-Structure in Peele's Plays as a Test of Authorship', *PMLA*, 51 (1936), 689–701; see also his earlier '"Verbal Tests" for Peele's Plays', *Studies in Philology*, 30 (1933), 473–96.

[3] Ravenscroft attempts an improvement here by giving Aaron a share in the dialogue in Act 1 (Ravenscroft, pp. 5, 11, 13, 14).

ture is marked by episodes at the end of the play which match some in the beginning: in Act 4 as in Act 1 Tamora controls the rage of Saturninus while she plots her own more devious course (1.1.442–58; 4.4.27–38); in Act 5 Tamora, who knelt to Titus when the general alighted from his triumphal chariot, appears in a chariot as Revenge to confront Titus again (1.1.104–20; 5.2.1–8); at the very end a new emperor is chosen for the second time (1.1.230–3; 5.3.140).

If, as Maxwell says, 'the structure of the whole play suggests Shakespeare rather than Peele' (p. xxxiii), it is hard to believe that Peele revised the first act, and what seemed to Maxwell suggestions of Peele's style might be better explained as Peele's influence. It may be worth pointing out that the first act, where the characteristics of Peele have most often been felt, consists almost entirely of public ceremonies, and that models of the elevated diction appropriate for such occasions were to be found in Peele's earlier plays, from which Dover Wilson and others have quoted parallel passages.

In an important article Hereward T. Price, who devoted many years to *Titus Andronicus*, asserted that 'the best parallel by which we can test authorship is construction', and that the closest parallels to the structure of *Titus Andronicus* were in other plays by Shakespeare. As he showed, the ruthless exploitation of a good man's folly in *King Lear* is remarkably similar in broad outlines to the persecution of Titus, and in both cases a noble mind is unhinged.[1] Price returned to the subject in a lecture on 'Construction in Shakespeare', where he discussed the opening of *Titus Andronicus* as a characteristically Shakespearian exposition of the idea underlying the design of the whole play – violence versus just desert.[2] Like Sampley, he found no examples of this sort of construction in Peele.

Another striking parallel may be observed between *Titus Andronicus* and Shakespeare's last tragedy. Coriolanus is again a great general, the chief support of Rome against her enemies, but driven by the treatment he is given to seek revenge against the city. When

---

[1] 'The Authorship of "Titus Andronicus"', *Journal of English and Germanic Philology*, 42 (1943), 55–81.

[2] Ann Arbor, 1951; see also Ruth Nevo's excellent analysis, 'Tragic Form in *Titus Andronicus*', in *Further Studies in English Language and Literature*, ed. A. A. Mendilow (Jerusalem, 1975), 1–18.

Titus' son Lucius marches against Rome, an allusion to Coriolanus makes the parallel between the stories explicit (4.4.66). Detailed analysis of the themes and style of *Titus Andronicus* leads A. C. Hamilton to describe it as 'a central and seminal play in the canon of Shakespeare's works'.[1] His belief that its closest relationship is with the Henry VI plays (p. 85) receives support from Gary Taylor's tests described above.

I believe that the evidence I have presented points to the con- clusion that *Titus Andronicus* is entirely by Shakespeare, that, by a conservative estimate, it was first performed in the years 1590–2, and was revised for the first recorded performance of January 1594. No compelling evidence associates any other playwright with it or justifies a date earlier than the second and third parts of *Henry VI*. There is none to prove that the earlier version of the play was very different from the one printed in Q1. The one question raised by this interpretation of the evidence is why, if the added scene had been performed by Sussex's Men before the play was entered in the Stationers' Register, it was not included in the first edition. A possible explanation will be offered in the section on Text.

The Peacham Drawing

The Peacham drawing now in the library of the Marquis of Bath at Longleat provides a unique glimpse of actors performing a Shakespeare play. Often described, and reproduced here (Fig. 4), it is in many regards a puzzling document.[2] It is a pen drawing, executed in fine detail in brown ink on one page of a folded folio sheet. The most important questions, for which there are no universally accepted answers, are what action and which charac- ters the artist has represented. Beneath the drawing, in a secretary hand, is an invented stage direction, 'Enter Tamora pleadinge for her sonnes going to execution', followed by lines from the play: Tamora's plea to Titus (1.1.104–20), one line of Titus' answer (1.1.121), two invented lines addressed to Aaron, and Aaron's

[1] *The Early Shakespeare* (San Marino, 1967), p. 67.
[2] See especially E. K. Chambers, 'The First Illustration to "Shakespeare"', *The Library*, IV, 5, (1924–5), 326–30; J. Q. Adams, Introduction to his facsimile edition of Q1, *Shakespeare's Titus Andronicus* (New York, 1936), pp. 31–40; J. Dover Wilson, '"Titus Andronicus" on the Stage in 1595', *Shakespeare Survey* 1 (Cambridge, 1948), 17–22.

Fig. 4. Henry Peacham's drawing, beneath which is his transcript of passages from *Titus Andronicus*, c.1595 (Longleat Portland Papers, vol. I, fol. 159^{v})

boastful catalogue of crimes from the last act (5.1.125–44). An 'et cetera' after Aaron's speech seems to show that there was no intention of transcribing any more, but on the next line is the name of Tamora's son Alarbus, seemingly written as a speech prefix, though Alarbus has no lines in the play.

There can be no doubt that Tamora is shown pleading with Titus, and the two figures kneeling behind her, their hands tied, are surely Chiron and Demetrius. The figures behind Titus have

21

sometimes been interpreted as two of his sons, but Dover Wilson argues convincingly that they are attendant soldiers. He calls attention to the discrepancy between their Elizabethan costume and the classical attire of all the other men, even the Gothic princes and Aaron the Moor. The Queen of the Goths is in a regal robe which, if not exactly classical, is un-Elizabethan. Thus some effort seems to have been made to suggest time and place in the costuming of upper-class characters, while the lower classes were given 'modern dress' (Wilson, 'Stage', p. 21). The sons of Titus, if they were present, would have been dressed more like their father.

At the moment in the play when Tamora makes her plea, however, Titus' sons are present, as well as Alarbus. Their absence in the drawing is hard to explain, as is the portrayal of Aaron as brandishing a sword and pointing to Chiron and Demetrius. At this time he is still a prisoner of war. John Munro suggests that the drawing should be understood in the tradition of 'comprehensive' illustration, where more than one episode appears in a single picture.[1] The omissions would then be less surprising and Aaron could be seen as he is in Act 5 when he gives the speech transcribed below the drawing. Although on this occasion he speaks from the ladder he has been forced to climb, Munro's explanation is probably right. Not only are there many examples from classical times to the seventeenth century of this style of illustration, but it was used specifically in the wood-cuts adorning plays in print. The famous title-page of the 1615 edition of *The Spanish Tragedy* shows on the left side Hieronymo discovering Horatio, hanging in the arbour, and on the right side the immediately preceding action of Lorenzo stifling Belimperia's outcries. Words issuing from their mouths in balloons identify the precise moments depicted, which, in the play, are separated by the exit of Lorenzo, dragging Belimperia with him. The woodcut following the title-page of William Sampson's *The Vow Breaker* (1630) shows four figures speaking lines (some of them slightly altered) from the third and fourth acts of the play. When a late edition of *The Witch of Edmonton* was published in 1658 it was similarly provided with a woodcut depicting three characters who are speaking lines from two acts of the play. Although the *Titus Andronicus* drawing is a more unified composition than either of the last two woodcuts, the speeches written below it show that it, too, combines episodes from two

---

[1] 'Titus Andronicus', *The Times Literary Supplement*, 10 June 1949.

widely separated points in the play. Aaron's gesture of pointing to Chiron and Demetrius may be explained by the fact that when he speaks the lines chosen by the artist he has just finished boasting that he instructed the princes to rape and mutilate Lavinia. In both the drawing and the text we have a conflation of Tamora's plea to Titus and Aaron's unrepentant answer to Lucius. A visual clue to the separation between the two episodes may be given by the placing of Aaron in a slightly different plane from the rest of the figures. It may also be significant that Aaron is rather elegantly dressed, as he apparently is not in the first scene, since in his soliloquy at the opening of Act 2 he says, 'Away with slavish weeds . . .! I will be bright, and shine in pearl and gold' (2.1.18–19). There remains the mystery of the speech prefix 'Alarbus' following his speech, and to date no one has offered a satisfactory solution.

In the lower left margin is the signature 'Henricus Peacham' in non-cursive Italian script, and a date, 'Anno m° q° g [or q?] q^to', the form of which has so far defied explanation. The first and second parts of the date presumably stand for *millesimo quingentesimo* and the last for *quinto*. If the final letter were for *quarto* there would probably be one of various possible symbols for 'r' in addition to the 'to'.[1] Since a date in the 1590s is most probable, one would expect for the third letter an 'n' for *nonogesimo*. A 'g' is unknown as a numerical symbol, and another 'q' (as it has sometimes been read) makes no sense. It is possible that the writer, intending to make an 'n', inadvertently repeated the 'q'.[2] The most satisfactory interpretation of the letters is '1595'. (According to the legal calendar then in use in England, in which the starting-point of the year was 25 March, 1595 would have included what would now be thought of as 1 January to 24 March 1596.)

Confirmation of this date seems at first to be given on another page of the folded sheet, where someone has written in what resembles Renaissance handwriting 'Henrye Peachams Hande 1595', but this may be a forgery by John Payne Collier, and is, in any case, only a guess. Among other pencilled annotations in a relatively modern hand is one above the figure of Tamora: 'Written by Henry Peacham – author of the Complete Gentleman.' This too may be by Collier. Adams (pp. 33–4) points out that another pencilled annotation opposite the lines from Act 1, 'So far from

---

[1] For this observation I am indebted to Professor Clarence Miller.
[2] The suggestion was made to me by Professor Miller.

Shakspear Titus Andronicus Sc. 2', refer to a scene-division which Collier adopted in his edition of the play. None of these annotations can be taken as authoritative, but they may be correct.

About 'Henricus Peacham' there has been much controversy. Was it indeed the author of *The Complete Gentleman* (1622), who was eighteen or nineteen in 1595? And if he made the drawing, did he also copy the verses beneath it, or was that done later by someone else, as Dover Wilson believes ('Stage', p. 19)? The case for Peacham rests on the authenticity of the signature and on his known ability as a draughtsman. He drew several collections of emblems, one of which, *Minerva Britanna*, was printed in 1612. Those which survive in manuscript are, however, more useful in judging his technique in drawing. Three of these, done between 1603 and 1610, were based on the 1603 edition of *Basilicon Doron* by James I. The earliest, in the Bodleian Library (MS Rawlinson Poetry 146), was dedicated to Prince Henry; the other two, in the British Library (MS Harleian 6855, art. 13, and MS Royal 12 A lxvi), were dedicated, respectively, to the King and to the Prince.[1] A later collection, *Emblemata Varia* (c. 1621), is in the Folger Library. Though several distinguished scholars have thought it unlikely that the artist who drew these emblems could have done the drawing of *Titus Andronicus*,[2] my examination of the manuscripts in the Bodleian Library and the British Library has given me no reason to be sceptical. The emblems, belonging to a tradition in which human figures are used to symbolize ideas, are bound to differ from sketches of actors on a stage. Of the kind of figure-drawing found in the Longleat manuscript, where all the characters are seen in profile, Peacham writes in his *The Art of Drawing with the Pen* (1606): 'The half face of all other is most easy, insomuch that if you will, you may draw it only with one line, never removing your hand' (p. 21).[3] In the Address 'To the Reader' prefixed to this work (sig. A3) he says that he was born with the ability to draw, and taught himself. To have done the sketch of *Titus Andronicus* at the age of eighteen or nineteen was certainly not beyond him.

Since Peacham's writing in the emblem manuscripts is in an

---

[1] See Alan Young's Note prefixed to the facsimile edition of *Emblemata Varia* (Menston, 1976).

[2] See Adams, pp. 34–6; Wilson, 'Stage', pp. 21–2.

[3] Repr. Amsterdam, 1970.

Italian hand it is difficult to compare with the secretary hand of the text of *Titus Andronicus* beneath the drawing, but Peter Croft, Librarian of King's College Library, Cambridge, is inclined to think that Peacham was again the writer, using the Longleat manuscript 'as an exercise in "writing fair" in the secretary script' as the emblem books were exercises in 'fair writing in the italic style'. He is the more drawn to this opinion by his belief that 'the probabilities are in favour of the signature on the Longleat MS being in the same hand as those in the two emblem books' (the two in the British Library). He notes that the italic 'Anno' in the date 'looks as though it is in the same hand as the text and also in the same hand as the signature'.[1]

If, then, Henry Peacham made the drawing and wrote out the text beneath it, it remains to ask where he saw the play, why he made the drawing, why he made certain alterations in the text, and how the document came into the Harley papers at Longleat. Since the only recorded performance in 1595/6 was the one on 1 January 1596 at Sir John Harington's country house, it is tempting to suppose that the young Peacham was invited there for the Christmas holiday celebrations, but there is no evidence to support this guess. He might have attended an unrecorded performance in London. If he was one of the guests at Burley-on-the-Hill, he might have made the drawing for his host or hostess, or otherwise for a friend. Its presence in a collection of papers belonging to someone else makes it unlikely that he was drawing purely for his own amusement.

Most of the alterations in the lines below the drawing are slight changes of spelling, but a few appear to be more significant. Some critics place the change from 'haystalks' to 'haystackes' in this category, but the Q1 reading is either a dialectal variant or a printer's error which any transcriber might well alter to the standard form; in Q2 it became 'haystakes', and then 'haystackes' in Q3 and F1. The change from 'But' to 'Tut' four lines from the end is more surprising. The same change, with the addition of a comma, was made in Q2 and kept in Q3 and F1. It is conceivable that some copies of Q1 had this reading as the result of a press

[1] I am happy to acknowledge the generous assistance of Mr Croft, whose opinion I quote with his permission from a letter to me. Professor Alan Young, who inclines to a similar opinion, has also kindly answered my queries about Peacham and has helped me by sharing xeroxes he made of Peacham manuscripts; see his *Henry Peacham* (Boston, 1979), p. 20.

correction, or alternatively that both Peacham and the Q2 compositor misread the 'B', which is somewhat smudged in the one surviving copy of Q1. Most striking of all is the change from 'sonne' to 'sonnes' in two lines of Tamora's speech (1.1.106, 108), and the use of the plural form in the invented stage direction. It is difficult to see how anyone who had watched the performance could have supposed that more than one of Tamora's sons was executed, and indeed, in the last line of the speech, Peacham correctly copies 'my first borne sonne', and then, after Aaron's speech, adds the son's name, 'Alarbus'. Confusion in copying Tamora's speech might have arisen from a misreading of 'sonne:' in line 106, where the colon could be taken for a broken 's'. Seeing the plural form in the next line might then have misled a copyist into 'correcting' the singular form in line 108, as the Folio compositor also did. But only if the recollection of what happened on stage was indistinct could this confusion have resulted in devising a stage direction about 'sonnes going to execution'. Did the image of Titus' sons going to execution in 3.1 intrude? Whatever the explanation may be, these errors suggest that the drawing was made some little time after the performance. Given the 'comprehensive' nature of the drawing and the fact that every character is seen precisely in profile, it is in any case obvious that Peacham was not sketching while the actors were on stage. The evidence of these mistakes does not, however, require us to conclude with Adams (p. 38) and Dover Wilson ('Stage', p. 19) that the lines were copied years later from the Folio. No edition of the play is consistently followed, and any copyist could have made the same mistakes that were later made by the compositors of Q2 and F1. If the date of 1595 is accepted, it is virtually certain that the manuscript was completed before 25 March when, in the old legal calendar, 1596 began.

In the Marquis of Bath's library the drawing is among the Harley papers brought to Longleat by Lady Elizabeth Bentinck, granddaughter of Edward Harley, 2nd Earl of Oxford, and daughter of William Bentinck, 2nd Duke of Portland, when she married Viscount Weymouth, who was created 1st Marquis of Bath. This particular group of papers had been collected by Sir Michael Hicks, secretary of the first Lord Burghley. Since the collection consists mainly of state papers and of letters from prominent political figures, young Peacham's record of a dramatic performance seems out of place, but Hicks was also praised for his wide learning and his interest in music.¹ If he knew Peacham, who was at Trinity College, Cambridge, where Hicks had been many years earlier, it is possible that the drawing was presented to him. Or it could have come into his collection through Burghley, who was a patron of the arts and also, as it happens, a friend of Sir John Harington of Exton.² If the drawing was inspired by the performance at Burley-on-the-Hill, it might have come into the hands of the Lord Treasurer. Although these are no more than guesses, they suggest some of the ways in which Peacham's drawing may have come into the collection of Sir Michael Hicks.

For reasons I have given, the drawing cannot be taken as an accurate representation of any one moment in a performance of the play. Yet there is no reason to doubt that the portrayal of each figure is based on the physical appearance of actors in these roles. Their gestures and costumes give us a more vivid impression of the visual impact of Elizabethan acting than we get from any other source.

Sources

Four analogues of the story dramatized in *Titus Andronicus* deserve special attention.³

(i) In the sixth book of Ovid's *Metamorphoses* is the best-known version of the story of Philomela, daughter of the King of Athens (see Bullough, vi. 48–58). Her sister Procne marries Tereus, King of Thrace, and gives birth to a son named Itys, but after five years she longs to see Philomela, and persuades her husband to arrange for her sister's visit. When Tereus returns to get Philomela he is so inflamed with desire for her that, after bringing her to Thrace, he takes her 'to a hut deep hidden in the ancient woods'⁴ where he rapes her and cuts out her tongue to prevent her telling her story. He tells Procne that she is dead. Philomela then weaves her story into a cloth which she manages to send her sister; Procne finds her,

¹ See Alan G. R. Smith, *Servant of the Cecils: The Life of Sir Michael Hicks* (1977), p. 167.

² His cousin, Sir John Harington, the translator of Ariosto, writes of meeting him with Burghley at Bath in 1598 (Henry Harington, *Nugae Antiquae* (1769), p. 49).

³ They are among the sources and analogues reprinted in Bullough, vi. 34–79.

⁴ *Metamorphoses*, trans. F. J. Miller, Loeb Library (London and Cambridge, Mass., 1956), vi. 521.

and together they plot revenge. So incensed is Procne that she decides to sacrifice Itys, whom she and Philomela kill. After cooking his flesh they serve it to Tereus; he attempts to kill them, but as he is pursuing them Philomela is changed into a nightingale, Procne into a swallow, and Tereus into a hoopoe. Ovid's telling of this famous legend is repeatedly recalled in the play, where both the rape of Lavinia and the revenge for it are so strikingly similar. A copy of the *Metamorphoses* is even brought on stage in 4.1. No one doubts that this is an important source.

(ii) Ovid also underlies the closest of all analogues, *The History of Titus Andronicus, the Renowned Roman General, Newly Translated from the Italian Copy printed at Rome*, a chapbook printed by Cluer Dicey sometime between 1736 and 1764.[1]

(iii) As already noted, John Danter entered a ballad of Titus Andronicus in the Stationers' Register in 1594. The earliest printed version that has survived, 'Titus Andronicus' Complaint', was published by Richard Johnson in his *Golden Garland* (1620).[2] It was presumably published before this date, and certainly several times later, one version appearing in the chapbook following the prose history (see Bullough, vi. 44–8). The story told in the ballad is very similar to that of the prose history, though in certain details more closely resembling the play. The controversial relationship of the prose history and the ballad to the play will be discussed below.

(iv) A popular tale of a wicked Moorish servant, published in several languages in the sixteenth century, provides an analogue to the portrayal of the Moor in the prose history and the play (see Bullough, vi. 13–15). An English version entered in the Stationers' Register in 1569 and 1570 has not survived, but a seventeenth-century ballad is in the Roxburghe collection.[3] A 'noble man', as he is called in the ballad, marries and has two children. One day, when he is hunting, he rebukes his blackamoor servant, who then vows to revenge himself. He has his opportunity when his master

---

[1] See Adams, p. 8; the text of the prose history, in modernized spelling and punctuation, is reprinted in Appendix A; also see Bullough, vi. 34–44.

[2] This version, in modernized spelling and punctuation, is reprinted in Appendix B.

[3] The earliest entry for the ballad is 14 December 1624; the Roxburghe ballad may date from 1693. See Hyder Rollins, *An Analytical Index to the Ballad-Entries in the Registers of the Company of Stationers of London* (Chapel Hill, N.C., 1924), Nos. 1234, 2677; Donald Wing, *Short-Title Catalogue, 1641–1700*, 2nd edn. (New York, 1972–), ii (1982), 390; *Roxburghe Ballads*, vol. ii (1872; repr. New York, 1966), p. 49; Bullough, vi. 71–6.

again goes hunting, leaving him behind. Knowing that his mistress and her two children are in a moated tower, he draws up the bridge, bolts the gates, and assaults the lady. Her cries alarm the neighbours, who bring her husband back, but he is unable to enter the tower. On the battlements the Moor kills first one child, then the other, dropping their bodies in the moat. When the nobleman offers to do anything to save his wife, the Moor demands that he cut off his nose, but after he has done so, the Moor tosses her to her death. The nobleman dies of shock, and the Moor, after laughing at the grieving neighbours, jumps to his death to avoid torture. It seems likely that this story influenced the story of the play.

When the chapbook history turned up at the Folger Library, it seemed that the main source of *Titus Andronicus* had been identified. J. Q. Adams stated his opinion (pp. 7–9) that this chapbook, like many issued in the eighteenth century by this publisher and others, was a reprint of a much older pamphlet, possibly of one covered by the 1594 entry in the Stationers' Register (discussed in Appendix F). Richard Farmer had seen the title of the chapbook in a catalogue – very likely that of 1764 mentioned by Adams (p. 8) – and J. O. Halliwell-Phillipps later had such a chapbook in his library,[1] but it had been lost to sight until the unique Folger copy was found. Geoffrey Bullough, who agrees with Adams that the prose history was probably in existence before the play, has an excellent analysis of Shakespeare's indebtedness to it (vi. 7–20). Since, however, the priority of the prose history is not universally accepted, it will be necessary to consider the arguments that it followed the play in order to determine its status as source or analogue. It will then be possible to discuss, much more briefly than Bullough, other possible sources of the play.

After Adams had argued that the prose history was the source of the play and that the ballad, mainly based on the prose history, also took some details from the play (p. 8), Ralph M. Sargent attempted to prove in greater detail the dependence of the play on the prose history and also to reduce the dependence of the ballad on the play.[2] His conclusions were challenged by Marco Mincoff, who proposed instead the sequence play–ballad–history.[3] In

[1] See Farmer's letter to Steevens in Appendix II of the Johnson-Steevens edition of Shakespeare (10 vols., 1773), vol. x, sig. Qq2ᵛ; Halliwell-Phillipps, *Memoranda on All's Well that Ends Well . . . and on Titus Andronicus* (Brighton, 1879), p. 73.

[2] 'The Sources of *Titus Andronicus*', *Studies in Philology*, 46 (1949), 167–83.

[3] 'The Source of "Titus Andronicus"', *N. & Q.*, 216 (1971), 131–4.

his eagerness to prove his point he made several misstatements (three of which are listed in Appendix D). G. Harold Metz attacked Mincoff and reasserted the priority of the prose history, but, most recently, G. K. Hunter has shown the weakness of some of Metz's points and has urged the reconsideration of 'the literary consequences of assuming Mincoff's order'.[1] The chief argument used by Metz is that Mincoff is wrong in denying that some material present in the play and the history is not in the ballad. Metz offers several examples of 'story elements common to the play and the *History* not in the ballad' (p. 166), but, as Hunter shows, some of these elements are indeed in the ballad, some are standard *topoi*, and some do not constitute genuine connections.

Hunter makes the excellent point that the different demands of a play, a ballad, and a history (or story) account for many of the differences between these three versions of *Titus Andronicus*. The ballad-writer is less concerned with motivation and fullness of characterization than either the playwright or the story-teller. Thus, for example, the omission in the ballad of Titus' invitation to the Emperor and Empress proves nothing about indebtedness ('Sources', p. 116). The story-teller seeks to give convincing explanations, and this author, who has a special interest in late Roman history, dilates on the historical background which is given much more briefly in the play and minimally in the ballad ('Sources and Meanings'). Once the differences between generic requirements are fully taken into consideration it becomes more difficult to use either the presence or absence of material in one version as proof of its chronological position, but certain sequences are more probable than others. The three accounts of the principal crimes against the Andronici (summarized in Appendix C) provide a useful basis for comparison. In the play the rape of Lavinia and the murder of her husband, with the ensuing arrest and execution of her brothers, are firmly united. When Aaron hears about the lust of Chiron and Demetrius he recommends rape (2.1), and by the time he speaks with the Empress, has planned the murder of Bassianus and the trap for Quintus and Martius as well (2.3). In one scene (3.1) Titus is confronted successively with the

[1] Metz, '"The History of Titus Andronicus" and Shakespeare's Play', *N. & Q.*, 220 (1975), 163–6; Hunter, 'Sources and Meanings in "Titus Andronicus"', in *The Mirror up to Shakespeare*, ed. J. C. Gray (Toronto, 1983), pp. 171–88; and 'The "Sources" of *Titus Andronicus* – once again', *N. & Q.*, 228 (1983), 114–16.

threat to the lives of his sons, the spectacle of the mutilated Lavinia, the loss of his hand, and the sight of his sons' heads. Given the desire for revenge on the parts of the Empress and Aaron, the sexual appetite of the Gothic princes serves to set the entire scheme in motion. In the history the atrocities are differently motivated and take place in three stages. In Chapter III the Gothic Queen, eager for her sons to inherit the throne, is angered by Lavinia's betrothal to the Emperor's son (not his brother, as in the play). She therefore plans the murder of the Prince, which is carried out by her sons and the Moor. In Chapter IV Lavinia sends her brothers to look for the Prince, and they 'unluckily' fall in the pit where the body is hidden. Observed by the Moor and the Queen's sons, the young Andronici are then caught and imprisoned, Titus is tricked into losing his hand, and the bodies of his beheaded sons are sent to him. In Chapter V Lavinia, having gone into the woods to mourn the deaths of her betrothed and her brothers, is raped and mutilated by the Queen's sons with the connivance of the Moor. When Marcus brings her to Titus, he at last vows revenge. The ballad also separates the murder from the rape.[1] The Queen arranges the murder after Lavinia's betrothal to 'Caesar's son', and then the Moor, as in the play, leads Titus' sons to the 'den' where the body lies. After they are in prison Lavinia is raped and mutilated, and only after Marcus has brought her to Titus does he lose his hand and receive the heads of his sons.

Hunter is surely right in saying that the ballad-writer, caring little about the connections between events, may reorder them so as to focus attention on the emotions of the hero. If we accept Mincoff's hypothesis, however, and imagine that the ballad-writer had only the play to go on, it is hard to see what gain in emotional intensity he could expect from separating the incidents of the murder and the rape, or from having Lavinia betrothed to 'Caesar's son' rather than married to his brother. As for the author of the prose history, who, if he wrote last, is likely to have known both the ballad and the play, he might have wished to emphasize political motivation by showing Lavinia's betrothal as a threat to the succession of the Queen's sons. If he wrote after the play, that is, he had more reason to make this change than did the ballad-writer. But of course political as well as personal motivation for the

---

[1] Mincoff says that 'the ballad-writer does not seem to have intended to separate them' (p. 133), but in fact he has done so.

Queen's actions is also strong in the play. To drop the sacrifice of Alarbus, substitute Lavinia's betrothal to the Emperor's son, and then to separate the murder and rape is not to tell a more convincing story but a somewhat different one, in which the Queen and the Moor are rather less calculating. Instead of working out one fiendishly clever scheme for the rape, murder, and execution of the young Andronici, they appear to improvise, once the murder has taken place, exploiting first Lavinia's despatch of her brothers into the woods and their accidental fall, and then her own flight to the woods to mourn. It is much easier to imagine Shakespeare improving on this story than the history-writer disassembling the tightly-knotted strands of Shakespeare's plot or choosing the version of the ballad-writer, who had already done so. The combination in the ballad of resemblances to both the play and the prose history is most easily explained by the assumption that the ballad-writer knew both.

The three accounts of the Gothic Queen's affair with the Moor also differ significantly. In the play their baby is not born until after the murder and rape (4.2), although just before these crimes are committed, on the day following the Queen's arrival in Rome, Lavinia and Bassianus taunt her with the scandal of her affair with Aaron, which has made the Emperor to be 'noted long' (see note on 2.3.86). There is no such illogicality in the history or the ballad, where the blackamoor child is born before the main plots against the Andronici get under way (Appendix A, pp. 199–200). The taunts of Lavinia and Bassianus suggest that Shakespeare knew a version of the story in which the affair had already gone on for a long time, although with his time scheme he obviously could not produce the baby until a later scene. Considerations of generic requirements do not make clear why the writers of the ballad and the history should have wanted to introduce the baby earlier. If the author of the history knew the play, he omitted the telling episode of Aaron's defence of his child and substituted for it the fantastic one in which the Queen persuades the Emperor that her black baby was 'conceived by the force of imagination' (Appendix A, p. 199).

The other significant difference is to be found in the treatment of Titus' sons. In the play he has four sons with him in Rome and refers to twenty-one who were slain in the service of their country (1.1.195), though later he speaks of twenty-two who 'died in honour's lofty bed' (3.1.10), a phrase which hardly applies to the additional son whom he has killed. There is evidence that Shakespeare added the ceremony of burial for Mutius after writing the rest of the scene (see section on 'Text' and notes on 1.1.287–8, 290–9, 341–90), and this suggests that Mutius may not have been in his original plan. Neither history nor ballad has an episode corresponding to the death of Mutius, and both speak of twenty-two sons slain in battle (Appendix A, p. 197; Appendix B, p. 204). More important, however, is Shakespeare's use of Lucius, the son who survives and is elected emperor after aiding his father by marching on Rome with the Goths. There are no such episodes in the history or the ballad, where Titus is aided in his revenge only by friends (Appendix A, p. 203; Appendix B, p. 207). The history is inconsistent in its account of Titus' sons, all three of whom are beheaded, though only two are said to fall in the pit (Appendix A, pp. 200–1). In the ballad the number of sons who fall in is the same as the number killed, but in some versions it is three, while in others it is two, though with nothing said of a surviving son. If the original ballad-writer or the history-writer had only the play for a source, it is strange that the surviving son would have been dropped in favour of 'friends', and strange that such confusion would have arisen. If the history came first, however, its careless inconsistency could have led to the two versions of the ballad, and the prominent 'Loss of two and twenty of his valiant sons' in the heading of Chapter II would initially have fixed that figure in Shakespeare's mind. Once again it is easier to see Shakespeare improving on the plot of the history than to understand what the history-writer would have thought to gain by altering these details. My conclusion is that the most probable order is history–play–ballad.[1]

A most interesting section of Hunter's essay on 'Sources and Meanings' concerns the historical background of the play and the prose narrative. Although the 'history' is imaginary, scholars have pointed to a number of historical sources which may have furnished the names and suggested certain incidents in both the narrative and dramatic versions of the story.[2] The narrative writer gives more detail than Shakespeare, and much of the pseudo-

[1] For a discussion of the evidence in the Stationers' Register bearing on the question of the early existence of the prose history see Appendix F on 'Copyright'.

[2] See especially Bullough, vi. 8–11, 23–6; Wolfgang Keller, 'Titus Andronicus', *Shakespeare-Jahrbuch*, 74 (1938), 137–62; Robert A. Law, 'The Roman Background of *Titus Andronicus*', *Studies in Philology*, 40 (1943), 145–53.

historical information in his opening chapter about wars with the Goths 'in the time of Theodosius' seems to have been assembled from accounts of widely scattered events in the fifth and sixth centuries in the reigns of Honorius and of Justinian. The name 'Andronicus' comes from the history of the Eastern Empire in the twelfth century. Hunter believes that the relative inaccessibility in the sixteenth century of the historians of these periods of the Roman Empire makes it unlikely that the prose history was written at that time. It is true that one of the chief authorities, Pedro Mexia's *Historia Imperial y Cesarea*, was not available in English at that time, nor were the works of other historians of the late Roman Empire such as Paulus Diaconus, Zosimus, Procopius, or Zonaras, but Mexia and the others I have named, with the exception of Zosimus, had been translated into Italian, and Procopius into French as well. The chapbook author claims to be translating from Italian, and such a story could well have been written in sixteenth-century Italy. It could also have been written by an Englishman with a knowledge of Italian or Spanish.

For centuries after its decline and fall Rome exerted a powerful imaginative force in Western Europe. In the medieval *Gesta Romanorum* the deeds of fabulous Romans, when 'Andronicus' or 'Titus', 'Saturninus' or 'Theodosius' was emperor, furnished preachers with material for homiletic allegory – 'Good friends, this emperor is our Lord Jesus Christ . . .'.[1] Later the histories of Rome were mined for model orations[2] and for episodes on which to base declamations, the popular exercises in forensic oratory derived from the Roman *controversiae*, in which the student invented speeches for and against an accused person. The title-page of one collection of declamations published in France in 1581 and translated into English in 1596 proclaimed its indebtedness to '*Titus Livius* and other ancient writers',[3] though even where there was some genuine foundation in history, the law cases were largely imaginary. Here, as in the *Gesta* (some of which derive from declamations), Roman history might be twisted into a fictional shape. Such blendings of history with invented material are interesting in relation to *Titus Andronicus*, and the *novelle* provide

---

[1] See, for example, the EETS edition (1879), pp. 9, 48, 65, 72, 172.

[2] See Lorich's edition of *Orations* from Livy and other historians (Marburg, 1541) and Remigio Nannini, *Orationi Militari* (Venice, 1546).

[3] Alexandre Sylvain, *Epitomes de Cent Histoires Tragicques* (Paris, 1581); [Lazarus Pyott], *The Orator* (1596).

one more category of examples. Bandello, one of the most influential of the writers of these popular stories, mixed incidents taken from Livy with those from other historians of ancient and modern times,[1] and William Painter did the same in his *Palace of Pleasure* (1566), where he carefully listed his sources.

From this evidence it is clear that in the Middle Ages and in the Renaissance authentic or imaginary Roman history was often used as a background for stories. Frequently these stories are somewhat similar in nature to *Titus Andronicus*, as, for example, the rape of Lucretia in Bandello (ii. 21), or Horatius' murder of his sister in Sylvain (no. 88), both taken from Livy. The controversial episodes chosen for declamations sometimes raise problems very like those that arise in the story of Titus Andronicus, as when, in another of Sylvain's selections from Livy, the senators of Capua ungratefully persecute Pacuvius, who has saved their lives (*Epitomes*, no. 3). Since models of these kinds were available in the late sixteenth century, it is not inherently improbable that the author of the prose history made use of them and of his reading of Ovid and the Roman historians to produce his version of the story before Shakespeare wrote his play.

If Shakespeare knew this story he made important changes in it and added material drawn from several other sources. Hunter is justifiably concerned to dispel the persistent myth of an unlearned Shakespeare who picked up his plots ready-made instead of 'inventing' them in the modern sense of that word. But Shakespeare's 'finding' of a story (the *inventio* of rhetoricians) never inhibited his creative power to transform it, and Hunter's valuable analysis of the 'opposed images of Republican austerity and Imperial decadence' not to be found in the prose history ('Sources and Meanings') loses none of its force if we suppose that Shakespeare added them to the story he had found. Two major episodes of Act I which are not in the chapbook – the sacrifice of Alarbus and the killing of Mutius – contribute to precisely that paradoxical opposition, and hence suggest how Shakespeare may have reshaped the material to bring out a new meaning. His reading of Livy, Herodian, and other historians probably formed his ideas and also furnished him with some of the names which are not in the chapbook ('Sources and Meanings'), such as Saturninus, Bassianus, and Mutius. Plutarch's *Life of Scipio Africanus* contains

[1] See T. G. Griffith, *Bandello's Fiction* (Oxford, 1955), pp. 43–70.

several of these names (see Law, p. 147), while his *Life of Coriolanus*, to which Shakespeare would return for his last tragedy, provided a model for the situation of Lucius, exiled from Rome and returning with a foreign army (see Bullough, vi. 24–5). The quarrel between Titus and the Queen of the Goths, motivated in the prose history entirely by his opposition to her growing political power, is based in the play on the more subtle contradiction in Titus' character between cruelty and piety, between inhumanity and love of family and country. Plutarch's Coriolanus was a model for the portrayal of such contradictions.

It is well to recall here what was said about the possibility that there was an old Titus play by another playwright (which might then stand between the prose history and Shakespeare's play): if there was such a play, it is likely that Shakespeare transformed it as he did the old play of *King Leir*. Similarly, it can be said that if there was no such play, but if the prose history existed essentially as we have it in the eighteenth-century chapbook, this was only the basis for a very different treatment of the events. Thus, if Shakespeare did not make the entire story up, he made it what it is in the play.

In Shakespeare's mind the tale of Titus Andronicus seems to have become associated with several other stories. The name Lavinia would have suggested the *Aeneid*, from which it was presumably taken. In the play, much more clearly than in the prose history, the rape and dismemberment of Lavinia are equated with the destruction of the Roman political order as, in the *Aeneid*, the winning of Lavinia makes possible the line of Roman rulers prophesied by Anchises (vi. 76 ff.). The episode of the rape, however, was clearly based on the legend of Philomela, best known through Ovid's version in the *Metamorphoses*, a poem that Shakespeare knew well. Ovid's emphasis on the transforming power of grief and rage profoundly influenced the play and probably suggested to Shakespeare the related example of Hecuba, referred to on two occasions (1.1.136; 4.1.20).[1] It is possible that he also knew the *Hecuba* of Euripides, which had been translated into Latin and Italian.[2] Philomela's revenge would surely have recalled Seneca's

[1] See my 'The Metamorphosis of Violence in *Titus Andronicus*', *Shakespeare Survey* 10 (Cambridge, 1957), 39–49.

[2] See Emrys Jones, *The Origins of Shakespeare* (Oxford, 1977), pp. 90–102; *Hecuba* was translated by Lodovico Dolce in 1543.

Thyestes, where Atreus kills his brother's sons and serves them to their father at a feast of reconciliation. There are allusions to other Senecan plays as well, but Ovid was by far the more important influence, affecting not only the treatment of character but often the poetic style, as in Act 2, Scene 4.[1] In the years when Shakespeare was apparently working on the play, he was also engaged in writing *Venus and Adonis*, based mainly on the *Metamorphoses*, and *Lucrece*, based mainly on the *Fasti*. There are close links between the play and both poems. The story of the rape of Lucrece, with its political implications, was especially relevant to *Titus Andronicus*, and may in turn have suggested the story of Virginia.

The fiendish revengefulness of Aaron the Moor is probably derived in part from the tale of the wicked Moorish servant, mentioned above, but Bullough is right in saying that Shakespeare need never have read the tale if he had the prose history, since the characteristics of Aaron that most resemble the Moorish servant were already incorporated there.

If the sources mentioned so far suggested the main outlines of the story, and Ovid in particular exerted a powerful influence on the poetry, Kyd's *The Spanish Tragedy* (1587–90) and Marlowe's *The Jew of Malta* (1589–90) provided crucially important dramatic models. When Jonson made his famous gibe at '*Jeronimo*' (i.e. *The Spanish Tragedy*) and '*Andronicus*', he bracketed them as examples of unchanging and unenlightened popular taste, but the resemblances between the two plays go far beyond the fact that both succeeded on the stage, and one of the more striking resemblances points, ironically, to their authors' appeal to the learned in their audiences. Although *The Spanish Tragedy* is basically unlike any play by Seneca or by the imitators of Seneca who wrote for aristocratic or academic audiences in the sixteenth century,[2] Kyd larded his play with Latin tags and with longer passages of Latin which are pastiches, partly derived from Seneca and other Roman authors, and partly invented. Like a classical façade on a modern building, they claim kinship with a respected tradition. *Titus Andronicus* also has a considerable number of Latin speeches. Here they are at least appropriate to the Roman setting if not always to

---

[1] See Bullough, vi. 26–9 and note on 2.4.16–32.

[2] See G. K. Hunter, 'Seneca and the Elizabethans', *Shakespeare Survey 20* (Cambridge, 1967), 17–26, and 'Seneca and English Tragedy', in *Seneca*, ed. C. D. N. Costa (London and Boston, 1974), 166–204.

the characters who make them; it comes as a surprise when one of the Gothic princes quotes Seneca, or when Aaron spots a quotation from Horace. Though there are fewer of these adornments than in *The Spanish Tragedy*, they serve a similar purpose of bidding for serious attention from the well-read.

The great distinction of *The Spanish Tragedy* is Kyd's theatrically effective portrayal of an admirable magistrate driven to commit murder by his desire for revenge. Grief for a murdered son and frustration at his inability to obtain justice are more than Hieronymo can bear; madness and the terrible ingenuity of his reprisal are the result. To anyone seeking to exploit the success of this play the story of Titus Andronicus offered another public official unable to obtain justice and driven to madness and revenge. Shakespeare made his hero more responsible for what happens to him, and delineated in greater detail the process by which he is transformed into a man obsessed with revenge. Some of the most startling features of the play are probably due in part to the model provided by Kyd. Like *The Spanish Tragedy, Titus Andronicus* is sensational, serious, learned, and spectacular.

The Jew of Malta, if not precisely a revenge play, is a play of many revenges, carried out by one of the prototypical Machiavellian schemers of the Elizabethan stage. That Barabas was a popular villain we know. Part of his appeal is due to his sardonic humour and the zest with which he pursues his criminal career. Marlowe's portrayal of him suggests a characteristic interest in the outsider and even a certain sympathy. Shakespeare's treatment of the outsider, Aaron, is in some respects remarkably similar. The sardonic humour is there (notably in 5.1); the speech in which Aaron boasts of his crimes immediately recalls Barabas (see note on 5.1.128–40), and the episodes with Aaron's baby present a sympathetic view unlike any in the prose history. The fact that Shakespeare clearly had *Tamburlaine* in mind at about the same time, when writing some of Gloucester's speeches in *3 Henry VI*, makes it all the more likely that he thought of Barabas in creating the role of Aaron.

That Shakespeare was also familiar with the work of George Peele can be taken for granted, and we have seen that his style and even his vocabulary in some sections of the play may have been influenced by Peele, but of far greater consequence were the impressions made on him by Kyd and Marlowe. For this play they provided the most important dramatic precedents.

Text

The First Quarto edition of *Titus Andronicus* (Q1, 1594) has several characteristics which suggest that it was printed from the author's 'foul papers' – the rough draft from which a fair copy would be made: the stage directions are sometimes vague (e.g. 'and others as many as can be', 1.1.69.6–7) and often descriptive, while showing familiarity with the theatre (e.g. '*Enter Aaron, Chiron, and Demetrius at one door; and at the other door young Lucius and another with a bundle of weapons, and verses writ upon them*', 4.2.0.1–3); speech prefixes vary (e.g. '*Saturninus*' alternates with '*King*' and '*Emperor*').[1] There are several indications that Shakespeare had second thoughts while composing this text, whether or not he was revising an older play. The most striking instance is the three and a half lines describing the sacrifice of 'the noblest prisoner of the Goths' as already accomplished, although the episode of the sacrifice of Alarbus immediately follows (see notes on 1.1.35, 69.5, 86–8, and 96–149). The episodes with Mutius may also have been added (see notes on 1.1.287–8, 290–9, 341–90); the possibility that this character was not in the original plan is discussed above in the section on Sources. Some lines of Titus' dialogue with the Clown in 4.3 appear to duplicate others (see note on ll. 104–5 and Appendix E) and a few lines may have been added to 5.2 (see note on l. 61). In some of these passages there may have been no clear indication of what was to be cancelled and in some other passages there are repetitions (e.g. at 1.1.344) which might have been eliminated if the manuscript had been more carefully prepared. In spite of this occasional untidiness, however, the text of Q1 presents no major problems and is clearly the authoritative text for all but 3.2.

The Second Quarto (Q2, 1600) was printed from a copy of Q1 in which the last three leaves of the K gathering were damaged, as Joseph S. G. Bolton shows.[2] Where the compositor of Q2 was unable to read his copy he made guesses which produced variant readings at 5.3.25.2, 59, 92–6, 129–32, 163–8, and 199–200 (see notes and collations); in the last instance he added four lines. Maxwell notes that a comparable injury to the top of sig. I4 prob-

[1] See W. W. Greg, *The Editorial Problem in Shakespeare* (Oxford, 1951), pp. 27 ff., and *Folio*, p. 203.

[2] 'The Authentic Text of *Titus Andronicus*', *PMLA*, 44 (1929), 776–80; see also Adams, pp. 24–8.

ably accounts for the divergent readings of Q2 at 5.2.71 and 106. Since each of the subsequent seventeenth-century editions was printed from its predecessor, these Q2 variants became part of the accepted text of the play until the rediscovery of Q1 in December 1904. Bolton and Adams show that, as might be expected, a few errors are corrected in Q2 and many more introduced (Bolton, pp. 766–8; Adams, pp. 20–4). The most notable improvement made by Q2 is the omission of the contradictory lines following 1.1.35.

The Third Quarto (Q3, 1611) again corrected a few errors and introduced a number of new ones (see Bolton, pp. 782–5). In general, this compositor was more careless than his predecessor, in two instances omitting entire lines. One of these omissions and an accompanying addition are important in determining the basis of the Folio text and will be discussed below.

The First Folio text of this play (F1, 1623), though printed from Q3 (see Bolton, pp. 785–8), differs significantly in several ways. Most conspicuous are the division into acts, presumably in deference to the tradition of five-act structure, and the addition of an entire scene (3.2). A line (1.1.398) is added; the words 'What booke?' are inserted as a separate line after 4.1.36; there is some normalization of speech prefixes, and stage directions are both altered and augmented. The superfluous 'What booke?' can be explained as a printer's error, caused by glancing ahead to l. 41, but the other additions show that Q3 was not the sole basis for F1, and the changes in the stage directions make it reasonably certain that a playhouse text, annotated by the prompter, was used in preparing the copy. The prompter's touch is indicated by the addition of several trumpet flourishes, by such added directions as 'A table brought in' (5.3.25.1), and, as Greg points out, by the duplication of 'wind horns' at 2.2.10.1, where the words, already in the text, were probably placed in the margin of the prompt-book and incorporated in the text by the F1 printer (*First Folio*, p. 205). It is natural to suppose that the text of *Titus Andronicus* annotated by the prompter would have been a fair copy of the foul papers from which Q1 was printed. It is quite possible that it contained the line (1.1.398) appearing in F1 for the first time, and that this line was also in the foul papers but was overlooked by the printer of Q1. The added scene (3.2), however, was presumably inserted in the prompt-book. The same rare-word test which links the play as a whole to the first tetralogy (see above, p. 10) suggests that this scene is later but not much later – approximately contemporary with such plays as *Romeo and Juliet* and *Richard II*. When copy for the Folio edition of *Titus Andronicus* was being prepared, then, someone may have collated a copy of Q3 with the prompt-book, entering the prompter's added or altered stage directions and speech prefixes, making a few alterations in the dialogue (such as the added line, 1.1.398), and copying out the additional scene.[1] What kept Greg and others from adopting this hypothesis as an explanation of the F1 text was that such an editor ought to have noticed the important differences between Q3 and the prompt-book at those places where Q2 had introduced variant readings. It appears, however, from other Folio texts printed from quartos that consultation of another authoritative text was often sporadic rather than thorough.[2] It is also possible, as Greg himself admitted, that the editor, noticing the variant readings, saw no reason to alter them. As Greg pointed out, 'The editor of Q2 did his work skilfully and his reconstruction is in no obvious way inferior to the original' (*Folio*, p. 209). For one reason or another the Folio printer's copy of Q3, though greatly altered by collation with the prompt-book, was by no means identical with it. In William Jaggard's printing house it was apparently worked on mainly by an apprentice known as Compositor E, who has been tentatively identified as John Leason.[3] He was the least expert of the Folio compositors and, confronted with this heavily marked-up quarto and an inserted manuscript sheet containing the additional scene, he made many errors. The fate of one passage (3.1.33–7) in successive editions illustrates the occasionally very puzzling transmission of the text from Q1 to F1:

> Q1. *Titus.* Why tis no matter man, if they did heare
> They would not marke me, if they did marke,

[1] In an article on 'The Copy for the Folio Text of *Love's Labour's Lost*' Stanley Wells suggests that differences between the quarto and folio texts of that play may best be explained by assuming a similar consultation of a playhouse manuscript (*Review of English Studies*, NS 33 (1982), 137–47).

[2] See, for example, Greg, *Folio*, p. 159; Wells, pp. 146–7.

[3] *The First Folio of Shakespeare*, The Norton Facsimile, ed. Charlton Hinman (New York, 1968), Introduction, pp. xviii–xix. Largely as a result of the work of T. Howard-Hill, Compositor E is now believed to have set all of *Titus Andronicus* except for Folio pages cc4 (beginning of the play to 1.1.70), dd3^v (3.1.216–3.2.38), and ee2^v (5.3.146 to the end).

>   They would not pittie me, yet pleade I must,
>   And bootlesse vnto them.
>   Therefore I tell my sorrowes to the stones,
>   (E3ᵛ)

Q2.   *Titus.* Why tis no matter man, if they did heare
>   They would not marke me, or if they did markè,
>   They would not pitty me, yet pleade I must,
>   And bootlesse vnto them.
>   Therefore I tell my sorrowes to the stones,
>   (E2ᵛ)

Q3.   *Titus.* Why tis no matter man, if they did heare
>   They would not marke me, or if they did marke,
>   All bootlesse vnto them.
>   Therefore I tell my sorrowes bootles to the stones,
>   (E2ᵛ)

F1.   *Ti.* Why 'tis no matter man, if they did heare
>   They would not marke me: oh if they did heare
>   They would not pitty me.
>   Therefore I tell my sorrowes bootles to the stones.
>   (dd2ᵛ, TLN 1169–72)

The Q2 addition of 'or' in l. 34 is such an improvement to both the metre and the flow of the sentence that it is tempting to think that the word was in the original manuscript; it might have stood in a lost press-corrected state of Q1, via which it found its way into the text of Q2. The Q3 printer, whose eye skipped l. 35, seems to have altered l. 36 to make more sense of the truncated sentence, and then inadvertently repeated 'bootless' in the following line. The Folio text is the hardest to explain. Since half of l. 35 was restored, this must be one of the places where the editor noticed a discrepancy between Q3 and the prompt-book and wrote in the additional words. It is hard to believe that he would not, in that case, have tried to restore the entire passage, but it is possible that in so doing he made this page very difficult to decipher. Compositor E apparently misread 'or' as 'oh' and carelessly repeated 'heare' in l. 34. Then, skipping not only the second half of l. 35 but all of

l. 36, he set l. 37 with the Q3 'bootles', which the editor may have failed to strike out.[1]

An important question raised by the Folio text remains to be considered: why, if 3.2 was written before the publication of Q1, was it not printed there? No certain answer can be given, but since the scene was presumably written on a separate sheet and was required for performance, it would naturally have been kept in the prompt-book. When Shakespeare's foul papers were given to the printer in 1594 it may be that no copy of the added scene was made to accompany them. Thus the added scene would not have reached the printer.

Since, with the exceptions noted, each edition after Q1 was based on the preceding one, Q1 is inevitably the prime authority. The great value of the Folio text to a modern editor lies in its indications, derived from the prompt-book, of how the play was performed, and in the text it provides of the added scene. Except in that scene the basis for the text of this edition is Q1, from which all substantive departures are noted in the collations.

The Play in Performance

The evidence of the earliest performances of *Titus Andronicus* has already been presented in the first section of this introduction. The first production of which we have definite knowledge, the one on 23 January 1594 by Sussex's Men, probably took place at the Rose Theatre on the Bankside (Chambers, *Stage*, ii. 94). Q1, which presumably gives us the text (except for 3.2) on which this production was based, calls for an unusually large cast. If we assume that there were to be at least two each of the senators, tribunes, attendants, and 'others' called for in various scenes, and if Saturninus and Bassianus in the opening scene have not only two soldiers each (a drummer and a flag-bearer) but also two other 'followers', then, making the fullest allowance for doubling (see chart, Appendix G), at least twenty-six actors will be required for

---

[1] The changes in this passage led Greg to suppose that the prompt-book was an annotated copy of Q2 (*Folio*, pp. 206–7). He thought that only if such a text had been used to correct a copy of Q3 could the combination in F1 of dependence on Q3, evidence of the prompter's hand, the restoration of part of 3.1.35, and the retention of the Q2 variant readings be explained. The hypothesis of sporadic consultation of the manuscript prompt-book makes his more complicated explanation unnecessary.

43

this scene. There are many possible schemes for doubling. In the one I have presented diagrammatically all the roles with more than three-line speeches are divided among fifteen actors – twelve men, and three boys (to play Tamora, Lavinia, and Young Lucius). Most of the twelve extras are mute most of the time, speaking only an occasional line as members of a crowd. Several of the extras who exit early in the first scene are needed to fill out the triumphal procession which enters after l. 69. The total number of actors required is brought to twenty-seven by Young Lucius, who is not present in the first scene, and it seems likely that the boy playing that part joined the 'others' in the procession. All the other characters who appear for the first time in later scenes can be played by actors from the first scene. I assume that a man could play the Nurse and that the Clown might have doubled in the first scene as the Captain.

It is less clear how many actors are required for the last scene, but with twenty-seven actors available, it is likely that most of them reappeared as Goths or Romans (the 'others' who enter with the Emperor). That such numbers of actors were sometimes mustered for a performance is shown by the 'plot' for *Tamar Cam*, where twenty regular actors were apparently required plus nine others, as Greg says, for the final 'march past'.[1]

Although we have no specific knowledge about the stage of the Rose, it may be assumed that in a general way it resembled the Swan, the one public theatre of which we have a sketch, and therefore had two entrances in the tiring-house wall at the back of the thrust stage beneath an overhanging gallery, which could be used as a playing space when action 'above' was stipulated. In the floor of the stage there would be at least one trap door, probably in the centre not far from the back wall. Such few properties as the text seems to require are mentioned in the notes of this edition. One sizeable structure to represent the tomb of the Andronici may have been set up against the centre of the tiring-house wall for the first act and removed before or during the second scene of Act 2.

After the three performances by Sussex's Men the only recorded public performances in the sixteenth century are the two by the combined Admiral's and Chamberlain's Men at Newington Butts, a theatre of which almost nothing is known. Then comes the

[1] *Dramatic Documents from the Elizabethan Playhouses*, 2 vols. (Oxford, 1931), i. 28; vol. ii, p. vii.

private performance at Burley-on-the-Hill on 1 January 1596. Although we have records of only these six performances before the Restoration, the title-pages of Q2 and Q3 suggest frequent revivals, and Jonson's derogatory allusion to the play in the Induction to *Bartholomew Fair* shows that it was still popular in 1614. For the years immediately following the Restoration we have the word of the prompter John Downes that it was among the old plays 'acted but now and then' by His Majesty's Company of Comedians, 'yet being well performed, were very satisfactory to the town'.[1] *Titus Andronicus* is one of twenty-one such plays, which are distinguished from the fifteen 'Principal Old Stock Plays' of the company. It appears again (as '*Andronicus*') in a 1669 list of plays formerly acted at Blackfriars and now allowed to the King's Company,[2] but no performance is recorded before 1678. In the autumn of that year Ravenscroft's alteration, *Titus Andronicus, or The Rape of Lavinia* (see p. 1), was probably acted for the first time, though it was not published until 1687. To judge by the prologues and the epilogue printed with it, this version of the play was revived in the season of 1685–6 or 1686–7 (*London Stage*, i. 273, 352). From the time of Ravenscroft's alteration until 1923 *Titus Andronicus* seems to have been performed in England only in radically altered versions.

According to Ravenscroft, his version became 'confirmed a stock-play',[3] and in the absence of other evidence we must take his word for it. When it was put on in August 1704, it was said not to have been acted for six years,[4] which might imply that it was given more regularly before 1698. During the 1704–5 season it was played twice more and then not again until August 1717, when James Quin, who was to be for many years the reigning favourite of the London stage, played Aaron. During the course of the seven seasons beginning with 1717–18 *Titus Andronicus* was performed ten more times, usually with Quin as Aaron. In March of 1724 he chose it as a benefit for himself, and͜   ͞ed in another benefit performance in April.[5]

[1] *Roscius Anglicanus* (1708), p. 9.

[2] *The London Stage, 1660–1800*, Part I: 1660–1700, ed. W. Van Lennep (Carbondale, Ill., 1965), pp. 151–2.

[3] 'To the Reader', *Titus Andronicus* (1687), sig. A2ᵛ.

[4] *The London Stage*, Part II: 1700–1729, ed. E. Avery (Carbondale, Ill., 1960), p. 73.

[5] *London Stage*, ii. 76, 80, 458–9, 499, 544, 605, 606, 613, 634, 683, 766, 772.

The fact that Aaron was considered to be the starring part in these years points up the brilliance of Shakespeare's characterization and the opportunities it offers to an actor. But the prominence given to it was probably due in part to Ravenscroft's alterations. Merely a conspicuous onlooker in Shakespeare's long opening scene, Aaron has several important speeches in the corresponding section of the adaptation, taking over lines originally given to Demetrius and Tamora. In the last act his defiance of his captors and the boasting confession he finally makes to save the life of his baby are moved to a climactic position at the conclusion of the cannibalistic banquet. Their theatrical effectiveness is further heightened by means of the newly-developed techniques of the Restoration stage. After the Emperor and Empress have begun their meal and Titus has stunned them by killing Lavinia, he orders a screen at the back of the stage to be drawn back, revealing Aaron on a rack, refusing to talk. Next a curtain is drawn to 'discover' the bodies of Demetrius and Chiron in chairs, their heads and hands hanging on the wall. Only after the stabbing of Tamora, the deaths of Titus and the Emperor, and Marcus' threat to kill Aaron's child, does Aaron confess his crimes. His death in flames as he continues to curse his enemies follows the choice of Lucius as emperor and ends the play. Of this restructuring and staging George Odell said, 'I know of no more interesting specimen of early stage usage.'[1] Undeniably melodramatic, the scene provides a final virtuoso turn for the interpreter of Aaron's part. In his tragic roles Quin was known for his melodic declamation and dignified bearing. John Hill uses his rendition of a speech in Ambrose Philips' *The Distressed Mother* as an example of the 'power of communicating sentiments of greatness, and lifting us up, as it were, above ourselves'.[2] We may guess how this power was applied to the interpretation of Aaron when we read of Quin's success as Zanga, the fierce Moor of Edward Young's *The Revenge*, a play compounded of *Othello* and Aphra Behn's *Abdelazer, or The Moor's Revenge*. The role continued to be popular with actors well into the nineteenth century, when George Daniel wrote, 'Zanga is a noble being – pursuing dark and crooked ways, only as they lead to vengeance.'[3] To such a charac-

---

[1] *Shakespeare from Betterton to Irving*, 2 vols. (New York, 1920), i. 191.

[2] *The Actor* (1755), p. 188.

[3] 'Remarks,' p. 7, prefixed to *The Revenge* in *Cumberland's British Theatre*, vol. 15 (1827).

ter Quin's special virtues were certainly suited, and because of them some of Zanga's nobility may have shone through Ravenscroft's Aaron.

The long absence of any version of the play from the London stage was probably due to distaste for its horrors and to the closely related doubts about Shakespeare's authorship discussed above. Before it was put on again in England an adventurous American actor-playwright, N. H. Bannister, appeared in *Titus Andronicus* for four nights in 1839 at the Walnut St. Theatre in Philadelphia, playing the part of the hero to his wife's Lavinia. Although the play was advertised as 'retaining the language of the immortal Bard',[1] the following notice was printed on the playbill for 31 January: 'The manager, in announcing this play, adapted by N. H. Bannister from the language of Shakespeare alone, assures the public that every expression calculated to offend the ear, has been studiously avoided, and the play is presented for their decision with full confidence that it will merit their approbation.' The playbill for the following day announces that it has been received 'with the decided approbation of the audience'. Charles Durang later wrote that 'Bannister, with much tact and poetical conception, ably preserved the beauties of its poetry, the intensity of its incidents, which work up the plot and the argument by very judicious modifications. He excluded the horrors with infinite skill, yet preserved all the interest of the drama in the moral deductions that Shakspere ever draws in his dramas.'[2] It is unfortunate that we do not know exactly which horrors were excluded nor which offensive expressions were avoided.

Another American actor was responsible for the only production of *Titus Andronicus* in the British Isles during the nineteenth century. Ira Aldridge, 'the African Roscius', had come to England in 1824 or 1825 and had made a considerable reputation in such tragic roles as Oroonoko, Zanga, and Othello.[3] When he was acting Zanga in London at the Surrey Theatre in 1848 the *Douglas Jerrold Newspaper* (25 March) commented on the 'force and vigour

---

[1] Playbill for 28 January; this and the playbill for 31 January are in the Harvard Theatre Collection.

[2] *History of the Philadelphia Stage Between the Years 1749 and 1855*, arranged and illustrated by Thompson Westcott (1868), iv. 157. These volumes are in the Furness Shakespeare Library of the University of Pennsylvania.

[3] Herbert Marshall and Mildred Stock, *Ira Aldridge, the Negro Tragedian* (New York, 1958), p. 48.

Fig. 5. Ira Aldridge as Aaron in Act 4, Scene 2 of his adaptation

in his passionate enunciation' and on his 'natural dignity of movement' (Marshall and Stock, p. 163) and the *Illustrated London News* (1 April) spoke of his excellent voice, commanding figure, and expressive countenance, to which he added 'the advantages of education and study'. The reviewer for *The Sunday Times* (26 March) found that in the last moments of the play 'the late remorse of a noble heart was expressed with deep feeling and pathos'. Aldridge's interpretation apparently had some of the characteristics for which Quin was praised, but, unlike Quin, Aldridge was also said by *The Sunday Times* to be 'exceedingly natural'. As he looked for other roles to increase his repertoire he hit upon Aaron and seems to have decided to give the character some of the admirable qualities of Zanga, for in collaboration with C. A. Somerset, the author of many plays, including one called *Shakespeare's Early Days*, he made more drastic alterations in Shakespeare's play than Ravenscroft had done. According to *The Era* (26 April, 1857), 'Aaron is elevated into a noble and lofty character'. The rape and mutilation of Lavinia are omitted, Tamora is chaste though 'strongminded', Chiron and Demetrius are 'dutiful children', and only Saturninus is a truly villainous character (Marshall and Stock, p. 172). If the memory of one spectator is to be trusted, Aldridge and his collaborator even incorporated 'one great scene from a play called *Zaraffa, The Slave King* (written in Dublin for Mr. Aldridge)'.[1] This *rifacimento*, which was played in Scotland, Ireland, and the English provinces from 1849 to 1860, and at the Britannia Theatre in London in 1852 and 1857, was considered a highly successful vehicle for the actor. *The Sunday Times* (26 April 1857) said: 'The part of Aaron gives full scope to Mr. Aldridge for his fiery genius, and his delineation of the character is a master-piece of powerful and impressive acting.' An engraving of Aldridge (Fig. 5) shows Aaron in a heroic stance, a scimitar in his right hand, guarding his child, who lies at his feet (and who, in this version, had been stolen from him). Once again Aaron (however transformed) took over the play.

The reviewers for both *The Sunday Times* and *The Era* believed that the original play was unfit for presentation and should never have been ascribed to Shakespeare, though *The Sunday Times* found that the play was 'vigorously written' and *The Era* noted that Aldridge 'thoroughly appreciates the recondite beauties of the author, whenever they exist'. It is noteworthy that in these years, when the play was repellent to so many critics, performances elicited a grudging recognition of its poetic and dramatic force.

In the autumn of 1923 the Old Vic mounted a production of *Titus Andronicus* which was remarkable for several reasons. The play had not been seen in England in any form since the days of Ira Aldridge and not as Shakespeare wrote it since the early years of the Restoration. In the staging, as in the text, this production exemplified the renewed concern for authenticity characteristic of the period. The director, Robert Atkins, was a disciple of William Poel, who had led the revolt against the elaborately realistic scenery popular in the nineteenth century. In five seasons (1920–1 to 1924–5) Atkins staged *Pericles* and all but two of the First Folio plays[2] in a manner approximating to the Elizabethan. A false proscenium of black velvet with doors in each pediment had been constructed, leaving the acting space in front of it (but behind the

[1] J. J. Shehan in *N. & Q.*, IV, 10 (1872), 132.

[2] The exceptions were *Measure for Measure* and *Cymbeline*, which had been done at the Old Vic in 1918 with other directors.

curtain) as a kind of apron stage, on which, with a minimum of props, the action moved swiftly.[1] The style of the production can be guessed from Doris Westwood's description of the first moments; the set consisted of 'a tall flight of red steps leading up to red doors' with the senators in red robes stationed on the top steps and Saturninus and Bassianus on pedestals at the right and left of the foot of the stairs as the curtain rose. At the conclusion of Bassianus' speech the senators came down and began marching around the stage until they were interrupted by the arrival of Titus' triumphal procession, headed by dancing girls with tambourines and soldiers carrying a coffin.[2] Atkins obviously made the most of the opportunities for pageantry. Wilfred Walter as Titus gave a 'grand performance', according to Gordon Crosse,[3] though some critics found him monotonous; Hay Petrie won three lines of praise from Herbert Farjeon for his performance as the Clown, and the critics agreed that George Hayes was splendid as Aaron.[4] Atkins gave him a striking piece of business, presumably inspired by his boasting in the last act (5.1.112–17): at the end of 3.1 Hayes appeared 'to fill the vacant stage with peals of laughter' (Crosse, p. 79). While some critics were contemptuous of the play, Crosse found it 'thoroughly enjoyable' and Montague Summers, who was lyrical in praise of both the play and the performance, observed correctly that even the more reluctant critics acknowledged the power of the tragedy.[5]

During the same theatrical season, in the spring of 1924, some Yale students in the Alpha Delta Phi fraternity, which had a tradition of presenting the least frequently performed Elizabethan plays, put on *Titus Andronicus* under the direction of John M. Berdan and E. M. Woolley. The horrors which inhibited other producers recommended the play to this group, and the recollections of members of the cast suggest that full justice was done to them.[6] While there was extensive cutting in the middle of the play (in 3.2 and 3.4), the rest was left largely intact. The perfor-

[1] Harcourt Williams, *Old Vic Saga* (1949), p. 51.

[2] *These Players: A Diary of the 'Old Vic'* (1926), pp. 29, 31, 32, 37.

[3] *Fifty Years of Shakespearean Playgoing* (1941), p. 79.

[4] *The Times*, 9 October; *The Saturday Review*, 13 October; Crosse, p. 79; Westwood, p. 40.

[5] Introduction to his edition of John Downes, *Roscius Anglicanus* (1929), p. 127.

[6] I am indebted to Morris Tyler and James W. Cooper of Tyler, Cooper, Grant, Bowerman, & Keefe of New Haven, Connecticut, for sharing with me their recollections, a marked copy of the play, and a photograph of the cast.

mance was greeted with enthusiasm and, in ignorance of Bannister's production, was thought to be the first in America. C. F. Tucker Brooke, who believed that Shakespeare made only a few revisions in a 'striking but inartistic play', conceded that spectators could understand, as readers hardly could, 'what a tremendous interest the acted story developed'.[1]

With the exception of a production in Denver, Colorado, in 1928, the play was again absent from the theatre in England and America until 1951. Since that year there has been such a large number of performances that no adequate description of each one can be given here.[2] Discussion of certain kinds of twentieth-century production and of a few outstanding examples will suggest what seeing the play may contribute to its understanding. Its theatrical effectiveness, commented on repeatedly in this century as it was earlier, has undoubtedly been responsible in part for the wider acceptance of Shakespeare's authorship.

The gleeful emphasis on horrors in the Yale production has characterized several others as well. This is obviously one way of dealing with a conspicuous feature of the play, and it was the way chosen by Kenneth Tynan and Peter Myers when they made a thirty-minute version to be part of a programme of Grand Guignol at the Irving Theatre in London in 1951. Tamora's ferocity was applauded by the reviewers, and Harold Hobson (*Sunday Times*, 11 November 1951) found 'practically the whole company waving gory stumps and eating cannibal pies . . . really splendid'. This 'selection of the bloodier scenes' made the *Times* reviewer (7 November) wonder whether a first-class production of the original play 'might discover something in extenuation of its barbarities'. The remarkable elimination of Aaron, however, led J. C. Trewin to write in the *Illustrated London News* (24 November) that 'A "Titus" without the figure of Aaron the Moor can hardly be counted.' The sense of something missing was also Mel Gussow's response to a later production which emphasized horror. At the CSC Repertory in New York in 1972 Christopher Martin presented the play as Theatre of Cruelty, trimming the text by cutting 'to the gore and gristle', according to Gussow (*New York Times*, 9 February 1972).

---

[1] *Yale Daily News*, 15 April 1924, and see Brooke, *The Tudor Drama* (Boston, New York, and Chicago, 1911), p. 218.

[2] For an account of these performances see the comprehensive 'Stage History of *Titus Andronicus*' by G. Harold Metz, *Shakespeare Quarterly*, 28 (1977), 154–69.

As a result there were 'no seething rages or intellectualized furies, but a succession of chopped limbs and severed heads'. He knew from other productions that the play could be more than this. When the Bristol New Vic performed *Titus Andronicus* in 1978 the setting suggested a bear pit, according to Eric Shorter, where 'we sat more or less all round the horrid action and peered into a well of sub-Shakespearian sensations' (*Drama*, 129 (1978), 65–6). The best he could say of the experience was that it 'proved surprisingly unlaughable . . . until the closing cannibalistic supper' and that one remembered the intensity. It seems fair to conclude from these experiments that although the terrible violence of the play has a certain appeal to the sensibility which produced Antonin Artaud and then was influenced by him, productions which have concentrated on this element have not been entirely successful.

The Irving Theatre *Titus Andronicus* of 1951 also exemplifies the experimentation with extensive cutting which has characterized other productions. In 1957 the Old Vic put on an hour-and-a-half performance on a double bill with a much-cut *Comedy of Errors* as part of a five-year programme of producing again all the plays in the Folio. The setting was a 'nondescript wooden structure of steps and slats and basketry' on which an Elizabethan travelling company was supposed to be performing (*Theatre World*, June 1957, 7–8). Muriel St. Clare Byrne wrote that 'The dominant notes of Walter Hudd's workmanlike production were simplicity, speed and vigour. There was a suitable Elizabethan relish in the playing, and the costuming was credibly Elizabethan-theatrical, with a nice admixture of ruffs and breastplates' (*Shakespeare Quarterly*, 8 (1957), 463). Barbara Jefford as Tamora, Robert Helpmann as Saturninus, and Keith Michell as Aaron received the best notices, though one critic noted that Aaron raised a laugh with his final repentance for any good deed he might have done. The play was clearly presented as a historical reconstruction, and as such was received with respect if not enthusiasm.

John Barton took a somewhat similar tack in Stratford-upon-Avon in 1981 when he directed a version from which 850 lines had been cut. Again it was a double bill, this time with *The Two Gentlemen of Verona*, and again both Elizabethanism and theatricality were stressed. Stanley Wells noted that the small playing area was defined by coat-racks and property baskets, and that the actors, who seemed to be a group of touring players, were visible

Fig. 6. Peter Brook's production, Stratford-upon-Avon, 1955. Act 1, Scene 1 : Tamora (Maxine Audley) kneels before Titus (Laurence Olivier), watched by Lucius (Michael Denison) and Aaron (Anthony Quayle)

Fig. 7. Brook's production, 1955. Act 2, Scene 4: the mutilated Lavinia (Vivien Leigh) with Chiron (Kevin Miles) and Demetrius (Lee Montague)

throughout, sitting in the shadows when they were supposed to be off stage (TLS, 18 September, 1981). Both Wells and Michael Billington found moments of great theatrical power (*Guardian*, 5 September), and Wells thought that although the omissions detracted from the 'steady-paced grandeur' of other productions, the evening worked well. Ned Chaillet had more reservations. He thought laughter was occasionally courted by the open theatricality of hobby horses, the greenery representing the 'ruthless woods', and Titus' manic glee as he stirred up the pie (*The Times*, 4 September). The smiles of the 'offstage' actors seemed to him to undermine the seriousness of certain tragic moments, and the ultimate effect was 'partially to reclaim a relish in gory excess, and partially to bury genuine horrors'.

The landmark production of this century, with which all later ones have been, implicitly or explicitly, compared, was Peter Brook's at Stratford in 1955 with Laurence Olivier as Titus, Vivien Leigh as Lavinia, Anthony Quayle as Aaron, and Maxine Audley as Tamora. With this production all the Shakespeare plays had been seen at Stratford as they already had at the Old Vic. Not only did Peter Brook assemble a strong cast; he saw to it that every aspect of the production contributed to a single overwhelming impression which made this theatrical experience unforgettable. He designed the scenery and costumes and devised a musical accompaniment (in part electronic) which Muriel St. Clare Byrne well described as 'strangely horrible' and 'ominous' (*Theatre Notebook*, 10 (1955–6), 46). 'The staging was powerfully simple', as Richard David wrote: 'three great squared pillars, set angle-on to the audience, fluted, and bronzy-grey in colour. The two visible sides could be swung back, revealing inner recesses that might be used as entrances or, in the central pillar, as a two-storeyed inner stage' ('Drams of Eale', *Shakespeare Survey 10* (Cambridge, 1957), 126). Against this sombre background there were occasional notes of bright red, as in the robes of the senators, the rusty crimson of Titus' military garments in the first scene, or the interior walls of his house when Tamora visits him in disguise. Although Brook did not alter the text in the manner of Ravenscroft or Aldridge, he cut over 650 lines, combined the third-act 'banquet' with the first scene of Act 4, and rearranged the sequence of later scenes in that act.

Olivier's acting was universally admired. J. C. Trewin described him in the first scene:

When Titus appeared, in triumph from the Goths, he was a veteran white-haired warrior, a man desperately tired. The lines of his body drooped; his eyes, among the seamed crowsfeet, were weary. Standing in mid-stage like some crumbling limestone crag, he greeted Rome because it was a thing of custom, but there was no spring in his voice, no light . . . At once Titus became real to us; and, having fixed him as a man, Olivier was able to move out into a wider air, to expand him to something far larger than life-size, to fill the stage and theatre with a swell of heroic acting.[1]

His rendition of 'I am the sea' (3.1.224) was a striking example of this heroic acting, which reminded more than one critic of King Lear. Quayle's energy and versatility made him equally impressive in his villainous scheming and the defence of his baby. Like some of his predecessors, he showed what an eminently actable role it is. Vivien Leigh received her share of praise, and Maxine Audley was said to give a 'flaming splendour to Tamora's wickedness' (Byrne, p. 47). Of the style of the acting as a whole David wrote: 'It was as if the actors were engaged in a ritual at once fluent from habitual performance and yet still practised with concentrated attention' (p. 126).

The physical manifestation of the play's atrocities was muted: the severed heads were encased in baskets; the severed hand, decently wrapped, was carried not in Lavinia's teeth but in her arms; Chiron and Demetrius were murdered off-stage. Yet there was no diminution of the impression of horror. The entrance of the raped and mutilated Lavinia was a moment of extraordinary power, mentioned by most of the reviewers. Her arms swathed in gauze, with scarlet streamers attached to her mouth and wrists, she was left upstage by Chiron and Demetrius, considerably distanced from the audience. As Muriel Byrne said, 'Vivien Leigh, utterly motionless, fixed in despair, seemed the very incarnation of woe' (p. 47; see Fig. 7). Marcus' long Ovidian speech was cut, as if Brook were substituting visual for verbal effect – the transforming power of costume and lighting for that of metaphor and simile.

Commenting on the success *Titus Andronicus* enjoyed on the Continent when he took his production on tour, Peter Brook wrote: 'The real appeal of *Titus* (over theoretically "greater" plays like *Hamlet* and *Lear*) was that abstract – stylised – Roman – classical though it appeared to be, it was obviously for everyone in the

---

[1] *Shakespeare on the English Stage 1900–1964* (1964), pp. 235–6.

audience about the most modern of emotions – about violence, hatred, cruelty, pain – in a form that, because *unrealistic*, transcended the anecdote and became for each audience *quite abstract and thus totally real.*'[1] Jack E. Reese makes a persuasive argument that what Brook did was directly inspired by a 'formalization' already present in the text.[2]

In 1967 Gerald Freedman directed a remarkable production for Joseph Papp's Shakespeare Festival at the outdoor Delacorte Theatre in New York's Central Park. In determining the style of the production Freedman reacted against a realistic and updated staging earlier that year by Douglas Seale at the Center Stage in Baltimore, where costumes recalled Mussolini, the Nazis, and the Allied armies of World War II. For Freedman that production failed in its

effort to draw positive and obvious parallels between the violence and wholesale murder of our times and the time of Titus Andronicus. It failed by also bringing into play our sense of reality in terms of detail and literal time structure. 'How could Lavinia suffer such loss of blood and still live?' 'Why doesn't Marcus take her to a hospital instead of talking?' 'Titus can't really be cutting off his hand on stage – what a clever trick.' Such questions and concerns are obviously not those of the play or playwright, but they are inevitable if you are invoking a reality embedded in a contemporary parallel.[3]

Freedman sought instead to capture the audience's imagination 'in a snare of made-up theatre conventions':

The solution had to lie in a poetic abstraction of time and in vivid impressionistic images rather than in naturalistic action, and this led me to masks and music and ritual . . . The setting was non-literal but inspired by the forms and sense of decay and rot seen in the ruins of Roman antiquity. The costumes recreated an unknown people of a non-specific time. The inspiration was Roman-Byzantine and feudal Japanese . . . The music eschewed electronics, which though non-literal are distinctly of our time. What I needed were those sounds that are part of our inherited primitive consciousness . . . (p. 4)

---

[1] 'Search for Hunger', *Encore* (July–August, 1961), p. 16.

[2] 'The Formalization of Horror in *Titus Andronicus*', *Shakespeare Quarterly*, 21 (1970), 77–84.

[3] Introduction to the Folio Society edition (1970), p. 4; repr. in *Introductions to Shakespeare* (1977), p. 24.

Suggestions of the theatrical conventions of Greece and the Orient enabled him to avoid a kind of realism which might limit, rather than widen, the appeal of the play, and in seeking to shock in the manner of Grand Guignol might, paradoxically, 'appear ludicrous or stagey' (p. 3).

Ming Cho Lee's sets suggested the moon to one reviewer (*New York Times*, 10 August 1967). Their cool green and blue were at the opposite end of the spectrum from the bronze and red of Brook's scenes. Theoni Aldredge designed half-masks and long black and silver priest-like robes for the cast, who shared the stage with musicians playing percussive instruments. The slaughter at the final banquet was accomplished symbolically by a chorus enveloping each victim in a red cloth which unwound to reveal a black shroud. For some reviewers Freedman went too far in the direction of pure theatrical artifice; for Mildred Kuner 'Symbolism rather than gory realism was what made this production so stunning.'[1]

Although Freedman's production did not receive such unreserved acclaim as did Peter Brook's, it stands out from all others in accounts of twentieth-century productions. It is a curious fact that the actors of the principal roles in New York were praised in much the same terms as their opposite numbers in Stratford. Olympia Dukakis as Tamora was 'an almost impersonal force'; Moses Gunn as Aaron was both 'evil feasting upon itself' and a human father; Jack Hollander as Titus not only rose to the heroism of the role with impressive vocal power, but was even more impressively calm when grief left him nothing to say; Erin Martin conveyed 'the dumb grief of a creature trapped in a hostile, senseless world'.[2] The actors in both productions were praised for pushing their interpretations into the realm of the heroic or of the personification of abstractions such as evil, revenge, or grief, though, again in both cases, the interpreters of Titus and Aaron were also commended for bringing out the character's humanity. The achievement of somewhat comparable effects was doubtless due in part to the choice of both directors to bring out the suggestion of ritual present in the many ceremonious scenes, especially those of the first and last acts. This way of staging the play seems to have worked better than the attempt to make the physical horrors shocking in the

---

[1] *New York Times*, 10 August 1967; Mildred Kuner, 'The New York Shakespeare Festival, 1967', *Shakespeare Quarterly*, 18 (1967), 414.

[2] *New York Times*, 10 August; Kuner, pp. 414–15.

manner of Grand Guignol and these productions have therefore given support to critics who see the play as something more than Shakespeare's attempt to outdo his fellow playwrights in the 'tragedy of blood'. The 'something more' is not only the effectiveness of certain roles and certain scenes, noticed by reviewers of most productions, but also a coherence which bespeaks an informing idea such as the productions of Brook and Freedman successfully projected.

Reception and Interpretation

Critical response to productions is an invaluable aid in forming a proper appreciation of the worth of *Titus Andronicus*. Although there have been exceptionally long periods when it was not staged, strong performances or imaginative direction have always elicited, even from unsympathetic critics, some recognition of its dramatic viability and some indication of where its strength lies. Again and again reviewers have been struck by the spectacular opening scene, by the expression of Titus' agony in the third act, and by Aaron's blend of the diabolical and the paternal. The scenes of horror, sometimes viewed as assets, sometimes as liabilities, inevitably affect every review. It is a reasonable inference that the distinguishing qualities of this tragedy are related to Shakespeare's use of spectacle, to his characterization of Titus and Aaron, and to his treatment of the violence perpetrated by his revengers and counter-revengers.

Ceremonies provide an almost uninterrupted series of spectacles in the first act – the confrontation of Saturninus and Bassianus, the entrance of Titus drawn in a chariot in a procession which is both triumph and funeral, the sacrifice of Alarbus following the unsuccessful intercession of Tamora, the burial of Titus' sons, the election of an emperor, preparations for a wedding, the burial of Mutius after the successful intercession of his uncle and brothers, and the seeming reconciliation of the Andronici with Saturninus and Tamora. Another procession and another unsuccessful intercession mark the opening of the first scene of the third act, which closes as the Andronici formally vow revenge and file out, carrying the severed hand and heads. The most spectacular of the remaining ceremonies are the shooting of arrows with messages to the gods; the masque-like visitation of Tamora and her sons disguised as Revenge, Rape, Murder; the final banquet; and the election of Lucius as emperor to restore order in Rome. We know that for at least one viewer at the private performance in 1596 the *'monstre'*, or spectacle, was worth more than the *'sujet'* – the subject matter or theme (see above, p. 3), but on many in that age of dumb shows and welcoming pageants the contribution of the spectacles to the meaning of the play would not have been lost.[1] The ceremonies of triumph, sacrifice, burial, and election immediately establish the solemnity of public occasions on which an ideal political order is affirmed and individuals are valued to the extent that they support it. The repeated interruptions of the ceremonies suggest the fragility of that order while the mention of Titus' dead sons and the deaths of Alarbus and Mutius emphasize the terrible cost of maintaining it. More disturbing are the questions raised about Titus, the upholder of political order. In the moment commemorated by Henry Peacham's drawing, his rigidity as he rejects Tamora's plea for mercy contrasts unfavourably with her self-abasement and lends force to her anguished protest, 'O cruel, irreligious piety!' It is the virtue of this tableau to present simultaneously two very different ideas: of Titus, the pious father and devoted servant of Rome (an idea probably reinforced by some representation of the tomb of the Andronici behind Titus), and of the cruel conqueror, incapable of compassion.

Some of the potential meanings of the stage images in Act I derive from a dramatic tradition extending back to the 'first English tragedy', *Gorboduc* (1561), where the dangers of civil disorder are enacted in the fatal struggle between two brothers, co-heirs to the throne. In this play and in several of those that follow it a large share of the meaning is projected in dumb shows. In *Jocasta* (1566), for example, a play by Gascoigne and Kinwelmersh based on Euripides' *The Phoenician Women*, the overweening ambition of Eteocles, who seeks to wrest control of Thebes from his brother, is represented by a dumb show of the Egyptian King Sesostris, drawn about the stage in a splendid chariot by four conquered kings. In

[1] For detailed discussions of the spectacles see Alice Venezky, *Pageantry on the Shakespearean Stage* (New York, 1951), pp. 34–6, 200; Hamilton, pp. 73 ff.; G. K. Hunter, 'Flatcaps and Bluecoats: Visual Signs on the Elizabethan Stage', *Essays and Studies*, 33 (1980), pp. 18–21; Ann Haaker, *'Non sine causa*: The Use of Emblematic Method and Iconology in the Thematic Structure of *Titus Andronicus'*, *Research Opportunities in Renaissance Drama*, 13–14 (1970–1), 143–68; E. M. Waith, 'The Ceremonies of *Titus Andronicus'*, in *The Mirror up to Shakespeare*, pp. 159–70.

more than one play funeral processions signify the price of civil war.[1] Two of Shakespeare's immediate predecessors seem to have remembered the symbolism of King Sesostris – Marlowe in a famous scene of the second part of *Tamburlaine* (4.3) and Lodge in *The Wounds of Civil War* (3.3), where the Roman general Sulla enjoys a similar triumph. The ambiguities of Titus' behaviour in the opening scene are thus intensified by suggestions inherent in the images of the triumphal chariot and the funeral procession.

If stage images sometimes add to the complexity of meaning they also make the structure of the play more obvious by providing (often ironic) links between the scenes. The spectacle of the Gothic queen kneeling before Titus to beg mercy for her son (see Figs. 4 and 6) is followed shortly by the supplication of Titus' brother and sons for the burial of the son Titus has killed. In the next act Lavinia kneels before Tamora to ask for her protection, and in the third act it is Titus himself who kneels to the judges as he begs them to spare his sons.[2] The image of Marcus in the opening scene, standing above the hostile factions to calm them and to urge an orderly election of a new emperor is almost duplicated at the end of the play when he calms the tumult following the banquet and lays the groundwork for the election of his nephew as emperor.

In *Gorboduc* and the tragedies which followed it spectacle was combined (though often not integrated) with the various sorts of declamatory rhetoric which Wolfgang Clemen describes in *English Tragedy before Shakespeare* (1955). In the more academic plays the rhetorical style was often framed to remind the spectators of Senecan tragedy, and even in plays written for the public theatre Seneca and other admired authors in the classical or native traditions served as models for passages of formal rhetoric. In the plays of Shakespeare's immediate predecessors, Kyd and Marlowe, not only were rhetoric and spectacle more thoroughly integrated but much of the rhetoric was in a more informal mode approaching that of conversation. In *Titus Andronicus*, although there are few set pieces of the sort found in earlier tragedies, two kinds of formal rhetoric occur with some frequency. One is what may be called the mode of public address, in which most of the dialogue of the first

---

[1] I discuss this tradition at greater length in '*Titus Andronicus* and the Wounds of Civil War', in *Literary Theory and Criticism*, ed. Joseph P. Strelka (forthcoming).

[2] See Judith M. Karr, 'The Pleas in *Titus Andronicus*', *Shakespeare Quarterly*, 14 (1963), 278–9.

act is written. The orotund style of this sequence of political speeches, pleas, prayers, and pronouncements is determined as much by the material as by the conventions of blank-verse tragedy. It is similar to the style used for such speeches in contemporary history plays, including Shakespeare's *Henry VI* trilogy. Another kind of formal rhetoric is closely related to Shakespeare's non-dramatic writing during these years, *Venus and Adonis* and *Lucrece*. Here Ovid is the prime source and influence. Tamora's seductive speech to Aaron (2.3.10–29), the only passage in the play that J. M. Mason[1] was willing to attribute to Shakespeare, is in the style of Ovidian love poetry and includes one specific parallel with *Venus and Adonis* (see note on l. 19). Even more markedly Ovidian are the lines Marcus addresses to his niece when he finds her in the forest (2.4.11–57). The discrepancy between the poetry and the spectacle of the raped and mutilated Lavinia is blatant and has been much discussed. For Nicholas Brooke the speech 'stands in the place of a choric commentary on that crime, establishing its significance to the play by making an emblem of the mutilated woman'.[2] Emphasizing the emblematic nature of both the poetry and the visual image in this scene, Brooke makes a persuasive argument that the combination, whether or not it is successful, is deliberate and characteristic of the play as a whole, which he regards as a stylistic experiment.

If the success of the experiment in 2.4 remains in doubt, a somewhat comparable experiment in 1.1 clearly succeeds. When Titus commits the bodies of his sons to the family tomb we are keenly aware of a discrepancy between the serenity of his solemn rhetoric and the unfeeling cruelty he has just shown to Tamora, who remains on stage as an observer. Titus' formally patterned words express an admirable contempt of a world where man is inhumane to man:

> In peace and honour rest you here, my sons,
> Rome's readiest champions, repose you here in rest,
> Secure from worldly chances and mishaps!
> Here lurks no treason, here no envy swells,

[1] John Monck Mason, *Comments on the Last Edition of Shakespeare's Plays* (Dublin, 1785), p. 306.

[2] *Shakespeare's Early Tragedies* (1968), p. 18; for other discussions of the Ovidian influence see Bradbrook, pp. 104–10; Waith, 'Metamorphosis', 39–49; Robert S. Miola, '*Titus Andronicus* and the Mythos of Shakespeare's Rome', *Shakespeare Studies*, 14 (1981), 85–98.

> Here grow no damnèd drugs, here are no storms,
> No noise, but silence and eternal sleep.
> In peace and honour rest you here, my sons!
>
> (1.1.150–6)

These noble wishes for the dead are directed back to their author by Lavinia as she enters: 'In peace and honour live Lord Titus long; . . .' The effectiveness of the passage, due in part to insistent repetition, is heightened by our ironic awareness that the hero's nobility is not quite all that it seems to be. Here response to the situation is enriched, rather than confused, by cross-currents of feeling.

Some of the most impressive poetry in the play lies outside the category of formal rhetoric. It can best be illustrated by some of Titus' speeches in 3.1. Both striking imagery and aphoristic economy lend force to his bitter outburst:

> Why, foolish Lucius, dost thou not perceive
> That Rome is but a wilderness of tigers?
> Tigers must prey, and Rome affords no prey
> But me and mine.
>
> (3.1.53–6)

A closely related image serves to express his grief for Lavinia a moment later:

> For now I stand as one upon a rock,
> Environed with a wilderness of sea.
>
> (ll. 93–4)

This speech is in turn linked by imagery to one of the most memorable speeches in the play, where Titus says:

> If the winds rage, doth not the sea wax mad,
> Threat'ning the welkin with his big-swoll'n face?
> And wilt thou have a reason for this coil?
> I am the sea.
>
> (ll. 221–4)

More than one reviewer commented on Laurence Olivier's moving rendition of this passage. When, at the conclusion of his speech, Titus is presented with the heads of his sons, eloquence is achieved not by the articulate expression of emotion but by the surprising brevity and seeming irrelevance of his question, 'When will this fearful slumber have an end?' (l. 251). Still more chilling is his burst of laughter when Marcus says: 'Now is a time to storm; why art thou still?' (l. 262).

Shakespeare's stylistic experiments in *Titus Andronicus* are not totally different from those of dramatists such as Kyd or even the author of *Locrine*, who combine the ornate with the simple, the learned with the popular, but the most successful of Shakespeare's experiments are more adventurous and result in moments of greater dramatic power. The intensity experienced by audiences at the productions by Peter Brook and Gerald Freedman was attributable not simply to the directors but also to the play.

A proper appreciation of the function of spectacle in the play thus leads naturally to the connection between spectacle and poetry, and finally to a greater awareness of a structure which they both support. The valuable studies of the play's structure by Hereward T. Price and by Ruth Nevo have been mentioned above in the section on Authorship (p. 19). Alan Sommers has shown how the structure is based on a contrast between Roman civilization and Gothic barbarism epitomized in Titus' line, 'Rome is but a wilderness of tigers' (3.1.54).[1] The fact that so much of both poetry and spectacle is clearly related to this central image goes far toward explaining the intensity achieved by sensitive directors.

The great majority of characters in *Titus Andronicus*, however clearly they are delineated, have only one facet. In this regard Titus and Aaron differ from the rest. The most conspicuous aspect of Shakespeare's characterization of his hero is the contradictions it contains. The spectacular scenes of the first act show both his devotion to Rome and cruel inflexibility, his pride and self-depreciation, his good intentions and faulty judgement. His insensitivity to Tamora's plea is matched by his blindness to the difference between Saturninus and Bassianus. Our response to his story is complicated not only by this contradictory mixture of characteristics but by the disproportion between his faults and the price he is made to pay for them. The sheer malevolence of his enemies, Tamora, Saturninus, and Aaron, leads to the outrages which make Titus a wholly sympathetic figure by the end of the third act. At that very moment, however, his obsession with revenge turns him into a madman, whom we watch with shocked

[1] '"Wilderness of Tigers": Structure and Symbolism in *Titus Andronicus*', *Essays in Criticism*, 10 (1960), 275–89.

amazement. His heroism is undeniable even though inseparable from horrifying fantasy. Laurence Olivier's performance showed how thoroughly this character can engage the feelings of the audience.

The fascination of Aaron, the other character who has repeatedly succeeded on the stage, derives from several sources. Most conspicuously, he is an embodiment of evil, his blackness readily seen as emblematic.[1] Long before he says a word or commits the first of the villainies of which he later boasts, he is ominously present on the stage. His aspiring soliloquy at the opening of the second act has, therefore, the effect of a carefully prepared entrance. That this sinister figure should become the chief engineer of the plots against the Andronici is less surprising on the stage than when the play is read.

The ingenuity of Aaron's schemes and his sheer vitality in carrying them out give him the ambiguous appeal of a Richard III, whose cleverness can be seen as admirable even though his downfall is desired. When such characters are presented from a comic perspective there is an even greater temptation to suspend moral judgement and join in their cruel laughter at the expense of their victims.[2] Shakespeare offers precisely this temptation in the first scene of the fifth act, where Aaron tells of his trickery with the relish of a Volpone. In so doing he becomes no less villainous but, for the moment, undeniably more attractive.

The two occasions on which Aaron defends his baby, first from Chiron and Demetrius (4.2) and later from Lucius (5.1), also affect response to the villain. Although the baby is further evidence of his wrongdoing, his spirited defence of it in the first scene and his bargaining with Lucius in the second project his humanity as a father in a memorable fashion, and thus give an additional complexity and solidity to the character (see Nevo, pp. 16–17). The comments on these scenes by numerous reviewers testify to their importance in making Aaron's role effective.

[1] See Eldred Jones, *Othello's Countrymen* (Oxford, 1965), pp. 49–60; G. K. Hunter, 'Othello and Colour Prejudice', *Proceedings of the British Academy*, 53 (1967), 139–49; Lemuel A. Johnson, *The Devil, the Gargoyle, and the Buffoon* (Port Washington, N.Y., and London, 1969), pp. 41–4.

[2] See Erich Segal, 'Marlowe's *Schadenfreude*', in *Veins of Humor*, ed. Harry Levin (Cambridge, Mass., 1972), 69–91; Richard Brucher, '"Tragedy, Laugh On": Comic Violence in *Titus Andronicus*', *Renaissance Drama*, NS 10 (1979), 71–91; Brooke, p. 37; E. M. Waith, 'The Appeal of the Comic Deceiver', *Yearbook of English Studies*, 12 (1982), 13–23 (p. 21).

Titus and Aaron are the poles of the contrast between civilization and barbarism which underlies the structure of the play.
Titus is the noble Roman father for whom it is pleasing and proper
to give up everything *pro patria*, Aaron the barbarian to whom the
exploitation of his environment comes as naturally as to a tiger.
Yet during the play Rome becomes 'a wilderness of tigers', and a
savage ferocity latent in even the noblest of the characters leads
him to commit the bloodiest of the crimes performed on stage.
Meanwhile, as Titus is being dehumanized by his commitment to
revenge, another equally surprising transformation takes place as
the barbaric Goths turn against their queen and Aaron and embrace the cause of the Andronici. Under Lucius they march on
Rome and become, as Ronald Broude says, 'instruments in Rome's
regeneration'.[1] At the end, with Titus dead and the death of Aaron
imminent, the healing process begins with the election of Lucius,
in whom the best of Titus' characteristics are preserved, as the new
emperor.

In presenting Titus and Aaron in such a way that each one elicits
varied, and even contradictory, responses, Shakespeare, possibly
influenced by Marlowe, created two roles on which he was to write
several variations. King Lear and Coriolanus are as clearly de-
scended from Titus as Richard III and Edmund are from Aaron.
From the vantage point of the later plays part of the interest in the
first tragedy lies in the examples it contains of Shakespeare's
manipulation of response to both heroes and villains.

Of the shocking violence of *Titus Andronicus* various explanations have been offered. There was certainly a tradition of bloody
incidents on the Elizabethan stage: in *Cambises* a man is supposed
to be flayed on stage; several murders are performed in *The Spanish
Tragedy* and the protagonist bites out his tongue. (We even have
information on how such horrors may have been performed on the
Elizabethan stage: see Fig. 8 and note on 3.1.190.) Shakespeare,
it is said, may have decided to outdo his predecessors. It would be
surprising if some such thought had not crossed the mind of a man
of the theatre, but it is a totally inadequate explanation of the
horrors in this play. In performance, as we have seen, they have
been valued most when they least resembled Grand Guignol and
took on a broader, even a symbolic, meaning. Some commentators
would claim that this perception was the product of a modern

[1] 'Roman and Goth in *Titus Andronicus*', *Shakespeare Studies*, 6 (1970), p. 31.

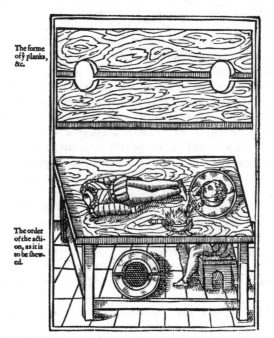

The forme of ẏ planks, &c.

The order of the acti- on, as it is to be shew- ed.

To cut off one's head, and to lay it in a platter, etc., which the jugglers call the decollation of John Baptist

To show a most notable execution by this art, you must cause a board, a cloth, and a platter to be purposely made, and in each of them holes fit for a boy's neck. The board must be made of two planks, the longer and broader the better; there must be left within half a yard of the end of each plank half a hole, so as both planks being thrust together, there may remain two holes, like to the holes in a pair of stocks; there must be made likewise a hole in the table-cloth or carpet. A platter also must be set directly over or upon one of them, having a hole in the middle thereof of the like quantity, and also a piece cut out of the same so big as his neck, through which his head may be conveyed into the midst of the platter; and then sitting or kneeling under the board, let the head only remain upon the board in the same. Then (to make the sight more dreadful) put a little brimstone into a chafing-dish of coals, setting it before the head of the boy, who must gasp two or three times so as the smoke enter a little into his nostrils and mouth (which is not unwholesome) and the head presently will appear stark dead, if the boy set his countenance accordingly; and if a little blood be sprinkled on his face, the sight will be the stranger.

This is commonly practised with a boy instructed for that purpose, who, being familiar and conversant with the company, may be known as well by his face as by his apparel. In the other end of the table, where the like hole is made, another boy of the bigness of the known boy must be placed, having upon him his usual apparel; he must lean or lie upon the board, and must put his head under the board through the said hole so as his body shall seem to lie on the one end of the board, and his head shall lie in a platter on the other end. ¶ There are other things which might be performed in this action, the more to astonish the beholders, which because they offer long descriptions, I omit: as to put about his neck a little dough kneaded with bullock's blood, which being cold will appear like dead flesh, and being pricked with a sharp round hollow quill, will bleed, and seem very strange, etc. ¶ Many rules are to be observed herein, as to have the table-cloth so long and wide as it may almost touch the ground. ¶ Not to suffer the company to stay too long in the place, etc.

Fig. 8. From Reginald Scot's *Discovery of Witchcraft* (1584), Book 13

sensibility and that 'the Elizabethan audience' delighted in gore for its own sake. It has often been pointed out that there were bloody public executions and that animal-baiting was a popular sport. The implication seems to be that Shakespeare, knowing what kind of audience he would have in the public theatre, catered to the crudity of their taste. But there is no longer any good reason to suppose that the unlettered groundling dominated the audience of the public theatre. As Ann Jennalie Cook says, 'the social and economic realities of Renaissance London decreed an audience more privileged than plebeian'.[1] Privileged playgoers may also have attended public executions and bear-gardens, and familiarity with the sight of blood may have made them more tolerant of stage-blood than most modern audiences, but it is hard to believe that they went to the theatre for this sort of thrill, and therefore unnecessary to suppose that playwrights felt compelled to provide it. It is much more reasonable to assume that Shakespeare, accepting the popular convention of on-stage violence, used it to support the leading ideas of his tragedy. His use of an elevated poetic style and his frequent references to classical literature suggest that he was writing for a mainly literate audience.

The most satisfying comments on the atrocities have come from those who have explored their relationship to the patterns of ideas and images which dominate the play. Nicholas Brooke does so in an essay already referred to. In two articles Albert Tricomi brings out the motif of mutilation in the imagery, and Huston Diehl writes of the symbolic significance of dismemberment and the cannibalistic banquet.[2] Emphasizing Aaron's sardonic humour, Richard Brucher contrasts this 'comic savagery' with 'the apparently sane Roman values of Lucius and Marcus' (Brucher, p. 80). The approach of these critics to the play's horrors has the advantage of corresponding to the experience of spectators for whom they were not simply horrors. Muriel Byrne, seeing the mutilated Lavinia in the Peter Brook production as 'the very incarnation of woe', clearly saw the terrible image as part of a larger pattern. When

[1] *The Privileged Playgoers of Shakespeare's London, 1576–1642* (Princeton, 1981), p. 271.
[2] Albert H. Tricomi, 'The Aesthetics of Mutilation in "Titus Andronicus"', *Shakespeare Survey 27* (Cambridge, 1974), 11–19; 'The Mutilated Garden in *Titus Andronicus*', *Shakespeare Studies*, 9 (1976), 89–105; Huston Diehl, 'The Iconography of Violence in English Renaissance Tragedy', *Renaissance Drama*, NS 11 (1980), 36–8.

Shakespeare wrote *Titus Andronicus* he did not have the easy assurance with which he later related the no-less terrible blinding of
Gloucester to the central themes of *King Lear* – 'I have no way, and
therefore want no eyes; I stumbled when I saw' (4.1.18–19) – but
he was writing in the same mode.

His strategies for presenting the most shocking episodes differ
considerably. If the horror of Lavinia's lacerated body is somewhat
distanced by the Ovidian poetry which denies immediacy to Marcus' emotions, nothing comes between the audience and the brutal
maiming of Titus. This is part of the series of intolerable injuries
which drive him beyond the bounds of reasonable control and
transform him into an obsessed revenger. After the refusal of the
judges to hear his plea for his sons comes his encounter with
Lavinia, treated in a totally different way from Marcus' encounter
in the preceding scene. Here horror and grief are given direct
expression: 'My grief was at the height before thou cam'st, | And
now like Nilus it disdaineth bounds' (3.1.70–1). If the audience is
to sense fully the effect on Titus of his enemies' cruelty, the horrors
of this scene cannot be muted. Thus the sight of his daughter is
followed by the loss of his hand and the return of the hand with the
heads of his sons. The accumulation of these atrocities supports
Marcus' statement, 'These miseries are more than may be borne'
(l. 242). The hero's transition into madness is marked not only by
his shocking laughter (3.1.263) but also by the grotesquerie of his
asking Lavinia to carry his severed hand in her teeth. The
likelihood that her actually doing so would be ludicrous has
troubled directors (Peter Brook altered the business) and may have
led Shakespeare himself or an early reviser to make an alteration
in the manuscript which produced a textual crux in Q1 (see note
on 3.1.280). Yet a combination of the ludicrous and the horrible
may have been intended. It is common enough in portrayals of
insane fantasies and is present in at least two later scenes in this
play: in one the Clown is sent to his death for delivering Titus' letter
(4.4); in another Titus enters costumed as a cook to serve the pasty
made of the Empress' sons (5.3). Somewhat similar in effect is
Aaron's murder of the Nurse, making fun of her cries. The mockery
accompanying this piece of violence testifies, not to the heartless-
ness of a madman, but to the moral imperviousness of the man
who also found the maiming of Titus laughable.

Brutal violence, occasionally tinged with comedy, serves several artistic purposes. It represents the political and moral degeneration of Rome when Saturninus becomes emperor. It also plays a major part in the presentation of the hero's metamorphosis into a cruel revenger. While no artistic device can be called inevitable, one can say with some assurance that Shakespeare's use of violence in *Titus Andronicus* is far from gratuitous. It is an integral part of his dramatic technique.

Consideration of the features of the play on which spectators most frequently comment continually suggests resemblances to the later tragedies and also to the contemporary history plays and narrative poems. These resemblances constitute a special attraction for students of Shakespeare, but even more important for an assessment of the worth of *Titus Andronicus* is the way in which each of the features we have examined supports the others and thus contributes to a single effect. However inferior this first of Shakespeare's tragedies may be to its successors, it is not the inchoate essay that it is sometimes thought to be. Experimental in style, it moves, unevenly at times, but often powerfully, toward a disaster for which the cause is established in the first minutes of action.

EDITORIAL PROCEDURES

EXCEPT for 3.2, for which the Folio is the only authority, the basis for the text of this edition is Q1. Spelling and punctuation have been modernized in accordance with the principles of the Oxford Shakespeare, described by Stanley Wells in *Modernizing Shakespeare's Spelling* (Oxford, 1979) and by Gary Taylor in his edition of *Henry V* (Oxford, 1982). The aim is to modernize more consistently than has been done in the past, with the result that what some editors would have preserved as distinctive Elizabethan forms of words have been treated here as variant spellings and have been altered. The object of modernization is to remove some of the differences between the experience of the modern reader and that of the reader for whom the text was printed. We cannot make ourselves into Elizabethan readers or spectators, and we should welcome the challenge to participate imaginatively in a period when the language differed somewhat from that spoken today, but the important differences are not those of spelling, and we should not be encouraged to confuse the quaintly archaic with the spirit of the times. Such alterations are not recorded unless they have been disputed or appear to be disputable, in which case they appear in the collations in this form:

swarthy] Q1 (swartie)

where the spelling of the control text is given in round brackets. In this edition the syllabic form of the past participle is indicated by an accent ('èd') and the non-syllabic form by the absence of that accent. The distinction between the two is based on Q1, which normally spells the non-syllabic form without an 'e' (e.g. 'kild' for 'killed'). Except in the case of this distinction, no attempt has been made to mark accentuations required by the metre, but in the notes the reader's attention is called to certain categories of words, such as those ending in '-tion', of which the pronunciation varies. One other convention should be noted: when 'and' means 'if', either by itself or in the phrase 'and if', it is silently changed to 'an' for the sake of clarity.

Departures from the original punctuation are noted only when they affect the meaning, as, for example, when a full stop is replaced by a comma or semicolon, or when the punctuation of the control text makes it uncertain whether a subordinate clause depends on a main clause preceding or following it. In such cases the modernized punctuation is treated as an emendation, recorded in the collations, and often discussed in the notes.

Speech prefixes have been silently normalized and are given in full. Significant variations in the copy text, such as '*Emperour*' or '*King*' for Saturninus, are noted in the collations, but not variant spellings such as Q1 'Aron' (throughout) or 'Bascianus' (here and there). The stage directions of F1 have often been adopted on the assumption that this text was based on prompt copy, and the directions of both Q1 and F1 have often been amplified for the sake of clarity. In many instances further directions have been added. All alterations of Q1's stage directions are recorded in the collations except for directions for a speech to be spoken 'aside' or 'to' another character; all of these (except for the '*Aside*' at 4.4.34) are to be understood as editorial; a dash is used to mark the end of an aside. Added stage directions are not bracketed if the specified action is clearly implied in the dialogue, nor are they attributed to a particular edition except in the case of directions added in the Folio. When the indications of action are sufficiently obvious in the dialogue no stage direction is added. Only stage directions which are editorial guesses are bracketed, and if the guess is a previous editor's, the attribution is given.

With the exception of the stage directions noted above ('aside' or 'to . . .'), all emendations (as distinguished from modernization) of the copy texts are recorded in the collations in the traditional form:

Pantheon] F2; Pathan Q1

where the lemma, representing the reading of this edition, is followed by the symbol for the source of the reading, and, after a semicolon, by the rejected reading of the control text. Citations of the early texts in the collations are given *literatim*, and preserve the early use of u, v, i, and j, but usually not long s nor the various ligatures. Rejected emendations in other editions are not recorded unless a strong case can be made for them. When the adopted reading is substantially, but not exactly, that of the edition from which it it taken, this fact is indicated by either '*subs.*' or the exact reading in round brackets following reference to the source:

1.1] F (*Actus Primus, Scoena Prima.*); *not in* Q1   *with attendant*] CAPELL (*subs.*); *not in* Q1

The indication '*not in* Q1', following attribution to a later edition, carries the further information that the reading is not in any intervening edition.

References to other plays of Shakespeare are keyed to Peter Alexander's edition (1951). Quotations in the commentary and introduction from the works of his contemporaries are normally taken from modern-spelling editions; when the original editions have been used, spelling and punctuation have been modernized except where reproduction of early documentary evidence (Stationers' Register entries, Henslowe's diary, title-pages) seemed desirable. There appears to be no good reason for treating the texts used to illuminate Shakespeare differently from the text of Shakespeare.

In calling attention to the many proverbs quoted or alluded to in the text of this play, I frequently give the form of a proverb as it appears in the *Oxford Dictionary of English Proverbs* or in M. P. Tilley's *Dictionary*, but do not do so when the form quoted in the play is almost identical.

Words are normally defined only when they first appear. All words that are glossed are listed in the index.

Abbreviations and References

EDITIONS OF SHAKESPEARE

Place of publication is London unless otherwise noted.

Q1	The First Quarto (1594)
Q2	The Second Quarto (1600)
Q3	The Third Quarto (1611)
F	The First Folio (1623)
F2	The Second Folio (1632)
F3	The Third Folio (1663)
F4	The Fourth Folio (1685)
Baildon	*Titus Andronicus*, ed. H. B. Baildon, The Arden Shakespeare (1912)
Barnet	*Titus Andronicus*, ed. Sylvan Barnet, The Signet Classic Shakespeare (New York, 1963)
Bevington	*Complete Works*, ed. David Bevington (Glenview, Ill., 1980)

73

Cambridge	*Works*, ed. W. G. Clark and W. A. Wright, The Cambridge Shakespeare, 9 vols. (Cambridge, 1863–6)
Capell	*Comedies, Histories, and Tragedies*, ed. Edward Capell, 10 vols. (1767–8)
Dyce	*Works*, ed. Alexander Dyce, 6 vols. (1857)
Dyce 1866	*Works*, ed. Alexander Dyce, 2nd edn., 9 vols. (1864–7); vol. 6 (1866)
Folio Society	*Titus Andronicus*, intro. by Gerald Freedman (1970)
Globe	*Works*, ed. W. G. Clark and W. A. Wright, The Globe Shakespeare (1864)
Hanmer	*Works*, ed. Thomas Hanmer, 6 vols. (Oxford, 1743–4)
Hudson	*Works*, ed. H. N. Hudson, 11 vols. (Boston, 1851–6)
Kittredge	*Complete Works*, ed. G. L. Kittredge (Boston, 1936)
Malone	*Plays and Poems*, ed. Edmond Malone, 10 vols. (1790)
Maxwell	*Titus Andronicus*, ed. J. C. Maxwell, new Arden Shakespeare (1953)
Maxwell 1961	*Titus Andronicus*, ed. J. C. Maxwell, new Arden Shakespeare, 3rd edn. (1961)
Munro	*The London Shakespeare*, ed. John Munro, 6 vols. (1957)
Pope	*Works*, ed. Alexander Pope, 6 vols. (1723–5)
Ravenscroft	*Titus Andronicus, or the Rape of Lavinia* (1687)
Riverside	*The Riverside Shakespeare*, textual editor G. B. Evans (Boston, 1974)
Rowe	*Works*, ed. Nicholas Rowe, 6 vols. (1709)
Rowe 1714	*Works*, ed. Nicholas Rowe, 8 vols. (1714)
Steevens	*Plays*, ed. Samuel Johnson and George Steevens, 10 vols. (1773)
Steevens 1803	*Plays*, ed. Samuel Johnson and George Steevens, 3rd edn., revised by Isaac Reed, 21 vols. (1803)
Theobald	*Works*, ed. Lewis Theobald, 7 vols. (1733)
Wilson	*Titus Andronicus*, ed. J. Dover Wilson, The New Shakespeare (Cambridge, 1948)

OTHER WORKS

| Adams | *Shakespeare's Titus Andronicus: The First Quarto, 1594*, introduction by J. Q. Adams (New York and London, 1936) |
| Arber | E. Arber, *A Transcript of the Registers of the Company of Stationers of London 1554–1640*, Text, 4 vols. (1875–7) |

Bolton	Joseph S. G. Bolton, 'The Authentic Text of *Titus Andronicus*', *PMLA*, 44 (1929), 776–80
Bradbrook	M. C. Bradbrook, *Shakespeare and Elizabethan Poetry* (1951; repr. Cambridge, 1979)
Braekman	W. Braekman, 'The Relationship of Shakespeare's *Titus Andronicus* to the German Play of 1620 and to Jan Vos's *Aran en Titus*', *Studia Germanica Gandensia*, 9 (1967), 9–117, and 10 (1968), 9–65
Brennecke	Ernest and Henry Brennecke, *Shakespeare in Germany* (Chicago, 1964)
Broude	Ronald Broude, 'Roman and Goth in *Titus Andronicus*', *Shakespeare Studies*, 6 (1970), 27–34
Brucher	Richard Brucher, '"Tragedy Laugh On": Comic Violence in *Titus Andronicus*', *Renaissance Drama*, NS 10 (1979), 71–92
Bullough	*Narrative and Dramatic Sources of Shakespeare*, ed. Geoffrey Bullough, 8 vols. (1964–75)
Cercignani	Fausto Cercignani, *Shakespeare's Works and Elizabethan Pronunciation* (Oxford, 1981)
Chambers, *Shakespeare*	E. K. Chambers, *William Shakespeare*, 2 vols. (Oxford, 1930)
Chambers, *Stage*	E. K. Chambers, *The Elizabethan Stage*, 4 vols. (Oxford, 1923)
Crosse	Gordon Crosse, *Fifty Years of Shakespearean Playgoing* (1941)
Dent	Robert W. Dent, *Shakespeare's Proverbial Language: an Index* (Berkeley, Calif., 1981)
EETS	Early English Text Society
Eyre and Rivington	G. E. B. Eyre and G. R. Rivington, *A Transcript of the Registers of the Worshipful Company of Stationers 1640–1708*, 3 vols. (1913–14)
Greg, *Bibliography*	W. W. Greg, *A Bibliography of the English Printed Drama to the Restoration*, 4 vols. (1939–59); vol. 1 (1939)
Greg, *Folio*	W. W. Greg, *The Shakespeare First Folio* (Oxford, 1955)
Hamilton	A. C. Hamilton, *The Early Shakespeare* (San Marino, Calif., 1967)
Henslowe's Diary	*Henslowe's Diary*, ed. R. A. Foakes and R. T. Rickert (Cambridge, 1961)

75

Hunter, 'Flatcaps'   G. K. Hunter, 'Flatcaps and Bluecoats: Visual Signs
on the Elizabethan Stage', *Essays and Studies*, 33 (1980),
16–47

Hunter, 'Sources'   G. K. Hunter, 'The "Sources" of *Titus Andronicus* –
once again', *N. & Q.*, 228 (1983), 114–16

Hunter, 'Sources and Meanings'   G. K. Hunter, 'Sources and Meanings
in *Titus Andronicus*', *The Mirror up to Shakespeare*, pp.
171–88

Jackson   Macdonald P. Jackson, *Studies in Attribution: Middleton and
Shakespeare*, Salzburg Studies in English Literature (Salzburg, 1979)

Jones   Emrys Jones, *The Origins of Shakespeare* (Oxford, 1977)

Kalendar of Shepherds   *Kalendar and Compost of Shepherds* [1518], ed.
G. C. Heseltine (1930)

London Stage   *The London Stage, 1660–1800*, Part I: 1660–1700, ed.
W. Van Lennep (Carbondale, Ill., 1965); Part II:
1700–1729, ed. E. Avery (Carbondale, Ill., 1960)

Manifold   J. S. Manifold, *The Music of English Drama* (1956)

Marshall and Stock   Herbert Marshall and Mildred Stock, *Ira Aldridge, the
Negro Tragedian* (New York, 1958)

Mirror up to Shakespeare   *The Mirror up to Shakespeare*, ed. J. C. Gray
(Toronto, 1983)

Nevo   Ruth Nevo, 'Tragic Form in *Titus Andronicus*', *Further
Studies in English Language and Literature*, ed. A. A. Mendilow (Jerusalem, 1975), 1–18

Nørgaard   Holger Nørgaard, 'Never Wrong But With Just Cause',
English Studies, 45 (1964), 138–9

ODEP   *Oxford Dictionary of English Proverbs*, 3rd edn., revised by
F. P. Wilson (Oxford, 1970)

OED   *Oxford English Dictionary*, 12 vols. and supplement
(Oxford, 1933)

Onions   C. T. Onions, *A Shakespeare Glossary*, 2nd edn. (1919;
repr. Oxford, 1953)

Parrott   T. M. Parrott, 'Shakespeare's Revision of "Titus
Andronicus"', *Modern Language Review*, 14 (1919),
16–37

Robertson, *Canon*   J. M. Robertson, *An Introduction to the Study of the
Shakespeare Canon* (1924)

Taylor and Warren   Gary Taylor and Michael Warren, eds., *The Division of the Kingdoms: Shakespeare's Two Versions of 'King Lear'* (Oxford, 1983)

Tilley   M. P. Tilley, *A Dictionary of the Proverbs in England in the Sixteenth and Seventeenth Centuries* (Ann Arbor, 1950)

Ungerer   Gustav Ungerer, 'An Unrecorded Elizabethan Performance of *Titus Andronicus*', *Shakespeare Survey 14* (Cambridge, 1961), 102–9.

Waith, 'Metamorphosis'   E. M. Waith, 'The Metamorphosis of Violence in *Titus Andronicus*', *Shakespeare Survey 10* (Cambridge, 1957), 39–49

Walker   W. S. Walker, *A Critical Examination of the Text of Shakespeare*, 3 vols. (1860)

Wilson, 'Stage'   J. Dover Wilson, '"Titus Andronicus" on the Stage in 1595', *Shakespeare Survey 1* (Cambridge, 1948), 17–22

Titus Andronicus

THE PERSONS OF THE PLAY

SATURNINUS, son of the late Emperor of Rome, afterwards Emperor

BASSIANUS, his brother

TITUS ANDRONICUS, Roman general, victorious over the Goths

MARCUS ANDRONICUS, his brother, a tribune

LUCIUS

QUINTUS

MARTIUS } his sons

MUTIUS

LAVINIA, his daughter

YOUNG LUCIUS, a boy, son of Lucius

PUBLIUS, son of Marcus

SEMPRONIUS

CAIUS } Titus' kinsmen

VALENTINE

AEMILIUS, a noble Roman

TAMORA, Queen of the Goths, afterwards Empress of Rome

ALARBUS

DEMETRIUS } her sons

CHIRON

AARON, a Moor, her lover

NURSE

CLOWN

MESSENGER

Senators, Tribunes, Roman Soldiers, Attendants, other Romans, Goths

1.1   ⌈*Flourish.*⌉ *Enter the Tribunes and Senators aloft; and*
       then enter below Saturninus and his followers at one
       door, and Bassianus and his followers at the other,
       with drums ⌈*and colours*⌉

SATURNINUS (*to his followers*)

  Noble patricians, patrons of my right,
  Defend the justice of my cause with arms;
  And, countrymen, my loving followers,
  Plead my successive title with your swords.

1.1] F (*Actus Primus. Scoena Prima.*): *not in* Q1   0.1 *Flourish*] F: *not in* Q1   0.2 *below*] *not in*
Q1   0.3 *at the other*] F: *not in* Q1   0.4 *drums and colours*] This edition: *Drums and Trumpets* Q1:
Drum & Colours F

1.1 The location is the Capitoline Hill in
Rome (see l. 12) near the senate house.
The tomb of the Andronici was probably
represented by a large property (Henslowe lists several tombs in his inventory
of properties: *Diary*, p. 319), set up in the
middle of the back wall of the stage; see
Introduction, p. 44.

0.1 *Flourish* fanfare of trumpets, commonly
used to signal the entrance of important
personages, especially royalty. Here, and
elsewhere, F has stage directions presumably derived from the prompt-book (see
Introduction, p. 40) and hence reflecting
stage practice, though not necessarily the
author's intention.
  Tribunes officials elected by the
plebeians, or common people, of ancient
Rome to protect their rights
  Senators members of the senate, chosen
originally from the patricians (see note on
l. 10) but later from the plebeians as well
  aloft on the upper stage

0.2 *Saturninus* One of several names which
Shakespeare may have taken from
Roman history (see Introduction, p. 35),
but may also have been influenced by
astrological theory that saturnine men
(those under the influence of Saturn)
were 'false, envious, . . . and malicious'
(*Kalendar of Shepherds*, pp. 141–2; see
Lawrence Babb, *The Elizabethan Malady*
(East Lansing, Mich., 1951), pp. 57–8).

0.2–3 *at one door . . . at the other* The wording of the F stage direction presupposes
two doors, one on each side of the main
stage, as in the Swan drawing (see
Introduction, p. 44).

0.3 *Bassianus* The name of a Roman emperor better known as Caracalla.

0.4 *drums* i.e. drummers
  colours flags or, in this case, flag-bearers;
here the F stage direction helps us to en-
visage the pageantry of the spectacular
entrances of the rival brothers, each accompanied by friends and soldiers (including a drummer and a flag-bearer).
The omission of trumpets in the prompt-
book on which F was based may mean
that the added 'flourish' for the entrance
of the tribunes and senators was substituted for trumpeters accompanying
the brothers (see collations).

1 SATURNINUS In Q1 the first seven speech-
prefixes are centred. At ll. 18, 63.3, and
156.1 a centred direction for entrance
also serves as a speech prefix.

1, 9 *to his followers* This direction has been
added on the assumption that both Saturninus and Bassianus address their supporters rather than the tribunes and
senators 'aloft'.

1 *patricians* the Roman aristocracy (the
brothers presumably have with them
supporters from this class)

4 *successive title* right of succession

I am his first-born son that was the last
That ware the imperial diadem of Rome;
Then let my father's honours live in me,
Nor wrong mine age with this indignity.

BASSIANUS (*to his followers*)

Romans, friends, followers, favourers of my right,
If ever Bassianus, Caesar's son,   10
Were gracious in the eyes of royal Rome,
Keep then this passage to the Capitol,
And suffer not dishonour to approach
The imperial seat, to virtue consecrate,
To justice, continence, and nobility;
But let desert in pure election shine,
And, Romans, fight for freedom in your choice.

     Enter Marcus Andronicus aloft with the crown

MARCUS

Princes that strive by factions and by friends
Ambitiously for rule and empery,
Know that the people of Rome, for whom we stand   20
A special party, have by common voice,
In election for the Roman empery,
Chosen Andronicus, surnamèd Pius

14 virtue consecrate,] ROWE 1714; vertue, consecrate Q1   17.1 *Enter . . . crown*] F; *Marcus Andronicus with the Crowne* Q1 (*centred*)   23–4 Pius . . . Rome.] Q2 (*subs.*); Pius: . . . Rome, Q1

5 **his . . . that** i.e. the first-born son of him who

6 **ware** wore

8 **age** i.e. seniority
   indignity i.e. to have a younger brother succeed to the throne

11 **Were gracious** found favour

12 **Keep** guard
   Capitol The hill on which stood the temple of Jupiter Capitolinus; often identified by Elizabethans with the Roman senate house, here imagined as adjoining the upper stage.

14 **consecrate** consecrated

15 **continence** restraint

16 **let . . . shine** i.e. let your choice be based on merit, not on primogeniture

17.1 *Enter . . . crown* The centred speech prefix in Q1 (see collations) may double as an entrance; there are other instances in Elizabethan drama where 'Enter' is understood but not printed, such as the centred '*Edmund alone with a sword and target*' in Marlowe's *Edward II* (sig. H3), also printed

in 1594. The F direction, presumably taken from the prompt-book, clearly suggests that performance tradition placed the entrance of Marcus here, even though it might seem more logical for him to enter with the other tribunes at the opening. His awareness of the strife between Saturninus and Bassianus does not prove that he has been on stage listening to their speeches, and his entrance at this point with the crown is more effective.

19 **empery** status of emperor

20–1 **people . . . party** See note on Tribunes, 1.1.0.1.

21 **voice** expression of opinion

22 **In election** i.e. as a candidate

23 **surnamèd** given as an honorary epithet. The surname of a general, such as Scipio Africanus, sometimes recalled the location of his victory.
   Pius Titus' surname refers to his devotion to patriotic duty, and recalls for any reader of Virgil '*pius Aeneas*', the heroic embodiment of that quality.

For many good and great deserts to Rome.
A nobler man, a braver warrior
Lives not this day within the city walls.
He by the senate is accited home
From weary wars against the barbarous Goths,
That with his sons, a terror to our foes,
Hath yoked a nation strong, trained up in arms.   30
Ten years are spent since first he undertook
This cause of Rome, and chastisèd with arms
Our enemies' pride; five times he hath returned
Bleeding to Rome, bearing his valiant sons
In coffins from the field.
And now at last, laden with honour's spoils,
Returns the good Andronicus to Rome,
Renownèd Titus, flourishing in arms.
Let us entreat, by honour of his name
Whom worthily you would have now succeed,   40
And in the Capitol and senate's right,
Whom you pretend to honour and adore,
That you withdraw you and abate your strength,
Dismiss your followers, and, as suitors should,
Plead your deserts in peace and humbleness.

SATURNINUS

How fair the tribune speaks to calm my thoughts!

BASSIANUS

Marcus Andronicus, so I do affy
In thy uprightness and integrity,
And so I love and honour thee and thine,

35–6 field. | And now] Q2 (*subs.*); field, and at this day, | To the Monument of that *Andronicy* | Done sacrifice of expiation, | And slaine the Noblest prisoner of the *Gothes*, | And now Q1

27 **accited** summoned
28 **Goths** See Introduction, p. 65.
30 **yoked** subdued
35 **field** The following three and a half lines in Q1 (see collations) conflict with the sacrifice of Alarbus (ll. 96–149), which they describe as already accomplished. They were omitted in Q2 and succeeding editions. In the manuscript from which Q1 was printed Shakespeare may have failed to mark these lines for deletion when he decided to stage the episode; see notes on ll. 69.5, 96–149, and

Introduction, p. 39.
39–40 **his name . . . succeed** i.e. the name of the candidate you favour. Capell emended 'succeed' to 'succeeded', assuming that the reference was to the dead emperor, but 'would have succeeded' makes little sense, whereas the wish to have one or the other brother succeed is precisely the matter Marcus is addressing.
41 **Capitol . . . right** the right of the Capitol and the senate
42 **pretend** claim
47 **affy** trust

Thy noble brother Titus and his sons,   50
And her to whom my thoughts are humbled all,
Gracious Lavinia, Rome's rich ornament,
That I will here dismiss my loving friends,
And to my fortunes and the people's favour
Commit my cause in balance to be weighed.

Exeunt his soldiers and followers

SATURNINUS

Friends that have been thus forward in my right,
I thank you all, and here dismiss you all,
And to the love and favour of my country
Commit myself, my person, and the cause.

Exeunt his soldiers and followers

(*To the Tribunes and Senators*)
Rome, be as just and gracious unto me   60
As I am confident and kind to thee.
Open the gates and let me in.

BASSIANUS

Tribunes, and me, a poor competitor.

⌈*Flourish.*⌉ *Saturninus and Bassianus go up into*
the senate house.
Enter a Captain

CAPTAIN

Romans, make way. The good Andronicus,
Patron of virtue, Rome's best champion,

55.1 *Exeunt . . . followers*] This edition; *Exit Soldiers* Q1   59.1 *Exeunt . . . followers*] *not in* Q1
63.1 *Flourish*] F; *not in* Q1   *Saturninus and Bassianus*] *They* Q1   64 CAPTAIN] F (*Cap.*); *not in* Q1

---

51 **all** entirely

55.1 *Exeunt . . . followers* The Q1 direction,
'*Exit Soldiers*' (see collations), tempts one
to suppose that some of the followers of
Bassianus, and later of Saturninus,
remain on stage to be addressed as
'Romans' by the Captain at l. 64, and
later as 'Patricians' by Saturninus (l.
204). The sheer numbers required for
Titus' triumphal procession, however,
make it more likely that both soldiers and
other followers leave the stage here to
return almost immediately in the
procession (see Introduction, p. 44).

62 **gates** presumably the gates of the off-
stage senate house

63 **competitor** rival

63.1–2 *Saturninus . . . house* Saturninus
and Bassianus leave the main stage by
the doors through which they entered,
and join the tribunes and senators on the
upper stage, from whence they all exit as
if to the senate house. The main stage,
and then the upper stage, are cleared just
before the Captain arrives to announce
the return of Titus. (See G. K. Hunter's
excellent discussion of the staging of this
scene: 'Flatcaps', pp. 18–20.) When he
calls on 'Romans' to 'make way' (l. 64) he
may, as Hunter suggests, address the
theatre audience; he did so in John Barton's 1981 production.

65 **Patron** (a) representative (b) pattern, of
which 'patron' was an alternative form

Successful in the battles that he fights,
With honour and with fortune is returned
From where he circumscrib̀ed with his sword,
And brought to yoke, the enemies of Rome.
> *Sound drums and trumpets, and then enter two of*
> *Titus' sons, Martius and Mutius, and then two men*
> *bearing a coffin covered with black; then two other*
> *sons, Lucius and Quintus; Titus Andronicus* ⌐in a
> *chariot⌐, and then Tamora, the Queen of Goths and her*
> *three sons, Alarbus, Chiron, and Demetrius, with*
> *Aaron the Moor, and others as many as can be. Then*
> *set down the coffin, and Titus speaks*

TITUS

Hail, Rome, victorious in thy mourning weeds!   70
Lo, as the bark that hath discharged his fraught
Returns with precious lading to the bay
From whence at first she weighed her anchorage,
Cometh Andronicus, bound with laurel boughs,
To re-salute his country with his tears,
Tears of true joy for his return to Rome.
Thou great defender of this Capitol,
Stand gracious to the rites that we intend.
Romans, of five-and-twenty valiant sons,
Half of the number that King Priam had,   80

69.2 *Martius and Mutius*] not in Q1   69.4 *Lucius and Quintus*] not in Q1   69.4–5 *in a chariot*] not in Q1   69.6 *three*] two Q1   *Alarbus*] not in Q1   78, 143 rites] Q1 (rights)

68 **circumscrib̀ed** brought within bounds
69.4 *Titus Andronicus* In this ceremonial procession Titus may be drawn in a chariot (compare l. 249).
69.5 *Tamora* Shakespeare may have derived the name from Tomyris, a Scythian queen famous for her cruelty (see Hamilton, p. 87).
69.6 *three . . . Alarbus* The stage direction in Q1 (followed in succeeding editions), specifying two sons and omitting Alarbus, suggests a stage of composition in which the episode of the sacrifice of Alarbus was not planned; see note on l. 35.
Alarbus The name may have been suggested, as Gary Taylor has pointed out to me, by a poem quoted in Puttenham's *Art of English Poesie* (1589, sig. V4ᵛ): 'the Roman prince did daunt | Wild Africans

and the lawless Alarbes.'
69.7 *Aaron* Given the influence of *The Jew of Malta* on the conception of Aaron's character (see Introduction, p. 38), it may be that a train of association led Shakespeare from the play to his name, for it has been noticed that the wicked slave, Ithamore, in Marlowe's play has a biblical name, and that Ithamar in Numbers 4:28 is 'the son of Aaron the priest' (see Bullough, vi. 20).
others . . . be The indefiniteness is characteristic of stage directions in an author's manuscript; see Introduction, p. 39.
71 **his fraught** its cargo
73 **anchorage** anchors
77 **defender** i.e. Jupiter Capitolinus
80 **Priam** King of Troy in the Trojan War

Behold the poor remains alive and dead.
These that survive let Rome reward with love –
These that I bring unto their latest home,
With burial amongst their ancestors.
Here Goths have given me leave to sheathe my sword.
Titus, unkind and careless of thine own,
Why suffer'st thou thy sons, unburied yet,
To hover on the dreadful shore of Styx?
Make way to lay them by their brethren.
    They open the tomb
There greet in silence, as the dead are wont,   90
And sleep in peace, slain in your country's wars.
O sacred receptacle of my joys,
Sweet cell of virtue and nobility,
How many sons hast thou of mine in store,
That thou wilt never render to me more!

LUCIUS

Give us the proudest prisoner of the Goths,
That we may hew his limbs, and on a pile
Ad manes fratrum sacrifice his flesh
Before this earthy prison of their bones,
That so the shadows be not unappeased,   100
Nor we disturbed with prodigies on earth.

TITUS

I give him you, the noblest that survives,
The eldest son of this distressèd queen.

98 *manes*] F3; *manus* Q1

83 **latest** last
84 **With** i.e. let Rome reward with
85 **Here . . . sword** (an ironical reference to his victory over them)
86–8 **Titus . . . Styx** Despite Titus' eagerness to give proper burial at last to the bodies of his sons, he is obliged to wait until the sacrifice of Alarbus has been completed. Shakespeare may originally have intended the burial to follow l. 95; see note on ll. 96–149.
88 **hover . . . Styx** Only when the body was properly buried could the soul cross this river into Hades.
89 **brethren** The pronunciation is trisyllabic here and wherever the metre requires it; in some instances the Q1 spelling is 'bretheren'.

89.1 **They . . . tomb** A door is opened or a curtain drawn back, and the pall-bearers prepare to lay the coffin in the tomb, when they are interrupted by Lucius' demand.
92 **receptacle** accented 'réceptácle'
96–149 **Give . . . souls** Dover Wilson (p. xxxv) points out that if these lines presenting the sacrifice of Alarbus are omitted, the text of Titus' speech 'runs straight on'. This is one more piece of evidence that the episode was not in the original plan; see note on l. 35.
98 *ad . . . fratrum* to the shades of [our] brothers (Latin)
100 **shadows** shades, ghosts
101 **prodigies** ominous happenings

TAMORA (*kneeling with her sons*)

    Stay, Roman brethren, gracious conqueror,
    Victorious Titus, rue the tears I shed,
    A mother's tears in passion for her son;
    And if thy sons were ever dear to thee,
    O, think my son to be as dear to me.
    Sufficeth not that we are brought to Rome
    To beautify thy triumphs, and return   110
    Captive to thee and to thy Roman yoke;
    But must my sons be slaughtered in the streets
    For valiant doings in their country's cause?
    O, if to fight for king and commonweal
    Were piety in thine, it is in these.
    Andronicus, stain not thy tomb with blood.
    Wilt thou draw near the nature of the gods?
    Draw near them then in being merciful;
    Sweet mercy is nobility's true badge;
    Thrice-noble Titus, spare my first-born son.   120

TITUS

    Patient yourself, madam, and pardon me.
    These are their brethren whom your Goths beheld
    Alive and dead, and for their brethren slain
    Religiously they ask a sacrifice.
    To this your son is marked, and die he must,
    T'appease their groaning shadows that are gone.

LUCIUS

    Away with him, and make a fire straight,
    And with our swords upon a pile of wood
    Let's hew his limbs till they be clean consumed.
            Exeunt Titus' sons with Alarbus

---

104 *kneeling with her sons*] *not in* Q1   129.1 *Exeunt*] *Exit* Q1

104 **kneeling with her sons** In a later aside to Saturninus Tamora threatens to 'make them know what 'tis to let a queen | Kneel in the streets' (ll. 454–5), and the Peacham drawing shows her on her knees with two of her sons (Fig. 4).
106 **passion** strong emotion, grief
109 **Sufficeth not** i.e. does it not suffice
117–18 **draw . . . merciful** Proverbial: 'It is in their Mercy that kings come closest to gods' (Tilley M898).

121 **Patient** control, calm
122 **their brethren** i.e. brothers of Titus' dead sons
124 **Religiously** i.e. out of piety to the dead
127 **fire** (disyllabic)
    straight straightway, at once
129 **clean** entirely
129.1 **Exeunt . . . Alarbus** They go off-stage to perform the sacrifice 'before' the tomb (see l. 99).

TAMORA (*rising with her sons*)

  O cruel, irreligious piety!   130

CHIRON

  Was never Scythia half so barbarous.

DEMETRIUS

  Oppose not Scythia to ambitious Rome.

  Alarbus goes to rest and we survive

  To tremble under Titus' threat'ning look.

  Then, madam, stand resolved, but hope withal

  The selfsame gods that armed the Queen of Troy

  With opportunity of sharp revenge

  Upon the Thracian tyrant in his tent

  May favour Tamora, the Queen of Goths

  (When Goths were Goths, and Tamora was queen),   140

  To quit the bloody wrongs upon her foes.

     Enter the sons of Andronicus again

LUCIUS

  See, lord and father, how we have performed

  Our Roman rites. Alarbus' limbs are lopped,

  And entrails feed the sacrificing fire,

  Whose smoke like incense doth perfume the sky.

  Remaineth nought but to inter our brethren,

  And with loud 'larums welcome them to Rome.

TITUS

  Let it be so, and let Andronicus

  Make this his latest farewell to their souls.

     ⌈*Flourish. Then*⌉ *sound trumpets, and lay the coffin*

       in the tomb

---

130 *rising with her sons*] not in Q1   138 his] Q1; her THEOBALD   149.1 *Flourish. Then*] F; *not*
in Q1   *coffin*] Q1; *Coffins* F

131 **Scythia** a region north of the Black Sea
    noted for its savage inhabitants
132 **Oppose** compare
136 **Queen of Troy** Hecuba, who avenged
    the death of her son by blinding his mur-
    derer, Polymestor, 'the Thracian tyrant'
    (l. 138). The story is told in Ovid's
    Metamorphoses, xiii. 533–75, and also in
    Euripides' *Hecuba*, where the heroine also
    kills Polymestor's two sons. Jones (pp.
    90–102) believes that Shakespeare knew
    this play, which Erasmus and others had
    translated into Latin. There, however, it
    is clear that the revenge is carried out in
    Hecuba's tent, and some editors have
    therefore emended 'his' (l. 138) to 'her'

(see collations). In Ovid the location of the
crime is less precise, though it is not
Polymestor's tent. Shakespeare was
probably following Ovid, and although it
is not clear why he should have written
'his tent', we cannot be sure that this is a
printer's error; see Holger Nørgaard,
'Never Wrong But With Just Cause', *Eng-*
lish Studies, 45 (1964), 138–9.
141 **quit** requite, avenge
142–3 **See . . . rites** They probably hold up
    bloody swords.
147 **'larums** military trumpet calls
149.1 **Flourish . . . trumpets** The F
    'Flourish' may duplicate the Q1 'Sound
    trumpets', but 'then sound trumpets' sug-

In peace and honour rest you here, my sons,   150
Rome's readiest champions, repose you here in rest,
Secure from worldly chances and mishaps!
Here lurks no treason, here no envy swells,
Here grow no damnèd drugs, here are no storms,
No noise, but silence and eternal sleep.
In peace and honour rest you here, my sons!
  Enter Lavinia

LAVINIA

In peace and honour live Lord Titus long;
My noble lord and father, live in fame!
Lo, at this tomb my tributary tears
I render for my brethren's obsequies,   160
And at thy feet I kneel, with tears of joy
Shed on this earth for thy return to Rome.
O bless me here with thy victorious hand,
Whose fortunes Rome's best citizens applaud.

TITUS

Kind Rome, that hast thus lovingly reserved
The cordial of mine age to glad my heart!
Lavinia, live, outlive thy father's days
And fame's eternal date, for virtue's praise!
  Lavinia rises.
  Enter above Marcus Andronicus, Saturninus,
  Bassianus, Tribunes, and others

MARCUS

Long live Lord Titus, my belovèd brother,
Gracious triumpher in the eyes of Rome!   170

---

157 LAVINIA] Q3 (*Laui.*); *not in* Q1   168.1 *Lavinia rises*] *not in* Q1   168.2–3 *Enter . . . others*] *not in* Q1

gests the possibility of two different trumpet calls.

coffin The F stage direction here (but not at l. 69.3) calls for more than one coffin, as one might expect, since there are several corpses. Several coffins, however, would crowd the stage and require more 'extras' in an already large cast. The Q1 stage direction is probably right; see Introduction, pp. 43–4.

150–6 **In peace . . . sons** Titus' sentiments

anticipate the famous dirge in *Cymbeline*, 'Fear no more the heat o'th'sun . . . Fear not slander, censure rash', etc. (4.2.259–82).

154 **drugs** poisonous plants
159 **tributary** of tribute
166 **cordial** comfort (literally: heart stimulant)
168 **date** duration
168.2 *Enter above* The F stage direction at l. 233.1 shows that the entrance here must be to the upper stage.

TITUS

Thanks, gentle tribune, noble brother Marcus.

MARCUS

And welcome, nephews, from successful wars,
You that survive, and you that sleep in fame!
Fair lords, your fortunes are alike in all,
That in your country's service drew your swords,
But safer triumph is this funeral pomp,
That hath aspired to Solon's happiness,
And triumphs over chance in honour's bed.
Titus Andronicus, the people of Rome,
Whose friend in justice thou hast ever been,   180
Send thee by me, their tribune and their trust,
This palliament of white and spotless hue,
And name thee in election for the empire
With these our late-deceasèd emperor's sons.
Be *candidatus* then, and put it on,
And help to set a head on headless Rome.

TITUS

A better head her glorious body fits
Than his that shakes for age and feebleness.
What should I don this robe and trouble you?
Be chosen with proclamations today,   190
Tomorrow yield up rule, resign my life,
And set abroad new business for you all?
Rome, I have been thy soldier forty years,
And led my country's strength successfully,
And buried one-and-twenty valiant sons,
Knighted in field, slain manfully in arms
In right and service of their noble country.
Give me a staff of honour for mine age,
But not a sceptre to control the world.
Upright he held it, lords, that held it last.   200

---

177 **aspired** risen

   Solon's happiness This Athenian law-
   giver said: 'Call no man happy until he is
   dead.'

182 **palliament** robe (one of two known oc-
   currences of the word; see Introduction,
   p. 14)

185 *candidatus* Literally, clad in white, as
   were Roman 'candidates' for office.

189 **What** why

190 **proclamations** Here, and wherever the
   metre requires it, the suffix '-tion' is
   disyllabic; a number of other suffixes are
   similarly variable: e.g. '-tient', '-cious',
   etc.

192 **set abroad** i.e. initiate

197 **In . . . of** to defend the rights of and to
   serve

MARCUS

Titus, thou shalt obtain and ask the empery.

SATURNINUS

Proud and ambitious tribune, canst thou tell?

TITUS

Patience, Prince Saturninus.

SATURNINUS   Romans, do me right. ·

Patricians, draw your swords, and sheathe them not

Till Saturninus be Rome's emperor.

Andronicus, would thou were shipped to hell,

Rather than rob me of the people's hearts!

LUCIUS

Proud Saturnine, interrupter of the good

That noble-minded Titus means to thee!

TITUS

Content thee, Prince; I will restore to thee   210

The people's hearts, and wean them from themselves.

BASSIANUS

Andronicus, I do not flatter thee,

But honour thee, and will do till I die.

My faction if thou strengthen with thy friends,

I will most thankful be, and thanks to men

Of noble minds is honourable meed.

TITUS

People of Rome, and people's tribunes here,

I ask your voices and your suffrages.

Will ye bestow them friendly on Andronicus?

TRIBUNES

To gratify the good Andronicus   220

And gratulate his safe return to Rome,

The people will accept whom he admits.

TITUS

Tribunes, I thank you, and this suit I make,

That you create our emperor's eldest son,

Lord Saturnine, whose virtues will, I hope,

201 **and ask** i.e. by asking

204 **Patricians** The senators may be among
    the 'others' who enter at l. 168.3.

206 **were** wert. 'Were' was the frequently
    used older form of the second person singu-

lar of the past subjunctive.

216 **meed** reward

218 **voices** votes

221 **gratulate** salute

93

Reflect on Rome as Titan's rays on earth,
And ripen justice in this commonweal.
Then if you will elect by my advice,
Crown him and say, 'Long live our emperor!'
MARCUS
      With voices and applause of every sort,   230
      Patricians and plebeians, we create
      Lord Saturninus Rome's great emperor,
      And say, 'Long live our Emperor Saturnine!'
            ⌈*A long flourish till they come down*⌉
SATURNINUS
      Titus Andronicus, for thy favours done
      To us in our election this day
      I give thee thanks in part of thy deserts,
      And will with deeds requite thy gentleness.
      And for an onset, Titus, to advance
      Thy name and honourable family,
      Lavinia will I make my empress,   240
      Rome's royal mistress, mistress of my heart,
      And in the sacred Pantheon her espouse.
      Tell me, Andronicus, doth this motion please thee?
TITUS
      It doth, my worthy lord, and in this match
      I hold me highly honoured of your grace,
      And here in sight of Rome to Saturnine,
      King and commander of our commonweal,
      The wide world's emperor, do I consecrate
      My sword, my chariot, and my prisoners,
      Presents well worthy Rome's imperious lord.   250
      Receive them then, the tribute that I owe,

226 Titan's] Q2; Tytus Q1   233.1 *A long ... down*] F; *not in* Q1   242 Pantheon] F2; Pathan
Q1

226 **Titan** the sun
231-2 **we create ... emperor** Since Marcus
      earlier held the crown, he may place it on
      Saturninus' head as he says these words.
233.1 The F stage direction shows that those
      on the upper stage now join Titus and the
      others on the main stage.
236 **in** as
237 **gentleness** nobility
238 **onset** beginning

240 **empress** Trisyllabic here and wherever
      the metre requires it; in some instances
      the Q1 spelling is 'emperesse'.
242 **Pantheon** temple dedicated to all the
      gods
243 **motion** proposal
249 **chariot** Titus may have been drawn on
      stage in a chariot.
250 **imperious** imperial

94

Mine honour's ensigns humbled at thy feet.

SATURNINUS

Thanks, noble Titus, father of my life.
How proud I am of thee and of thy gifts
Rome shall record, and when I do forget
The least of these unspeakable deserts,
Romans, forget your fealty to me.

TITUS (*to Tamora*)

Now, madam, are you prisoner to an Emperor –
To him that for your honour and your state
Will use you nobly and your followers.   260

SATURNINUS (*aside*)

A goodly lady, trust me, of the hue
That I would choose, were I to choose anew. –
Clear up, fair queen, that cloudy countenance;
Though chance of war hath wrought this change of
          cheer,
Thou com'st not to be made a scorn in Rome.
Princely shall be thy usage every way.
Rest on my word, and let not discontent
Daunt all your hopes. Madam, he comforts you
Can make you greater than the Queen of Goths.
Lavinia, you are not displeased with this?   270

LAVINIA

Not I, my lord, sith true nobility
Warrants these words in princely courtesy.

SATURNINUS

Thanks, sweet Lavinia. Romans, let us go;
Ransomless here we set our prisoners free.
Proclaim our honours, lords, with trump and drum.
          Flourish

BASSIANUS (*seizing Lavinia*)

Lord Titus, by your leave, this maid is mine.

---

264 chance] Q2; change Q1   270 this?] F; this. Q1   275.1 *Flourish] not in* Q1   276 *seizing*
Lavinia] not in Q1

252 **ensigns** tokens   267 **Rest** rely
256 **unspeakable** inexpressible   268 **he** he who
261 **hue** Not exclusively 'colour', but more 271 **sith** since
    generally 'appearance' or 'complexion'.   272 **Warrants** justifies
264 **cheer** countenance

TITUS

How, sir? Are you in earnest then, my lord?

BASSIANUS

Ay, noble Titus, and resolved withal

To do myself this reason and this right.

MARCUS

Suum cuique is our Roman justice;   280

This prince in justice seizeth but his own.

LUCIUS

And that he will and shall, if Lucius live.

TITUS

Traitors, avaunt! Where is the Emperor's guard?

Treason, my lord! Lavinia is surprised.

SATURNINUS

Surprised! By whom?

BASSIANUS   By him that justly may

Bear his betrothed from all the world away.

     Exeunt Bassianus and Marcus with Lavinia

MUTIUS

Brothers, help to convey her hence away,

And with my sword I'll keep this door safe.

     Exeunt Lucius, Quintus, and Martius

TITUS

Follow, my lord, and I'll soon bring her back.

MUTIUS

My lord, you pass not here.

TITUS   What, villain boy,   290

Barr'st me my way in Rome?

---

280 *cuique*] F2; *cuiqum* Q1   286.1 *Exeunt . . . Lavinia*] MALONE (*subs. after* Rowe; *not in* Q1
288.1 *Exeunt . . . Martius*] MALONE (*after* Capell); *not in* Q1   290–1 What . . . Rome] *divided
by* POPE; *one line in* Q1

---

280 **Suum cuique** to each his own (Latin);
compare 'And the country proverb
known, | That every man should take his
own' (*Dream*, 3.4.458–9).

283 **avaunt** be gone

284 **Treason . . . surprised** Saturninus,
having presumably headed for one of the
stage doors at l. 275, followed by some of
the lords, has not seen his brother's
manoeuvre.

287–8, 290–9 Gary Taylor has suggested
that these lines presenting the death of

Mutius may be additions to a first draft of
the scene. Without them the stage business is more readily comprehensible,
since Saturninus could then leave after l.
275. This would explain his not seeing
Bassianus' seizure of Lavinia and also
Titus' question, 'Where is the Emperor's
guard?' (l. 283); see notes on ll. 284 and
341–90. If Mutius was a second thought,
it is easy to understand the occasional
confusion about how many of Titus' sons
were killed in battle (see note on 3.1.10).

96

MUTIUS   Help, Lucius, help!

> *Titus kills him. During the fray, exeunt Saturninus,*
> *Tamora, Chiron, Demetrius, and Aaron.*
> *Enter Lucius*

LUCIUS

My lord, you are unjust, and more than so,

In wrongful quarrel you have slain your son.

TITUS

Nor thou, nor he, are any sons of mine;

My sons would never so dishonour me.

Traitor, restore Lavinia to the Emperor.

LUCIUS

Dead, if you will, but not to be his wife,

That is another's lawful promised love.   *Exit*

> *Enter aloft the Emperor with Tamora and her two sons,*
> *Chiron and Demetrius, and Aaron the Moor*

SATURNINUS

No, Titus, no, the Emperor needs her not;

Nor her, nor thee, nor any of thy stock.   300

I'll trust by leisure him that mocks me once,

Thee never, nor thy traitorous haughty sons,

Confederates all thus to dishonour me.

Was none in Rome to make a stale

But Saturnine? Full well, Andronicus,

Agree these deeds with that proud brag of thine,

That saidst I begged the empire at thy hands.

TITUS

O monstrous! What reproachful words are these?

SATURNINUS

But go thy ways; go, give that changing piece

To him that flourished for her with his sword.   310

A valiant son-in-law thou shalt enjoy –

291.1 *Titus kills him*] *He kills him* Q3; *not in* Q1   291.1–2 *During . . . Aaron*] GLOBE (*subs.*); *not in* Q1   291.3 *Enter Lucius*] CAPELL; *not in* Q1   298 *Exit*] *not in* Q1   298.2 *Chiron and Demetrius*] *not in* Q1   299 SATURNINUS] *Emperour* Q1

301 **by leisure** slowly
304 **to make** i.e. to be made
304 **stale** laughing-stock
306 **that proud brag** This is a figment of

Saturninus' imagination.
309 **changing piece** fickle wench
310 **flourished . . . sword** brandished his
sword to get her

One fit to bandy with thy lawless sons,
To ruffle in the commonwealth of Rome.

TITUS

These words are razors to my wounded heart.

SATURNINUS

And therefore, lovely Tamora, Queen of Goths,
That like the stately Phoebe 'mongst her nymphs
Dost overshine the gallant'st dames of Rome,
If thou be pleased with this my sudden choice,
Behold, I choose thee, Tamora, for my bride,
And will create thee Empress of Rome.   320
Speak, Queen of Goths, dost thou applaud my choice?
And here I swear by all the Roman gods,
Sith priest and holy water are so near,
And tapers burn so bright, and everything
In readiness for Hymenaeus stand,
I will not re-salute the streets of Rome,
Or climb my palace, till from forth this place
I lead espoused my bride along with me.

TAMORA

And here in sight of heaven to Rome I swear,
If Saturnine advance the Queen of Goths,   330
She will a handmaid be to his desires,
A loving nurse, a mother to his youth.

SATURNINUS

Ascend, fair queen, Pantheon. Lords, accompany
Your noble Emperor and his lovely bride,
Sent by the heavens for Prince Saturnine,
Whose wisdom hath her fortune conquerèd.
There shall we consummate our spousal rites.

Exeunt all but Titus

---

316 Phoebe] F2; *Thebe* Q1   333 queen, Pantheon. Lords,] POPE (subs.); Queene: Panthean
Lords Q1; *Pantheon Lords,* F4   337.1 *Exeunt . . . Titus*] *Exeunt Omnes* Q1

312 **bandy** brawl
313 **ruffle** swagger
316 **Phoebe** Diana, who, in Phaer's 1558
    translation of Virgil's *Aeneid* (i. 498–
    501), 'overshines' her attendant
    nymphs (noted by Ritson; see Steevens
    1803, xxi. 25).
325 **Hymenaeus** god of marriage
    stand Plural because 'everything' is

plural in sense; compare 'every one of
these letters are in my name' (*Twelfth
Night*, 2.5.153).
327 **climb** i.e. climb the stairs to
332 **mother** (suggesting the disparity be-
    tween their ages)
336 **Whose wisdom** Presumably refers to
    Tamora, who has overcome bad fortune
    by wisely accepting Saturninus.

TITUS

  I am not bid to wait upon this bride.

  Titus, when wert thou wont to walk alone,

  Dishonoured thus and challengèd of wrongs?   340

     Enter Marcus and Titus' sons, Lucius, Quintus, and
     Martius

MARCUS

  O Titus, see, O see what thou hast done!

  In a bad quarrel slain a virtuous son.

TITUS

  No, foolish tribune, no; no son of mine,

  Nor thou, nor these, confederates in the deed

  That hath dishonoured all our family,

  Unworthy brother, and unworthy sons!

LUCIUS

  But let us give him burial as becomes,

  Give Mutius burial with our brethren.

TITUS

  Traitors, away! He rests not in this tomb.

  This monument five hundred years hath stood,   350

  Which I have sumptuously re-edified.

  Here none but soldiers and Rome's servitors

  Repose in fame; none basely slain in brawls.

  Bury him where you can, he comes not here.

MARCUS

  My lord, this is impiety in you.

  My nephew Mutius' deeds do plead for him,

  He must be buried with his brethren.

340.1–2 *Lucius . . . Martius*] *not in* Q1

338 **bid** asked

340 **challengèd** accused

341–90 **O Titus . . . cause** Another passage which may, as Dover Wilson suggests (p. xxxvi), have been added after the rest of the scene was written; see Introduction, p. 39. Marcus' comment on Titus' 'dreary dumps' (l. 391), which seems inappropriate here, would be natural following l. 340, as would his question about Tamora.

344 **Nor . . . these** Dover Wilson and Maxwell have noted the echo of Titus' words to Lucius (l. 294) and of Saturninus' words to Titus (l. 300). These and other repetitions suggest a manuscript hastily completed.

347 **becomes** is fitting

350 **monument** tomb; compare the 'monument' in *Romeo*, 5.3

351 **re-edified** rebuilt

354 **Bury . . . can** Maxwell suggests that this also has the sense of 'wherever you bury him'.

⌈MARTIUS⌉

And shall, or him we will accompany.

TITUS

'And shall?' What villain was it spake that word?

⌈MARTIUS⌉

He that would vouch it in any place but here.   360

TITUS

What, would you bury him in my despite?

MARCUS

No, noble Titus, but entreat of thee

To pardon Mutius and to bury him.

TITUS

Marcus, even thou hast struck upon my crest,

And with these boys mine honour thou hast wounded.

My foes do I repute you every one,

So trouble me no more, but get you gone.

⌈QUINTUS⌉

He is not with himself; let us withdraw.

⌈MARTIUS⌉

Not I, till Mutius' bones be burièd.

Marcus, Lucius, Quintus, and Martius kneel

MARCUS

Brother, for in that name doth nature plead –   370

⌈MARTIUS⌉

Father, and in that name doth nature speak –

TITUS

Speak thou no more, if all the rest will speed.

MARCUS

Renownèd Titus, more than half my soul –

358 MARTIUS] MAXWELL (*conj.* Bolton); *Titus two sonnes speakes* Q1 (*centred*)   360 MARTIUS] CAPELL; *Titus sonne speakes* Q1 (*centred*)   364 struck] Q1 (*stroke*)   368 QUINTUS] CAPELL; 3. *Sonne* Q1   369, 371 MARTIUS] CAPELL; 2. *Sonne* Q1   369.1 *Marcus . . . Martius*] *The brother and the sonnes* Q1

358 MARTIUS Joseph Bolton ('Two Notes on *Titus Andronicus*', *Modern Language Notes*, 45 (1930), 140–1) interprets '*two sonnes*' in the Q1 stage direction (see collations) as the printer's misreading of '2. [for "*second*"] *sonne*' in the manuscript (as in the speech-prefixes at ll. 369, 371), and argues that Martius is meant. Titus answers as if to *one* person.

358 **shall** (has the force of a command)
360 **vouch** maintain
364 **struck** See Cercignani, p. 136, for an explanation of the Q1 variant spelling, 'stroke'.
368 **not with beside**
372 **if . . . speed** if the others are to succeed (in their plea). Titus is especially irritated with his more insistent son.

LUCIUS

Dear father, soul and substance of us all –

MARCUS

Suffer thy brother Marcus to inter

His noble nephew here in virtue's nest,

That died in honour and Lavinia's cause.

Thou art a Roman; be not barbarous:

The Greeks upon advice did bury Ajax,

That slew himself; and wise Laertes' son   380

Did graciously plead for his funerals;

Let not young Mutius, then, that was thy joy,

Be barred his entrance here.

TITUS   Rise, Marcus, rise.

    They rise

The dismall'st day is this that e'er I saw,

To be dishonoured by my sons in Rome.

Well, bury him, and bury me the next.

    They put Mutius in the tomb

LUCIUS

There lie thy bones, sweet Mutius, with thy friends,

Till we with trophies do adorn thy tomb.

    They all ⌈but Titus⌉ kneel and say:

MARCUS, LUCIUS, MARTIUS, QUINTUS

No man shed tears for noble Mutius;

He lives in fame, that died in virtue's cause.   390

    They rise, and all but Titus and Marcus ⌈stand aside⌉

383.1 *They rise] not in* Q1   386.1 *Mutius] him* Q1   388.1 *but Titus] not in* Q1   389 MARCUS, LUCIUS, MARTIUS, QUINTUS] *not in* Q1   390.1 *They . . . aside]* KITTREDGE; *Exit all but Marcus and Titus* Q1 ; *Exit* F

379 **upon advice** after deliberation

    Ajax The Greek warrior who killed himself after an insane fit in which he had slaughtered sheep, thinking them to be the Greek generals who had slighted him; though his countrymen at first refused to bury him, Odysseus, 'Laertes' son' (l. 380), persuaded them to do so. The story was dramatized by Sophocles in his *Ajax*, but Shakespeare may more likely have known it, as Maxwell says, from Lambrinus' commentary on Horace (*Satires*, II. iii. 187) often used in sixteenth-century English grammar schools.

387 **friends** perhaps 'friends' bones'

388 **trophies** memorials

388.1 **but Titus** It seems probable that 'all' in this stage direction does not include Titus. He has told the others to bury Mutius and he would hardly say that Mutius 'died in virtue's cause'.

390.1 **stand aside** Though the early texts have an 'exit' here for all but Marcus and Titus, the sons are addressed in l. 471. Kittredge's direction, 'stand aside', is good. They may close the tomb and move a few steps away from Marcus and Titus, who speak only to each other.

MARCUS

My lord, to step out of these dreary dumps,
How comes it that the subtle Queen of Goths
Is of a sudden thus advanced in Rome?

TITUS

I know not, Marcus, but I know it is.
Whether by device or no, the heavens can tell.
Is she not then beholding to the man
That brought her for this high good turn so far?
Yes, and will nobly him remunerate.

⌈*Flourish.*⌉
Enter the Emperor, ⎫ ⎧ Enter at the other
Tamora and her two ⎬ ⎨ door Bassianus and
sons, with the Moor, ⎭ ⎩ Lavinia, with
at one door.   others.

SATURNINUS

So, Bassianus, you have played your prize.
God give you joy, sir, of your gallant bride!   400

BASSIANUS

And you of yours, my lord! I say no more,
Nor wish no less, and so I take my leave.

SATURNINUS

Traitor, if Rome have law or we have power,
Thou and thy faction shall repent this rape.

BASSIANUS

'Rape' call you it, my lord, to seize my own,
My true betrothèd love, and now my wife?

398 Yes . . . remunerate] F; *not in* Q1   398.1 *Flourish*] F; *not in* Q1

391 **dumps** melancholy fits
395 **device** scheming
396 **beholding** beholden; 'beholding' was
   the commoner form in Elizabethan English.
398 **Yes . . . remunerate** On the addition of
   this line in F see Introduction, pp. 40–1.
   Malone suspected that it should have
   been given to Marcus, but the naïve confidence in Tamora's gratitude is more
   characteristic of Titus.
398.2–5 **Enter . . . others** The layout of the
   Q1 stage direction is reproduced since its
   unusual form emphasizes the symmetry
   of another spectacular entrance, comparable to the one which opens the play.

Again the two royal brothers enter, one
from each door, accompanied this time
by their brides and others (probably attendants); the Andronici are presumably
close to the tomb at centre-stage. Once
more it is a crowded scene, and this seg-
ment of the action begins, like the play
itself, with hostile exchanges between
Saturninus and Bassianus.
399 **played . . . prize** played (and won) your
   match. The phrase was often used of a
   fencing match.
400 **gallant** splendid
404 **rape** (in the broader sense of 'abduc-
   tion')

But let the laws of Rome determine all;
Meanwhile am I possessed of that is mine.

SATURNINUS

'Tis good, sir; you are very short with us;
But if we live we'll be as sharp with you.   410

BASSIANUS

My lord, what I have done, as best I may
Answer I must, and shall do with my life.
Only thus much I give your grace to know:
By all the duties that I owe to Rome,
This noble gentleman, Lord Titus here,
Is in opinion and in honour wronged,
That, in the rescue of Lavinia,
With his own hand did slay his youngest son
In zeal to you, and highly moved to wrath
To be controlled in that he frankly gave.   420
Receive him then to favour, Saturnine,
That hath expressed himself in all his deeds
A father and a friend to thee and Rome.

TITUS

Prince Bassianus, leave to plead my deeds;
'Tis thou and those that have dishonoured me.
Rome and the righteous heavens be my judge,
How I have loved and honoured Saturnine!
⌈*He kneels*⌉

TAMORA (*to Saturninus*)

My worthy lord, if ever Tamora
Were gracious in those princely eyes of thine,
Then hear me speak indifferently for all;   430
And at my suit, sweet, pardon what is past.

SATURNINUS

What, madam, be dishonoured openly,
And basely put it up without revenge?

427.1 *He kneels*] BEVINGTON (*subs.*); *not in* Q1

408 **that** that which (as at l. 420)
416 **opinion** reputation
420 **controlled** restrained
        frankly generously
427.1 *He kneels* Titus is told to rise in l. 459,
        but in the absence of a stage direction in

any early text it is not clear when he
kneels. The action would be a logical accompaniment to this assertion of loyalty.
430 **indifferently** impartially
433 **put it up** accept the disgrace (metaphor-
        ically sheathing a weapon)

TAMORA

Not so, my lord; the gods of Rome forfend
I should be author to dishonour you.
But on mine honour dare I undertake
For good Lord Titus' innocence in all,
Whose fury not dissembled speaks his griefs.
Then at my suit look graciously on him;
Lose not so noble a friend on vain suppose,   440
Nor with sour looks afflict his gentle heart.
(*Aside to Saturninus*)
My lord, be ruled by me, be won at last,
Dissemble all your griefs and discontents;
You are but newly planted in your throne;
Lest then the people, and patricians too,
Upon a just survey take Titus' part,
And so supplant you for ingratitude,
Which Rome reputes to be a heinous sin,
Yield at entreats; and then let me alone,
I'll find a day to massacre them all,   450
And raze their faction and their family,
The cruel father and his traitorous sons,
To whom I suèd for my dear son's life;
And make them know what 'tis to let a queen
Kneel in the streets and beg for grace in vain. –
Come, come, sweet Emperor; come Andronicus;
Take up this good old man, and cheer the heart
That dies in tempest of thy angry frown.

SATURNINUS

Rise, Titus, rise; my Empress hath prevailed.

TITUS (*rising*)

I thank your majesty, and her, my lord.   460
These words, these looks infuse new life in me.

442 My lord . . . last] QI *indents*   460 *rising*] *not in* QI

434 **forfend** forbid
435 **author** agent
436 **undertake** vouch
438 **fury not dissembled** unconcealed anger
440 **vain suppose** idle supposition
447–8 **ingratitude . . . sin** The theme of
  Rome's ingratitude to Titus anticipates a
  salient feature of Shakespeare's last

  tragedy, *Coriolanus*.
449 **at entreats** to entreaty
  let me alone leave it to me
451 **raze** The QI spelling 'race' suggests
  both 'raze' and the obsolete 'arace', to
  root out.
457 **Take up** raise to his feet

TAMORA

Titus, I am incorporate in Rome,
A Roman now adopted happily,
And must advise the Emperor for his good.
This day all quarrels die, Andronicus.
And let it be mine honour, good my lord,
That I have reconciled your friends and you.
For you, Prince Bassianus, I have passed
My word and promise to the Emperor
That you will be more mild and tractable.   470
And fear not, lords, and you, Lavinia;
By my advice, all humbled on your knees,
You shall ask pardon of his majesty.

    Marcus, Lavinia, Lucius, Quintus, and Martius kneel

⌈LUCIUS⌉

We do, and vow to heaven and to his highness
That what we did was mildly as we might,
Tend'ring our sister's honour and our own.

MARCUS

That on mine honour here do I protest.

SATURNINUS

Away, and talk not; trouble us no more.

TAMORA

Nay, nay, sweet Emperor, we must all be friends.
The tribune and his nephews kneel for grace;   480
I will not be denied; sweetheart, look back.

SATURNINUS

Marcus, for thy sake, and thy brother's here,
And at my lovely Tamora's entreats,
I do remit these young men's heinous faults;

473.1 *Marcus . . . kneel*] *not in* Q1   474 LUCIUS] ROWE; Q1 *continues to Tamora*; Q2 *indents but without a new speech prefix*; *All* Q3; *Son* F

462 **am incorporate in** have become a part of
463 **happily** fortunately
465 **die** (may, as Maxwell suggests, have the meaning 'let them die')
471 **lords** i.e. Marcus and Titus' sons
474 LUCIUS The Q3 emendation '*All*' is possible, but since F is probably based on a
prompt copy, its attribution to one 'son' is preferable (see collations). Lucius, as the eldest, is the natural spokesman.
475 **mildly . . . might** done as mildly as we could
476 **Tend'ring** having regard for

Stand up. (*They rise*) Lavinia, though you left me like a
    churl,
I found a friend, and sure as death I swore
I would not part a bachelor from the priest.
Come, if the Emperor's court can feast two brides,
You are my guest, Lavinia, and your friends.
This day shall be a love-day, Tamora.   490

TITUS

Tomorrow, an it please your majesty
To hunt the panther and the hart with me,
With horn and hound we'll give your grace *bonjour*.

SATURNINUS

Be it so, Titus, and gramercy too.

          Sound trumpets. Exeunt all but Aaron

2.1

AARON

Now climbeth Tamora Olympus' top,
Safe out of fortune's shot, and sits aloft,
Secure of thunder's crack or lightning flash,
Advanced above pale envy's threat'ning reach;

---

485 *They rise*] not in Q1   494.1 *Sound . . . Aaron*] *Exeunt.* | *sound trumpets, manet Moore.* Q1 ;
Exeunt F

  2.1] ROWE (subs.); *Actus Secunda.* | *Flourish. Enter Aaron alone* F ; *not in* Q1   4 reach;] reach,
Q1 ; reach: F

485 **Stand up** These words were omitted by
    Pope, who presumably supposed, as some
    later editors did, that they were a stage
    direction. In Q1, however, such direc-
    tions are usually in the form of state-
    ments (e.g. '*They open the tomb*', '*They all
    kneel*'). An exception is '*Stab him*'
    (2.3.116.1).
486 **sure as death** Proverbial (Tilley D136).
490 **love-day** day appointed to settle dis-
    putes; also day for love
491 **an** if
492 **panther . . . hart** The panther is an exo-
    tic touch; Shakespeare may have known
    that some Roman emperors hunted
    panthers in Africa and that they were
    imported for wild-animal shows in Rome.
    They were not, of course, hunted as deer
    were in the Roman woods.
493 *bonjour* good day (French)
494 **gramercy** thanks

494.1 *Sound . . . Aaron* The Q1 stage direc-
    tion, leaving Aaron on stage, shows that
    no break in the action was intended here.
    The act division introduced by F was
    probably literary, paying homage to the
    tradition of a five-act structure. If the F
    directions represent a later stage practice,
    the tomb might have been removed
    during the interval (see headnote for
    2.2).
2.1.1 **AARON** In F he is directed to enter
    alone after an inappropriate 'flourish',
    transferred from the preceding stage
    direction in Q1, where it accompanies the
    Emperor's departure.
    Olympus Mount Olympus was the home
    of the Greek gods.
  3 **of** from
  4 **reach;** The punctuation in Q1 and F here
    and at the end of l. 8 (see collations)
    differs significantly. The Q1 comma after

As when the golden sun salutes the morn,
And having gilt the ocean with his beams,
Gallops the zodiac in his glistering coach,
And overlooks the highest-peering hills,
So Tamora;
Upon her wit doth earthly honour wait,   10
And virtue stoops and trembles at her frown;
Then, Aaron, arm thy heart, and fit thy thoughts
To mount aloft with thy imperial mistress,
And mount her pitch, whom thou in triumph long
Hast prisoner held, fettered in amorous chains,
And faster bound to Aaron's charming eyes
Than is Prometheus tied to Caucasus.
Away with slavish weeds and servile thoughts!
I will be bright, and shine in pearl and gold,
To wait upon this new-made Empress.   20
To wait, said I? – To wanton with this queen,
This goddess, this Semiramis, this nymph,
This siren, that will charm Rome's Saturnine,
And see his shipwrack and his commonweal's.
Holla, what storm is this?
    Enter Chiron and Demetrius braving

8 highest-peering] THEOBALD; highest piering Q1   hills,] hills. Q1; hills: F   9 So Tamora;] So *Tamora.* Q1 *(centred)*   25 Holla] Q1 (Hollo)

'reach' and full stop after 'hills' make the simile 'as when . . . hills' refer only to the preceding four lines, and isolate the words 'So Tamora' (centred in Q1 but not in F), which clearly should refer back to 'As when . . .'. The F colons suggest that the simile refers both to what precedes and to what follows it; see note on l. 9.

7 **Gallops** i.e. gallops through
8 **overlooks** looks down on
9 **So Tamora;** I have changed the full stop of Q1 to a semicolon (see collations), since, as Maxwell says, those words may also 'look forward as well as backward'. The sense is: Tamora's climbing is like the sun's, and her wisdom and power place her as far above others as the sun is above the highest hills.
10 **wit** intelligence
14 **mount her pitch** rise to the highest point of her flight (a term from falconry)
16 **charming** bewitching

17 **Prometheus** A demigod who stole fire from Olympus; Zeus punished him by chaining him to a rock in the Caucasus.
18 **Away . . . weeds** Aaron may discard some of the drab clothing ('weeds') he has worn as a prisoner and put on the 'bright' robe referred to in l. 19; Tamburlaine transforms himself in a similar way in Act 1, Scene 2 of Marlowe's play.
22 **Semiramis** Legendary Assyrian queen, famous for her beauty, her military conquests, and her lust.
24 **shipwrack** older standard form of 'shipwreck'; 'wrack' alone means 'a wrecked ship' (*OED*).
25.1 **Enter . . . braving** During his soliloquy Aaron should probably move down-stage right or left so that he is at some distance from the door at which Chiron and Demetrius enter. They are unaware of him until he approaches and speaks to them at l. 45.
braving defying (each other)

DEMETRIUS

    Chiron, thy years wants wit, thy wits wants edge

    And manners, to intrude where I am graced,

    And may, for aught thou knowest, affected be.

CHIRON

    Demetrius, thou dost overween in all,

    And so in this, to bear me down with braves.   30

    'Tis not the difference of a year or two

    Makes me less gracious, or thee more fortunate;

    I am as able and as fit as thou

    To serve, and to deserve my mistress' grace,

    And that my sword upon thee shall approve,

    And plead my passions for Lavinia's love.

AARON (*aside*)

    Clubs, clubs! These lovers will not keep the peace.

DEMETRIUS

    Why, boy, although our mother, unadvised,

    Gave you a dancing-rapier by your side,

    Are you so desperate grown to threat your friends?   40

    Go to; have your lath glued within your sheath,

    Till you know better how to handle it.

CHIRON

    Meanwhile, sir, with the little skill I have,

    Full well shalt thou perceive how much I dare.

DEMETRIUS

    Ay, boy, grow ye so brave?

        They draw

AARON   Why, how now, lords?

    So near the Emperor's palace dare ye draw,

    And maintain such a quarrel openly?

    Full well I wot the ground of all this grudge.

---

37 AARON] Moore Q1 (*and so ll.* 45, 60, 75, 91, 96, 98)

26 **wants** In Elizabethan English the third person singular form is often used for the plural.
    edge sharpness

27 **graced** received with favour

28 **affected** loved

29 **thou dost overween** you are arrogantly presumptuous

30 **braves** defiant threats

32 **gracious** worthy of favour

35 **approve** prove

37 **Clubs, clubs** The cry used for calling the watch to stop a street fight by interposing clubs.

39 **dancing-rapier** ornamental sword worn in dancing

40 **to** as to

41 **lath** wooden sword (such as was carried by the Vice in a morality play)

48 **wot** know

I would not for a million of gold
The cause were known to them it most concerns,   50
Nor would your noble mother for much more
Be so dishonoured in the court of Rome.
For shame, put up.
DEMETRIUS   Not I, till I have sheathed
My rapier in his bosom, and withal
Thrust those reproachful speeches down his throat,
That he hath breathed in my dishonour here.
CHIRON
For that I am prepared and full resolved,
Foul-spoken coward, that thund'rest with thy tongue,
And with thy weapon nothing dar'st perform.
AARON Away, I say!   60
Now, by the gods that warlike Goths adore,
This petty brabble will undo us all.
Why, lords, and think you not how dangerous
It is to jet upon a prince's right?
What, is Lavinia then become so loose,
Or Bassianus so degenerate,
That for her love such quarrels may be broached
Without controlment, justice, or revenge?
Young lords, beware! And should the Empress know
This discord's ground, the music would not please.   70
CHIRON
I care not, I, knew she and all the world,
I love Lavinia more than all the world.
DEMETRIUS
Youngling, learn thou to make some meaner choice;
Lavinia is thine elder brother's hope.
AARON
Why, are ye mad? Or know ye not in Rome
How furious and impatient they be,
And cannot brook competitors in love?

53 **put up** sheathe your swords
62 **brabble** quarrel
64 **jet** encroach
68 **controlment** restraint
69–70 **And . . . please** It suits Aaron's argu-
    ment to say so, but in fact he counts on
    her approval (see ll. 121–6).
70 **ground** reason (with a pun on the musi-

cal meaning: bass over which melody is
played)
71 **knew she** if she knew. Maxwell points to
    an echo of Kyd's *Spanish Tragedy* (1588?):
    'On whom I doted more than all the
    world, | Because she loved me more than
    all the world' (2.6.5–6).
73 **meaner** lower

I tell you, lords, you do but plot your deaths
By this device.

CHIRON

Aaron, a thousand deaths would I propose   80
To achieve her whom I love.

AARON   To achieve her how?

DEMETRIUS

Why makes thou it so strange?
She is a woman, therefore may be wooed;
She is a woman, therefore may be won;
She is Lavinia, therefore must be loved.
What, man! More water glideth by the mill
Than wots the miller of, and easy it is
Of a cut loaf to steal a shive, we know:
Though Bassianus be the Emperor's brother,
Better than he have worn Vulcan's badge.   90

AARON (*aside*)

Ay, and as good as Saturninus may.

DEMETRIUS

Then why should he despair that knows to court it
With words, fair looks, and liberality?
What, hast not thou full often struck a doe,
And borne her cleanly by the keeper's nose?

AARON

Why then, it seems some certain snatch or so
Would serve your turns.

CHIRON   Ay, so the turn were served.

DEMETRIUS

Aaron, thou hast hit it.

AARON   Would you had hit it too!

---

80 **propose** undertake to face
82 **Why ... strange** Why do you seem surprised?
   makes for 'makest' (a common substitution in Elizabethan English)
83–4 **She ... won** Proverbial: 'All women may be won' (*ODEP*, p. 911; Tilley W681).
86–7 **More . . . of** Proverbial (*ODEP*, p. 870; Tilley W99).
87–8 **easy . . . shive** Proverbial (*ODEP*, p. 724; Tilley T34).
88 **shive** slice

90 **worn ... badge** been cuckolded, as Vulcan was by Venus. A short line unless 'worn' is disyllabic like 'fire' in 1.1.127. *OED* records the seventeenth-century spelling 'woren'.
92 **court it** play the suitor
94 **struck** i.e. struck dead
95 **cleanly** adroitly
96 **snatch** swift catch; also (colloquially) hasty copulation. 'Turns' and 'hit' in the following lines continue the sexual *double entendre*.

Then should not we be tired with this ado.
Why, hark ye, hark ye, and are you such fools   100
To square for this? Would it offend you then
That both should speed?

CHIRON

Faith, not me.

DEMETRIUS   Nor me, so I were one.

AARON

For shame, be friends, and join for that you jar.
'Tis policy and stratagem must do
That you affect, and so must you resolve
That what you cannot as you would achieve,
You must perforce accomplish as you may.
Take this of me: Lucrece was not more chaste
Than this Lavinia, Bassianus' love.   110
A speedier course than ling'ring languishment
Must we pursue, and I have found the path.
My lords, a solemn hunting is in hand;
There will the lovely Roman ladies troop.
The forest walks are wide and spacious,
And many unfrequented plots there are,
Fitted by kind for rape and villainy.
Single you thither then this dainty doe,
And strike her home by force, if not by words;
This way, or not at all, stand you in hope.   120
Come, come, our Empress, with her sacred wit
To villainy and vengeance consecrate,
Will we acquaint with all what we intend,
And she shall file our engines with advice,
That will not suffer you to square yourselves,

111 than] ROWE; this Q1

101 **square** quarrel
102 **speed** succeed
104 **for that you jar** to get what you quarrel
    for
105 **policy** Machiavellian scheming
106 **affect** aim at
107–8 **what . . . may** Proverbial: 'Men must
    do as they may (can), not as they would'
    (Tilley M554).
109 **Lucrece** Roman wife whose rape by Tar-
    quin and subsequent suicide form the
    subject of Shakespeare's poem *Lucrece*,

published the same year as *Titus Andronicus* (1594).
113 **solemn** ceremonial
116 **plots** places
117 **kind** nature
118 **Single** i.e. single out (hunting term)
121 **sacred** devoted
122 **consecrate** dedicated
124 **file our engines** sharpen our stratagems
125 **square yourselves** quarrel with each
    other

But to your wishes' height advance you both.
The Emperor's court is like the house of fame,
The palace full of tongues, of eyes and ears;
The woods are ruthless, dreadful, deaf, and dull.
There speak, and strike, brave boys, and take your turns;   130
There serve your lust, shadowed from heaven's eye,
And revel in Lavinia's treasury.

CHIRON

Thy counsel, lad, smells of no cowardice.

DEMETRIUS

Sit fas aut nefas, till I find the stream
To cool this heat, a charm to calm these fits,
Per Stygia, per manes vehor.   *Exeunt*

2.2   *Enter Titus Andronicus and his three sons, Lucius,*
         Quintus, and Martius, making a noise with hounds
         and horns, and Marcus

TITUS

The hunt is up, the morn is bright and grey,
The fields are fragrant, and the woods are green.
Uncouple here, and let us make a bay,
And wake the Emperor and his lovely bride,

2.2] ROWE (*subs.*); *not in* Q1   0.1–2 *Lucius . . . Martius*] *not in* Q1   0.3 *and Marcus*] F (*at end of direction*); *not in* Q1   1 morn] Q3; Moone Q1

127 **house of fame** house of rumour (the subject of a well-known poem by Chaucer)

129 **woods . . . dull** In rapid succession the same woods are described in sharply contrasting terms; compare 2.3.12–15, 93–7.

134 *Sit . . . nefas* be it right or wrong (Latin)

136 *Per . . . vehor* I am borne through the Stygian regions among shades (Latin, adapted from Seneca's *Hippolytus*, l. 1180); i.e. I am in hell. The fashion of introducing bits of Latin, often adaptations of Seneca, into tragedy is well exemplified in Kyd's *Spanish Tragedy*.

2.2 The location is outside the Emperor's palace. Before or during the scene the tomb is presumably dismantled and carried off.

0.2 *noise* Not pejorative; it was the standard

term for an assemblage of instruments (J. S. Manifold, *The Music in English Drama* (1956), p. 42).

0.2 *hounds* Dogs certainly appeared in some Elizabethan plays (Louis Wright, 'Animal Actors on the English Stage', *PMLA*, 42 (1927), 656–69), and probably added to the spectacle here; note Titus' command (l. 3) to 'uncouple' (unleash) them.

0.3 *horns* Not 'the noble French horn . . ., but a harsh stubby little thing like Robin Hood's bugle' (Manifold, p. 42).
and Marcus This F addition to the stage direction is justified by the speech ascribed to Marcus at l. 20.

1 **grey** The word conventionally used for the morning sky; compare 'the sun | In the grey vault of heaven' (*2 Henry IV*, 2.3.18–19).

3 **bay** deep, prolonged barking

And rouse the Prince, and ring a hunter's peal,
That all the court may echo with the noise.
Sons, let it be your charge, as it is ours,
To attend the Emperor's person carefully.
I have been troubled in my sleep this night,
But dawning day new comfort hath inspired.   10

> *Here a cry of hounds, and wind horns in a peal; then*
> *enter Saturninus, Tamora, Bassianus, Lavinia, Chiron,*
> *Demetrius, and their attendants*

Many good morrows to your majesty;
Madam, to you as many and as good.
I promisèd your grace a hunter's peal.

SATURNINUS
And you have rung it lustily, my lords,
Somewhat too early for new-married ladies.

BASSIANUS
Lavinia, how say you?

LAVINIA   I say no;
I have been broad awake two hours and more.

SATURNINUS
Come on, then; horse and chariots let us have,
And to our sport. (*To Tamora*) Madam, now shall ye see
Our Roman hunting.

MARCUS   I have dogs, my lord,   20
Will rouse the proudest panther in the chase,
And climb the highest promontory top.

TITUS
And I have horse will follow where the game
Makes way and runs like swallows o'er the plain.

DEMETRIUS (*to Chiron*)
Chiron, we hunt not, we, with horse nor hound,
But hope to pluck a dainty doe to ground.   *Exeunt*

---

11 Many] *speech prefix 'Titus' repeated in* Q1   16–17 I say . . . more] *so divided in* F; *one line in*
Q1   24 runs] Q1; runne F2

---

5 **hunter's peal** horn-blowing to set the
dogs barking; see J. W. Fortescue in
Shakespeare's England, 2 vols. (Oxford,
1916), ii. 347.
10.1 *cry* barking

10.1 *wind* blow
21 **chase** hunting-ground
23 **horse** i.e. horses
24 **Makes . . . runs** See note on 2.1.26.

2.3   *Enter Aaron alone with a bag of gold*

AARON

He that had wit would think that I had none,
To bury so much gold under a tree,
And never after to inherit it.
Let him that thinks of me so abjectly
Know that this gold must coin a stratagem,
Which, cunningly effected, will beget
A very excellent piece of villainy.
And so repose, sweet gold, for their unrest
That have their alms out of the Empress' chest.

> *He hides the gold.*
> *Enter Tamora alone to the Moor*

TAMORA

My lovely Aaron, wherefore look'st thou sad,   10
When everything doth make a gleeful boast?
The birds chant melody on every bush,
The snake lies rollèd in the cheerful sun,
The green leaves quiver with the cooling wind,
And make a checkered shadow on the ground.
Under their sweet shade, Aaron, let us sit,
And whilst the babbling echo mocks the hounds,
Replying shrilly to the well-tuned horns,
As if a double hunt were heard at once,
Let us sit down and mark their yellowing noise;   20
And after conflict such as was supposed

2.3] CAPELL (*subs.*); *not in* Q1   0.1 *with a bag of gold*] *not in* Q1   1 AARON] *Moore* Q1 (*and so ll.* 30, 52)   9.1 *He . . . gold*] *not in* Q1   13 snake] Q3; snakes Q1

2.3 The location is the forest. A trap door at centre stage is opened to represent a pit; near it are loose branches. A property 'elder tree' (see ll. 272–3) is set near the pit with 'nettles' at its base. Henslowe's mention of a bay tree and two moss banks (*Diary*, pp. 319–20) suggests the sort of properties required here.

2 **bury . . . tree** From ll. 271–3 it is clear that Aaron hides the gold in the 'nettles' under the tree, where he 'finds' it again at l. 280.

3 **inherit** take possession of

9 **That . . . chest** i.e. who find this gold from Tamora's treasury. Aaron's plan is in fact more complicated: the 'unrest' of his vic-

tims will be caused by the mere suspicion that the gold was left for their agent.

11 **everything . . . boast** as if all things were competing to express their happiness

13 **snake** The Q1 reading, 'snakes', is possible, but the Q3 correction seems right, since the singular form of the verb is not used with a plural subject in the preceding or following line.

19 **double hunt** Compare 'As if a second chase were in the skies' (*Venus*, l. 696, noted by Parrott, *Modern Language Review*, 14 (1929), p. 27).

20 **yellowing** yelping; 'app. extension of *yell* on the analogy of *bell, bellow*' (*OED*).

The wand'ring prince and Dido once enjoyed,
When with a happy storm they were surprised,
And curtained with a counsel-keeping cave,
We may, each wreathèd in the other's arms,
Our pastimes done, possess a golden slumber,
While hounds and horns and sweet melodious birds
Be unto us as is a nurse's song
Of lullaby, to bring her babe asleep.

AARON

Madam, though Venus govern your desires,   30
Saturn is dominator over mine.
What signifies my deadly-standing eye,
My silence, and my cloudy melancholy,
My fleece of woolly hair that now uncurls,
Even as an adder when she doth unroll
To do some fatal execution?
No, madam, these are no venereal signs;
Vengeance is in my heart, death in my hand,
Blood and revenge are hammering in my head.
Hark, Tamora, the empress of my soul,   40
Which never hopes more heaven than rests in thee,
This is the day of doom for Bassianus;
His Philomel must lose her tongue today,
Thy sons make pillage of her chastity,
And wash their hands in Bassianus' blood.
        He holds out a letter which Tamora takes
Seest thou this letter? Take it up, I pray thee,
And give the king this fatal-plotted scroll.
Now question me no more; we are espied.

45.1 *He . . . takes*] *not in* Q1

22 **wand'ring prince** Aeneas
23–4 **When . . . cave** In the *Aeneid*, iv. 160–72, Virgil tells the famous story of Dido and Aeneas taking refuge from the storm in a cave.
23 **happy** fortunate
31 **Saturn** Saturnine men, according to Elizabethan astrologists, are melancholy and 'will never forgive till they be revenged' (*Kalendar of Shepherds*, pp. 141–2); see note on Saturninus, 1.1.0.2.
    dominator i.e. the prime influence (according to astrology)

32 **deadly-standing** fixed with a murderous stare
37 **venereal** erotic (pertaining to Venus)
43 **Philomel** Philomela; for Ovid's account of her rape (*Metamorphoses*, vi), one of the most important sources of the play, see Introduction, pp. 27–8; also note the references to the legend at 2.4.26–7, 38–9; 4.1.47–8; 5.2.194–5.
46–7 **Seest . . . scroll** This plan is later changed; the letter is placed where Titus will find it; see ll. 294–5.
46 **Take it up** i.e. take it

Here comes a parcel of our hopeful booty,
Which dreads not yet their lives' destruction.   50
    Enter Bassianus and Lavinia

TAMORA
Ah, my sweet Moor, sweeter to me than life!
AARON
No more, great Empress; Bassianus comes.
Be cross with him, and I'll go fetch thy sons
To back thy quarrels, whatsoe'er they be.   *Exit*
BASSIANUS
Who have we here? Rome's royal Empress,
Unfurnished of her well-beseeming troop?
Or is it Dian, habited like her,
Who hath abandonèd her holy groves
To see the general hunting in this forest?
TAMORA
Saucy controller of my private steps,   60
Had I the power that some say Dian had,
Thy temples should be planted presently
With horns, as was Acteon's, and the hounds
Should drive upon thy new-transformèd limbs,
Unmannerly intruder as thou art!
LAVINIA
Under your patience, gentle Empress,
'Tis thought you have a goodly gift in horning,
And to be doubted that your Moor and you
Are singled forth to try thy experiments.
Jove shield your husband from his hounds today!   70
'Tis pity they should take him for a stag.

---

54 *Exit*] *not in* Q1   69 thy] Q1 ; *not in* Q2, F

49 **parcel** part
    hopeful booty i.e. hoped-for victims
56 **Unfurnished . . . troop** unaccompanied by
    suitable followers
57 **Dian** Diana, goddess of chastity and the
    hunt
    habited dressed
60 **Saucy** 'in Shakespeare's time often an
    epithet of more serious condemnation
    than at present' (Onions).
    controller critic
62 **presently** immediately
63 **Actaeon's** As punishment for seeing

Diana bathing Actaeon was transformed
into a stag and killed by his own hounds.
64 **drive** rush
66 **Under your patience** if you permit me to
    say so
67 **horning** i.e. giving your husband a
    cuckold's horns
68 **doubted** suspected
69 **thy experiments** Later editions achieve
    metrical regularity by dropping 'thy', but
    also lose something of Lavinia's personal
    venom; 'thy' was sometimes elided before
    a vowel (Cercignani, p. 290).

BASSIANUS

Believe me, Queen, your swarthy Cimmerian
Doth make your honour of his body's hue,
Spotted, detested, and abominable.
Why are you sequestered from all your train,
Dismounted from your snow-white goodly steed,
And wandered hither to an obscure plot,
Accompanied but with a barbarous Moor,
If foul desire had not conducted you?

LAVINIA

And, being intercepted in your sport,   80
Great reason that my noble lord be rated
For sauciness. (*To Bassianus*) I pray you, let us hence,
And let her joy her raven-coloured love;
This valley fits the purpose passing well.

BASSIANUS

The King my brother shall have notice of this.

LAVINIA

Ay, for these slips have made him noted long,
Good king to be so mightily abused.

TAMORA

Why, I have patience to endure all this.
        Enter Chiron and Demetrius

DEMETRIUS

How now, dear sovereign, and our gracious mother?
Why does your highness look so pale and wan?   90

TAMORA

Have I not reason, think you, to look pale?

72 swarthy] Q1 (swartie); swarth F   85 notice] Q1 ; note POPE

72 **swarthy** The F 'swarth' (see collations) makes the line regular, but it is not necessarily more correct.
Cimmerian i.e. Aaron; the Cimmerians, according to Homer, lived in total darkness.
74 **Spotted** smirched
abominable The Q1 spelling 'abhominable', common in Elizabethan texts, reveals a meaning derived from the false etymology, '*ab homine*', away from man, inhuman.
75 **sequestered** (accented 'séquestéred')

81 **rated** berated
83 **joy** enjoy
85 **notice** Pope substituted 'note' to avoid an extra syllable.
86 **noted** notorious
long In the chapbook story the Emperor has long been suspicious of the Empress, to whom he has been married for many months; in the play, as Maxwell notes, this reference to such a lapse of time gives the effect of a double time-scheme, as in *Othello*.

These two have 'ticed me hither to this place,
A barren detested vale you see it is;
The trees, though summer, yet forlorn and lean,
Overcome with moss and baleful mistletoe.
Here never shines the sun, here nothing breeds,
Unless the nightly owl or fatal raven;
And when they showed me this abhorrèd pit,
They told me here at dead time of the night
A thousand fiends, a thousand hissing snakes,   100
Ten thousand swelling toads, as many urchins,
Would make such fearful and confusèd cries
As any mortal body hearing it
Should straight fall mad, or else die suddenly.
No sooner had they told this hellish tale
But straight they told me they would bind me here
Unto the body of a dismal yew,
And leave me to this miserable death.
And then they called me foul adulteress,
Lascivious Goth, and all the bitterest terms   110
That ever ear did hear to such effect.
And had you not by wondrous fortune come,
This vengeance on me had they executed.
Revenge it, as you love your mother's life,
Or be ye not henceforth called my children.

DEMETRIUS

This is a witness that I am thy son.
    He stabs Bassianus

CHIRON

And this for me, struck home to show my strength.
    He also stabs Bassianus, who dies. Tamora threatens
    Lavinia

116.1 *He stabs Bassianus*] *Stab him* Q1   117.1–2 *He . . . Lavinia*] *not in* Q1

---

92 **'ticed** enticed
95 **Overcome** overgrown
97 **fatal** ominous
101 **urchins** hedgehogs
107 **dismal yew** Yew trees were associated
with graveyards; their berries were said
to be poisonous, and some thought that

the shadow of the tree would kill anyone
sleeping under it; see H. T. Price,
'The Yew-Tree in "Titus Andronicus"',
N. & Q., 208 (1963), 98–9.
110 **Lascivious Goth** Probably punning on
'goat' (as in *As You Like It*, 3.3.9), a
proverbially lecherous animal.

LAVINIA

Ay, come, Semiramis, nay, barbarous Tamora,

For no name fits thy nature but thy own!

TAMORA

Give me the poniard. You shall know, my boys,   120

Your mother's hand shall right your mother's wrong.

DEMETRIUS

Stay, madam; here is more belongs to her.

First thresh the corn, then after burn the straw.

This minion stood upon her chastity,

Upon her nuptial vow, her loyalty,

And with that painted hope braves your mightiness;

And shall she carry this unto her grave?

CHIRON

An if she do, I would I were an eunuch.

Drag hence her husband to some secret hole,

And make his dead trunk pillow to our lust.   130

TAMORA

But when ye have the honey ye desire,

Let not this wasp outlive, us both to sting.

CHIRON

I warrant you, madam, we will make that sure.

Come, mistress, now perforce we will enjoy

That nice-preservèd honesty of yours.

---

123 thresh] Q1 (thrash)   131 ye desire] F2; we desire Q1   132 outlive,] THEOBALD; out liue Q1

118 **Semiramis** See notes on 2.1.22 and 1.1.69.5; Tamora so far exceeds Semiramis that only her own name is appropriate.

122 **here ... her** she has more (that we can use) *or* here's more which concerns her

123 **First ... straw** This sounds proverbial, but is not recorded in *ODEP* or Tilley; it is very like the proverbs Demetrius spouts at 2.1.83–8.

124 **minion** hussy
stood upon made much of

126 **painted** false. The unusual metre has tempted some editors to substitute a monosyllable.

129–30 **Drag ... lust** This macabre refinement of cruelty is not carried out and is not part of Aaron's plan, as Chiron apparently knows (see ll. 185–6). It seems

to have been borrowed from or to have influenced Thomas Nashe's *The Unfortunate Traveller* (see Introduction, p. 6).

131 **ye desire** Although this F2 correction (see collations) at first seems to make much better sense, G. K. Hunter has suggested to me a plausible justification of Q1 'we': Tamora may refer to the general desire to have what we want. I accept 'ye' largely because a reference to the young men's lust seems more likely than a general reflection.

132 **outlive** survive (an unique instance of 'outlive' used intransitively; possibly an error for 'o'erlive', as Maxwell suggests)

133 **warrant** frequently monosyllabic

135 **nice-preservèd honesty** fastidiously guarded chastity

119

LAVINIA

  O Tamora, thou bearest a woman's face –

TAMORA

  I will not hear her speak; away with her!

LAVINIA

  Sweet lords, entreat her hear me but a word.

DEMETRIUS (*to Tamora*)

  Listen, fair madam, let it be your glory

  To see her tears, but be your heart to them   140

  As unrelenting flint to drops of rain.

LAVINIA

  When did the tiger's young ones teach the dam?

  O, do not learn her wrath; she taught it thee;

  The milk thou suck'st from her did turn to marble;

  Even at thy teat thou hadst thy tyranny.

  Yet every mother breeds not sons alike;

  (*To Chiron*) Do thou entreat her show a woman's pity.

CHIRON

  What, wouldst thou have me prove myself a bastard?

LAVINIA

  'Tis true, the raven doth not hatch a lark;

  Yet I have heard – O, could I find it now! –   150

  The lion, moved with pity, did endure

  To have his princely paws pared all away.

  Some say that ravens foster forlorn children

  The whilst their own birds famish in their nests.

  O, be to me, though thy hard heart say no,

  Nothing so kind, but something pitiful.

TAMORA

  I know not what it means; away with her!

LAVINIA

  O, let me teach thee for my father's sake,

153 Some] Q2; So me Q1   158 thee] Q1; thee: THEOBALD

140–1 **heart . . . flint** A proverbial comparison (Tilley H311).
143 **learn** teach
144 **suck'st** (for the unpronounceable past tense 'suck'dst')
149 **raven . . . lark** Compare 'An eagle does not hatch a dove' (*ODEP*, p. 211; Tilley E2).

150 **find it** i.e. find it so
151–2 **The lion . . . away** a well-known fable (Tilley L316)
154 **birds** i.e. young ones
156 **Nothing . . . pitiful** not nearly so kind as the raven, but somewhat pitying
157 **it** i.e. pity

That gave thee life when well he might have slain thee,
Be not obdurate; open thy deaf ears.   160

TAMORA

Hadst thou in person ne'er offended me,
Even for his sake am I pitiless.
Remember, boys, I poured forth tears in vain
To save your brother from the sacrifice,
But fierce Andronicus would not relent.
Therefore away with her, and use her as you will;
The worse to her, the better loved of me.

LAVINIA ⌈*embracing Tamora's knees*⌉

O Tamora, be called a gentle queen,
And with thine own hands kill me in this place;
For 'tis not life that I have begged so long;   170
Poor I was slain when Bassianus died.

TAMORA

What begg'st thou then, fond woman? Let me go.

LAVINIA

'Tis present death I beg, and one thing more
That womanhood denies my tongue to tell.
O, keep me from their worse-than-killing lust,
And tumble me into some loathsome pit,
Where never man's eye may behold my body;
Do this, and be a charitable murderer.

TAMORA

So should I rob my sweet sons of their fee.
No, let them satisfy their lust on thee.   180

DEMETRIUS

Away! For thou hast stayed us here too long.

---

159 slain thee,] Q1; slaine thee: F   160 ears] Q1 (yeares); eares Q3   168 *embracing . . . knees*]
not in Q1   172 then, . . . woman? . . . go] MAXWELL; then . . . woman . . . goe? Q1; then?
. . . woman . . . go? Q3   180 satisfy] Q2 (satisfie); satisfiee (*or* satisfice) Q1

160 **ears** The spelling 'yeares' in Q1 (see
    collations) reflects a variant pronunci-
    ation (see Cercignani, p. 362).
162 **Even** precisely
168 *embracing . . . knees* The transform-
    ation of Lavinia from righteous critic to
    suppliant may be emphasized by a piece
    of stage business: she probably kneels

and clutches Tamora.
172 **What . . . go** The punctuation of the
    early texts makes it uncertain whether
    'fond woman' goes with the first or
    second clause (see collations).
    fond foolish
174 **denies** forbids

LAVINIA

No grace, no womanhood? Ah, beastly creature,
The blot and enemy to our general name!
Confusion fall –

CHIRON

Nay, then I'll stop your mouth. (*To Demetrius*) Bring thou
her husband;
This is the hole where Aaron bid us hide him.
*Demetrius throws the body of Bassianus into the pit ⌈and
covers the opening with branches⌉; then exeunt Chiron
and Demetrius with Lavinia*

TAMORA

Farewell, my sons; see that you make her sure.
Ne'er let my heart know merry cheer indeed
Till all the Andronici be made away.
Now will I hence to seek my lovely Moor,   190
And let my spleenful sons this trull deflower.   *Exit*
*Enter Aaron with two of Titus' sons, Quintus and
Martius*

AARON

Come on, my lords, the better foot before;
Straight will I bring you to the loathsome pit
Where I espied the panther fast asleep.

QUINTUS

My sight is very dull, whate'er it bodes.

MARTIUS

And mine, I promise you. Were it not for shame,
Well could I leave our sport to sleep a while.
He falls into the pit

186.1–3 *Demetrius . . . Lavinia*] not in Q1 ; *Exeunt* F2   191 *Exit*] F; *not in* Q1   191.1–2 *Quintus
and Martius*] *not in* Q1   192 AARON] F; *not in* Q1   197.1 *He . . . pit*] *not in* Q1

183 **our general name** our reputation as
     women
184 **Confusion** destruction
185 **stop your mouth** i.e. with his hand or
     perhaps with a kiss; compare 'stop his
     mouth with a kiss', *Much Ado*, 2.1.322–3.
186.2 *covers . . . branches* This piece of busi-
     ness is required by l. 199.
187 **make her sure** render her harmless
188 **cheer** frame of mind
189 **made away** killed

191 **spleenful** lustful
     trull slut
192 **better foot before** Proverbial (Tilley
     F570); i.e. put your best foot forward,
     make haste.
194 **panther fast asleep** Shakespeare may
     have read that one method of hunting
     panthers was by luring them into a pit,
     but most of the details of this hunt are
     derived from stag-hunting.

QUINTUS

What, art thou fallen? What subtle hole is this,
Whose mouth is covered with rude-growing briers,
Upon whose leaves are drops of new-shed blood　　　200
As fresh as morning dew distilled on flowers?
A very fatal place it seems to me.
Speak, brother, hast thou hurt thee with the fall?

MARTIUS

O brother, with the dismal'st object hurt
That ever eye with sight made heart lament.

AARON (*aside*)

Now will I fetch the King to find them here,
That he thereby may have a likely guess
How these were they that made away his brother.　*Exit*

MARTIUS

Why dost not comfort me and help me out
From this unhallowed and bloodstainèd hole?　　　210

QUINTUS

I am surprisèd with an uncouth fear;
A chilling sweat o'erruns my trembling joints;
My heart suspects more than mine eye can see.

MARTIUS

To prove thou hast a true-divining heart,
Aaron and thou look down into this den,
And see a fearful sight of blood and death.

QUINTUS

Aaron is gone, and my compassionate heart
Will not permit mine eyes once to behold
The thing whereat it trembles by surmise.
O, tell me who it is, for ne'er till now　　　220
Was I a child to fear I know not what.

MARTIUS

Lord Bassianus lies berayed in blood,

208 *Exit*] F (*Exit Aaron*); *after l. 207 in* Q1　210 unhallowed] F; unhollow Q1　222 berayed in blood] WILSON; bereaud in blood Q1; embrewed here Q2

198 **subtle** ingeniously disguised, treacherous
202 **fatal** ill-omened
211 **surprisèd** bewildered
　　uncouth uncanny
219 **by surmise** even by imagining

222 **berayed in** defiled by. Dover Wilson's conjecture makes good sense of the line (see collations); 'embrewed here' (Q2) also makes sense, but if it had been the manuscript reading, could hardly have led to 'bereaud in blood' in Q1. It seems to

All on a heap, like to a slaughtered lamb,
In this detested, dark, blood-drinking pit.

QUINTUS

If it be dark, how dost thou know 'tis he?

MARTIUS

Upon his bloody finger he doth wear
A precious ring that lightens all this hole,
Which, like a taper in some monument,
Doth shine upon the dead man's earthy cheeks,
And shows the ragged entrails of this pit;   230
So pale did shine the moon on Pyramus
When he by night lay bathed in maiden blood.
O brother, help me with thy fainting hand –
If fear hath made thee faint as me it hath –
Out of this fell devouring receptacle,
As hateful as Cocytus' misty mouth.

QUINTUS

Reach me thy hand, that I may help thee out,
Or, wanting strength to do thee so much good,
I may be plucked into the swallowing womb
Of this deep pit, poor Bassianus' grave.   240
I have no strength to pluck thee to the brink.

MARTIUS

Nor I no strength to climb without thy help.

QUINTUS

Thy hand once more; I will not loose again
Till thou art here aloft or I below.
Thou canst not come to me; I come to thee.
    He falls in.
    Enter the Emperor and Aaron the Moor

---

231 Pyramus] Q2; *Priamus* Q1   236 Cocytus'] F2; *Ocitus* Q1   245.1 *He falls in*] *not in* Q1; *Boths fall in* F

be a guess like that of the early owner of
the Folger Q1, who wrote in 'heere reav'd
of lyfe'.

223 **on a heap** prostrate
227 **ring . . . lightens** Certain gems were
thought to shine in the dark.
228 **monument** tomb
229 **earthy** pallid
230 **ragged entrails** rough interior

231 **Pyramus** Lover of Thisbe, who killed
himself when he supposed her dead (the
story acted by the 'rude mechanicals' in
Dream).
235 **fell** savage
receptacle See note on 1.1.92.
236 **Cocytus** A river in Hades, used here for
hell; a smoking hell-mouth was a standard property in medieval drama.
238 **wanting** lacking

SATURNINUS

Along with me! I'll see what hole is here,
And what he is that now is leapt into it.
Say, who art thou that lately didst descend
Into this gaping hollow of the earth?

MARTIUS

The unhappy sons of old Andronicus,   250
Brought hither in a most unlucky hour,
To find thy brother Bassianus dead.

SATURNINUS

My brother dead! I know thou dost but jest;
He and his lady both are at the lodge,
Upon the north side of this pleasant chase;
'Tis not an hour since I left them there.

MARTIUS

We know not where you left them all alive,
But, out alas! here have we found him dead.

> *Enter Tamora, with attendants, Titus Andronicus,*
> *and Lucius*

TAMORA Where is my lord the King?

SATURNINUS

Here, Tamora, though grieved with killing grief.   260

TAMORA

Where is thy brother Bassianus?

SATURNINUS

Now to the bottom dost thou search my wound.
Poor Bassianus here lies murderèd.

TAMORA

Then all too late I bring this fatal writ,
The complot of this timeless tragedy,
And wonder greatly that man's face can fold
In pleasing smiles such murderous tyranny.

> *She giveth Saturnine a letter*

258.1 with . . . Titus] *not in* Q1   260 SATURNINUS] *King* Q1 (*and so for remainder of scene except*
l. 268)   grieved] Q1 (griude); grip'd MAXWELL

258.1 **attendants** Two are needed to bear off
the dead body at the end of the scene, and
two to guard Martius and Quintus.
262 **search** probe

265 **complot** plot
timeless untimely
266 **fold** hide (suggesting the folds of skin
made by 'smiles')

SATURNINUS (*reads the letter*)
  'An if we miss to meet him handsomely,
  Sweet huntsman – Bassianus 'tis we mean –
  Do thou so much as dig the grave for him;   270
  Thou know'st our meaning; look for thy reward
  Among the nettles at the elder tree
  Which overshades the mouth of that same pit
  Where we decreed to bury Bassianus.
  Do this and purchase us thy lasting friends.'
  O Tamora, was ever heard the like?
  This is the pit, and this the elder tree.
  Look sirs, if you can find the huntsman out
  That should have murdered Bassianus here.

AARON
  My gracious lord, here is the bag of gold.   280

SATURNINUS (*to Titus*)
  Two of thy whelps, fell curs of bloody kind,
  Have here bereft my brother of his life. –
  Sirs, drag them from the pit unto the prison;
  There let them bide until we have devised
  Some never-heard-of torturing pain for them.
      Attendants drag Quintus, Martius, and Bassianus' body
      from the pit

TAMORA
  What, are they in this pit? O wondrous thing!
  How easily murder is discoverèd!

TITUS (*kneeling*)
  High Emperor, upon my feeble knee
  I beg this boon, with tears not lightly shed,
  That this fell fault of my accursèd sons –   290
  Accursèd if the fault be proved in them –

---

268 SATURNINUS ... *letter*] Q1 (*subs.*; *centred*)   276 O,Tamora] Q1 *adds prefix* 'King.'   285.1–2
Attendants ... pit] *not in* Q1   288 *kneeling*] *not in* Q1   291 fault] THEOBALD; faults Q1

268 **handsomely** conveniently
275 **purchase** win
279 **should have** was to have
281 **kind** nature
287 **How ... discoverèd** Proverbial: 'Murder

will out' (*ODEP*, p. 551; Tilley M1315).
291 **fault** Theobald's emendation (see collations) is logical; Q1 'faults' is an understandable inconsistency since two persons are referred to.

SATURNINUS

    If it be proved! You see it is apparent.

    Who found this letter? Tamora, was it you?

TAMORA

    Andronicus himself did take it up.

TITUS

    I did, my lord, yet let me be their bail;

    For by my fathers' reverend tomb I vow

    They shall be ready at your highness' will

    To answer their suspicion with their lives.

SATURNINUS

    Thou shalt not bail them; see thou follow me.

    Some bring the murdered body, some the murderers.　　300

    Let them not speak a word – the guilt is plain;

    For by my soul, were there worse end than death,

    That end upon them should be executed.

TAMORA

    Andronicus, I will entreat the king.

    Fear not thy sons; they shall do well enough.

TITUS (*rising*)

    Come, Lucius, come, stay not to talk with them.

              Exeunt with Martius and Quintus under guard;

              attendants bearing the body of Bassianus

2.4　　*Enter the Empress' sons, Chiron and Demetrius, with*

        Lavinia, her hands cut off, and her tongue cut out, and

        ravished

DEMETRIUS

    So now go tell, an if thy tongue can speak,

    Who 'twas that cut thy tongue and ravished thee.

CHIRON

    Write down thy mind, bewray thy meaning so,

    An if thy stumps will let thee play the scribe.

---

296 fathers'] Q1 (Fathers)　　306 *rising*] *not in* Q1　　306.1–2 *Exeunt . . . Bassianus*] *not in* Q1; *Exeunt* F

  2.4] DYCE (*subs.*); *not in* Q1　　0.1 *Chiron and Demetrius*] *not in* Q1

---

292 **apparent** obvious

298 **their suspicion** suspicion of them

305 **Fear not** fear not for

2.4.3 **bewray** reveal

DEMETRIUS

See how with signs and tokens she can scrawl.

CHIRON

Go home, call for sweet water, wash thy hands.

DEMETRIUS

She hath no tongue to call, nor hands to wash,
And so let's leave her to her silent walks.

CHIRON

An 'twere my cause, I should go hang myself.

DEMETRIUS

If thou hadst hands to help thee knit the cord.   10

Exeunt Chiron and Demetrius

⌈*Wind horns.*⌉
Enter Marcus from hunting

MARCUS

Who is this? My niece, that flies away so fast?
Cousin, a word: where is your husband?
If I do dream, would all my wealth would wake me!
If I do wake, some planet strike me down,
That I may slumber an eternal sleep!
Speak, gentle niece, what stern ungentle hands
Hath lopped and hewed and made thy body bare
Of her two branches, those sweet ornaments,
Whose circling shadows kings have sought to sleep in,
And might not gain so great a happiness   20
As half thy love? Why dost not speak to me?
Alas, a crimson river of warm blood,
Like to a bubbling fountain stirred with wind,
Doth rise and fall between thy rosèd lips,

5 scrawl] Q1 (scrowl)   10.1 *Chiron and Demetrius*] *not in* Q1   10.2 *Wind horns*] F; *not in* Q1

5 **scrawl** gesticulate. The Q1 spelling 'scrowl' may imply a punning allusion to 'scroll', often spelt the same way (as at 4.4.16); the first instance in the *OED* of 'scroll' as a verb, meaning 'to write down', is 1606.

6 **sweet** perfumed

9 **cause** case

10.2 **Wind horns** i.e. off stage, as an indication that the hunt is in progress

10.3 *from hunting* May indicate that his costume and those of others were appropriate for hunting, but since the upper-class characters in the Peacham drawing appear in approximations of

classical dress, it is difficult to guess what sort of hunting costume may be implied.

12 **Cousin** Commonly used for a close relative other than parent, child, or sibling.

13 **would . . . me** i.e. I would give all I own to be awakened

14 **strike me down** exert its evil influence on me

16–32 **what . . . cloud** This highly ornamented description, resembling some passages in *Lucrece*, shows Shakespeare's indebtedness to Ovid's *Metamorphoses*; see Bradbrook, pp. 60–6, 108, and Waith, 'Metamorphosis', pp. 39–49.

Coming and going with thy honey breath.
But sure some Tereus hath deflowered thee,
And, lest thou shouldst detect him, cut thy tongue.
Ah, now thou turn'st away thy face for shame;
And notwithstanding all this loss of blood,
As from a conduit with three issuing spouts,   30
Yet do thy cheeks look red as Titan's face,
Blushing to be encountered with a cloud.
Shall I speak for thee? Shall I say 'tis so?
O, that I knew thy heart, and knew the beast,
That I might rail at him to ease my mind!
Sorrow concealèd, like an oven stopped,
Doth burn the heart to cinders where it is.
Fair Philomela, why she but lost her tongue,
And in a tedious sampler sewed her mind;
But, lovely niece, that mean is cut from thee.   40
A craftier Tereus, cousin, hast thou met,
And he hath cut those pretty fingers off,
That could have better sewed than Philomel.
O, had the monster seen those lily hands
Tremble, like aspen leaves, upon a lute,
And make the silken strings delight to kiss them,
He would not then have touched them for his life.
Or, had he heard the heavenly harmony
Which that sweet tongue hath made,
He would have dropped his knife and fell asleep,   50
As Cerberus at the Thracian poet's feet.
Come, let us go and make thy father blind,
For such a sight will blind a father's eye.
One hour's storm will drown the fragrant meads;
What will whole months of tears thy father's eyes?
Do not draw back, for we will mourn with thee;
O, could our mourning ease thy misery!   *Exeunt*

27 him] ROWE; them Q1   30 three] HANMER; their Q1

26 **Tereus** See note on 2.3.43.
27 **detect** expose
31 **Titan** See note on 1.1.226.
36–7 **like . . . is** The close connection between *Titus* and Shakespeare's narrative
   poetry is well illustrated by the use of this
   exact image for 'concealed sorrow' in
   Venus, ll. 331–3. The idea is proverbial
   (Tilley, F265; Dent, p. 187).

39 **tedious sampler** laboriously executed
   needlework
   sewed her mind i.e. revealed her story in
   her embroidery
51 **Cerberus** The three-headed watchdog at
   the entrance of Hades; Orpheus, 'the
   Thracian poet', charmed him with the
   music of his lyre.

3.1   *Enter the Judges, Tribunes, and Senators with Titus'*
       two sons, Martius and Quintus, bound, passing over
       the stage to the place of execution, and Titus going
       before, pleading

TITUS

Hear me, grave fathers. Noble tribunes, stay.
For pity of mine age, whose youth was spent
In dangerous wars, whilst you securely slept;
For all my blood in Rome's great quarrel shed,
For all the frosty nights that I have watched,
And for these bitter tears which now you see,
Filling the agèd wrinkles in my cheeks,
Be pitiful to my condemnèd sons,
Whose souls is not corrupted as 'tis thought.
For two-and-twenty sons I never wept,   10
Because they died in honour's lofty bed;

       Andronicus lieth down, and the Judges and others pass
       by him

For these, tribunes, in the dust I write
My heart's deep languor and my soul's sad tears.
Let my tears stanch the earth's dry appetite;
My sons' sweet blood will make it shame and blush.
O earth, I will befriend thee more with rain,

       Exeunt the Judges and others with the prisoners

3.1] ROWE (*subs.*); *Actus Tertius* F; *not in* Q1   0.1 *Tribunes*] *not in* Q1   0.2 *Martius and Quintus*]
not in Q1   *over*] This edition; *on* Q1   11.1 *and others*] *not in* Q1   16.1 *Exeunt . . . prisoners*]
not in Q1; *Exeunt* F

3.1 The location is once more a street in
Rome. There may have been a traverse (a
stage curtain) between the two entrances
(see note on ll. 233 ff.).

0.2 *over* Stanley Wells suggests this
emendation (see collations); he writes:
'"over" was often abbreviated, or written
with a superscript r; the misreading
would have been very easy, and I know
of no parallel to the Quarto reading.'

10 **two-and-twenty** If Mutius is added to the
'one-and-twenty' sons Titus says he has
buried (1.1.195), this total is correct, but
he would hardly refer to the son he killed
as having 'died in honour's lofty bed'. In
the chapbook narrative twenty-two of
Titus' twenty-five sons have been killed in

battle, and Shakespeare may originally
have planned to show only three sons in
Rome. In this case he simply failed to alter
'two-and-twenty' here, as he had done at
1.1.195, when he added a fourth son to
the number accompanying Titus to
Rome.

11.1 **lieth down** i.e. prostrates himself
13 **languor** grief
14 **stanch** satisfy
15 **shame** be ashamed
16.1 *Exeunt . . . prisoners* Many editors add
this stage direction to the one after l. 11,
but the placement of the F '*Exeunt*' after
'rain' allows time for the procession to
pass.

That shall distil from these two ancient urns,
Than youthful April shall with all his showers.
In summer's drought I'll drop upon thee still;
In winter with warm tears I'll melt the snow,   20
And keep eternal springtime on thy face,
So thou refuse to drink my dear sons' blood.
        Enter Lucius with his weapon drawn
O reverend tribunes! O gentle agèd men!
Unbind my sons, reverse the doom of death,
And let me say, that never wept before,
My tears are now prevailing orators.
LUCIUS
    O noble father, you lament in vain;
    The tribunes hear you not, no man is by,
    And you recount your sorrows to a stone.
TITUS
    Ah, Lucius, for thy brothers let me plead: 30
    Grave tribunes, once more I entreat of you –
LUCIUS
    My gracious lord, no tribune hears you speak.
TITUS
    Why, 'tis no matter, man; if they did hear,
    They would not mark me; if they did mark,
    They would not pity me, yet plead I must,
    And bootless unto them.
    Therefore I tell my sorrows to the stones,
    Who, though they cannot answer my distress,
    Yet in some sort they are better than the tribunes,
    For that they will not intercept my tale.   40
    When I do weep, they humbly at my feet
    Receive my tears and seem to weep with me;
    And were they but attirèd in grave weeds,

17 urns] HANMER; ruines Q1   21 on thy] Q2; out hy Q1   34 me; if] Q1; me, or if Q2

17 **urns** Though 'ruins', the reading of all
early texts, is possible (see collations),
Hanmer's emendation is plausible and
makes better sense.
19 **still** continually
22 **So** on condition that
24 **doom** sentence
26 **orators** advocates, as in a law court
34 **me; if** The Q2 addition of 'or' between
these two words (see collations) achieves

metrical regularity, though we cannot be
sure that 'or' was in the manuscript copy
for Q1.
36 **bootless** in vain; this half-line may, as
Maxwell suggests, be a false start. For a
discussion of the variant versions of this
passage see Introduction, pp. 41–2.
40 **intercept** interrupt
43 **grave weeds** sober garments

Rome could afford no tribunes like to these.
A stone is soft as wax, tribunes more hard than stones;
A stone is silent and offendeth not,
And tribunes with their tongues doom men to death.
But wherefore stand'st thou with thy weapon drawn?
LUCIUS
To rescue my two brothers from their death,
For which attempt the judges have pronounced   50
My everlasting doom of banishment.
TITUS ⌜*rising*⌝
O happy man! They have befriended thee.
Why, foolish Lucius, dost thou not perceive
That Rome is but a wilderness of tigers?
Tigers must prey, and Rome affords no prey
But me and mine. How happy art thou then
From these devourers to be banishèd!
But who comes with our brother Marcus here?
        Enter Marcus with Lavinia
MARCUS
Titus, prepare thy agèd eyes to weep,
Or if not so, thy noble heart to break.   60
I bring consuming sorrow to thine age.
TITUS
Will it consume me? Let me see it then.
MARCUS
This was thy daughter.
TITUS   Why, Marcus, so she is.
LUCIUS (*falling on his knees*) Ay me! This object kills me.
TITUS
Faint-hearted boy, arise, and look upon her.
        ⌜*Lucius rises*⌝
Speak, Lavinia, what accursèd hand
Hath made thee handless in thy father's sight?

---

52 *rising*] *not in* Q1   64 *falling on his knees*] *not in* Q1   65.1 *Lucius rises*] *not in* Q1

44 **afford** provide
52 **rising** Titus probably gets to his feet
   during this dialogue. His bitter indict-
   ment of Rome provides a good occasion.
64 **object** 'something presented to the sight'
   (*OED*)

65 **arise** Titus' command shows that Lucius
   has fallen to his knees, and, presumably,
   that he rises at this point.
66 **Lavinia** What appears to be an accent
   over the 'e' in Q1's 'Lavinea' is probably
   an imperfection in the paper.

What fool hath added water to the sea,
Or brought a faggot to bright-burning Troy?
My grief was at the height before thou cam'st,   70
And now like Nilus it disdaineth bounds.
Give me a sword, I'll chop off my hands too,
For they have fought for Rome, and all in vain;
And they have nursed this woe in feeding life;
In bootless prayer have they been held up,
And they have served me to effectless use.
Now all the service I require of them
Is that the one will help to cut the other.
'Tis well, Lavinia, that thou hast no hands,
For hands to do Rome service is but vain.   80

LUCIUS
Speak, gentle sister, who hath martyred thee?

MARCUS
O, that delightful engine of her thoughts,
That blabbed them with such pleasing eloquence,
Is torn from forth that pretty hollow cage,
Where like a sweet melodious bird it sung
Sweet varied notes, enchanting every ear.

LUCIUS
O, say thou for her, who hath done this deed?

MARCUS
O, thus I found her straying in the park,
Seeking to hide herself, as doth the deer
That hath received some unrecuring wound.   90

TITUS
It was my dear, and he that wounded her
Hath hurt me more than had he killed me dead;
For now I stand as one upon a rock,
Environed with a wilderness of sea,
Who marks the waxing tide grow wave by wave,
Expecting ever when some envious surge

---

68 **What . . . sea** Proverbial: 'To cast Water into the sea' (*ODEP*, p. 870; Tilley W106).
71 **Nilus** the River Nile, known for its annual flooding
75 **prayer** (disyllabic here)
76 **effectless** unproductive
81 **martyred** mutilated
82 **engine** instrument

83 **blabbed** freely spoke
89–90 **deer . . . wound** Proverbial: 'As the stricken Deer withdraws himself to die' (Tilley D189).
90 **unrecuring** incurable
96 **Expecting ever when** always waiting for the time when
envious malicious

Will in his brinish bowels swallow him.
This way to death my wretched sons are gone;
Here stands my other son, a banished man,
And here my brother, weeping at my woes;   100
But that which gives my soul the greatest spurn
Is dear Lavinia, dearer than my soul.
Had I but seen thy picture in this plight,
It would have madded me; what shall I do
Now I behold thy lively body so?
Thou hast no hands to wipe away thy tears,
Nor tongue to tell me who hath martyred thee.
Thy husband he is dead, and for his death
Thy brothers are condemned, and dead by this.
Look, Marcus. Ah, son Lucius, look on her.   110
When I did name her brothers, then fresh tears
Stood on her cheeks, as doth the honey-dew
Upon a gathered lily almost witherèd.

MARCUS
Perchance she weeps because they killed her husband,
Perchance because she knows them innocent.

TITUS (*to Lavinia*)
If they did kill thy husband, then be joyful,
Because the law hath ta'en revenge on them.
No, no, they would not do so foul a deed;
Witness the sorrow that their sister makes.
Gentle Lavinia, let me kiss thy lips,   120
Or make some sign how I may do thee ease.
Shall thy good uncle and thy brother Lucius
And thou and I sit round about some fountain,
Looking all downwards to behold our cheeks,
How they are stained, like meadows yet not dry,
With miry slime left on them by a flood?
And in the fountain shall we gaze so long
Till the fresh taste be taken from that clearness,
And made a brine-pit with our bitter tears?
Or shall we cut away our hands like thine?   130

97 **his** its
101 **spurn** contemptuous blow
105 **lively** living
109 **by this** by this time
112 **honey-dew** sweet dew
121 **do thee ease** bring you relief
129 **And made** i.e. and the clear pool made

Or shall we bite our tongues, and in dumb shows
Pass the remainder of our hateful days?
What shall we do? Let us that have our tongues
Plot some device of further misery,
To make us wondered at in time to come.

LUCIUS

Sweet father, cease your tears, for at your grief
See how my wretched sister sobs and weeps.

MARCUS

Patience, dear niece. Good Titus, dry thine eyes.

TITUS

Ah, Marcus, Marcus! Brother, well I wot
Thy napkin cannot drink a tear of mine,   140
For thou, poor man, hast drowned it with thine own.

LUCIUS

Ah, my Lavinia, I will wipe thy cheeks.

TITUS

Mark, Marcus, mark. I understand her signs;
Had she a tongue to speak, now would she say
That to her brother which I said to thee.
His napkin, with his true tears all bewet,
Can do no service on her sorrowful cheeks.
O, what a sympathy of woe is this,
As far from help as limbo is from bliss!
      Enter Aaron the Moor alone

AARON

Titus Andronicus, my lord the Emperor   150
Sends thee this word, that if thou love thy sons,
Let Marcus, Lucius, or thyself, old Titus,
Or any one of you, chop off your hand
And send it to the King; he for the same
Will send thee hither both thy sons alive,
And that shall be the ransom for their fault.

TITUS

O gracious Emperor! O gentle Aaron!

146 with his] F4; with her Q1   150 AARON] *Moore* Q1 (*and so ll. 174, 187*)

131 **dumb shows** An Elizabethan dumb
    show was 'a part of a play represented by
    action without speech' (*OED*), as in *Ham-
    let*, 3.2.

140 **napkin** handkerchief
148 **sympathy** shared feeling
149 **limbo** a region near hell for those who
    die unbaptized

Did ever raven sing so like a lark,
That gives sweet tidings of the sun's uprise?
With all my heart I'll send the Emperor my hand.   160
Good Aaron, wilt thou help to chop it off?
LUCIUS

Stay father, for that noble hand of thine,
That hath thrown down so many enemies,
Shall not be sent. My hand will serve the turn,
My youth can better spare my blood than you,
And therefore mine shall save my brothers' lives.
MARCUS

Which of your hands hath not defended Rome,
And reared aloft the bloody battle-axe,
Writing destruction on the enemy's castle?
O, none of both but are of high desert.   170
My hand hath been but idle; let it serve
To ransom my two nephews from their death;
Then have I kept it to a worthy end.
AARON

Nay, come, agree whose hand shall go along,
For fear they die before their pardon come.
MARCUS

My hand shall go.
LUCIUS   By heaven, it shall not go!
TITUS

Sirs, strive no more; such withered herbs as these
Are meet for plucking up, and therefore mine.
LUCIUS

Sweet father, if I shall be thought thy son,
Let me redeem my brothers both from death.   180
MARCUS

And for our father's sake, and mother's care,
Now let me show a brother's love to thee.
TITUS

Agree between you; I will spare my hand.
LUCIUS

Then I'll go fetch an axe.

---

167 **Which . . . hands** i.e. has either of you   178 **meet** fit
    a hand which   179 **shall** am to

MARCUS   But I will use the axe.
                              Exeunt Lucius and Marcus

TITUS
  Come hither, Aaron. I'll deceive them both;
  Lend me thy hand, and I will give thee mine.
AARON *(aside)*
  If that be called deceit, I will be honest,
  And never whilst I live deceive men so;
  But I'll deceive you in another sort,
  And that you'll say ere half an hour pass.   190
      He cuts off Titus' left hand.
      Enter Lucius and Marcus again

TITUS
  Now stay your strife; what shall be is dispatched.
  Good Aaron, give his majesty my hand;
  Tell him it was a hand that warded him
  From thousand dangers; bid him bury it.
  More hath it merited; that let it have.
  As for my sons, say I account of them
  As jewels purchased at an easy price,
  And yet dear too, because I bought mine own.
AARON
  I go, Andronicus; and for thy hand
  Look by and by to have thy sons with thee.   200
  (Aside) Their heads, I mean. O, how this villainy
  Doth fat me with the very thoughts of it!
      ⌐*Laughs as he moves to one side*⌐
  Let fools do good, and fair men call for grace;
  Aaron will have his soul black like his face.   *Exit*
TITUS *(kneeling)*
  O, here I lift this one hand up to heaven,

184.1 *Lucius and Marcus*] *not in* Q1   190 *left*] *not in* Q1   202.1 *Laughs . . . side*] *not in* Q1
205 *kneeling*] *not in* Q1

190 *He . . . hand* Juggling tricks to make it
seem that a hand or a head was chopped
off were often used on the Elizabethan
stage; see Fig. 8, and Louis B. Wright,
'Juggling Tricks and Conjury on the
English Stage before 1642', *Modern
Philology*, 24 (1926–7), 269–84.
Though Titus calls it the hand that
'warded' the emperor 'from thousand

dangers' (ll. 193–4), it is his left hand,
as we know from 3.2.7.
193 **warded** guarded
195 **that** i.e. burial
198 **dear** expensive
200 **Look** expect
202 **fat** feed, i.e. delight
202.1 *Laughs . . . side* See 5.1.112–13,
where Aaron describes his actions.

And bow this feeble ruin to the earth;
If any power pities wretched tears,
To that I call. (*To Lavinia, who kneels*) What, wouldst
    thou kneel with me?
Do then, dear heart, for heaven shall hear our prayers,
Or with our sighs we'll breathe the welkin dim   210
And stain the sun with fog, as sometime clouds
When they do hug him in their melting bosoms.

MARCUS

O brother, speak with possibility,
And do not break into these deep extremes.

TITUS

Is not my sorrows deep, having no bottom?
Then be my passions bottomless with them.

MARCUS

But yet let reason govern thy lament.

TITUS

If there were reason for these miseries,
Then into limits could I bind my woes;
When heaven doth weep, doth not the earth o'erflow?   220
If the winds rage, doth not the sea wax mad,
Threat'ning the welkin with his big-swoll'n face?
And wilt thou have a reason for this coil?
I am the sea. Hark how her sighs doth blow!
She is the weeping welkin, I the earth;
Then must my sea be movèd with her sighs;
Then must my earth with her continual tears
Become a deluge, overflowed and drowned;

208 *who kneels*] not in Q1   215 Is . . . sorrows] MAXWELL (*conj.* Dyce 1866); Is . . . sorrow Q1;
Are . . . sorrows DYCE 1866   224 blow] F2; flow Q1

206 **ruin** mutilated body
210 **breathe . . . dim** make the sky cloudy
211 **sometime** sometimes
213 **with** within the bounds of
215 **sorrows** The plural seems to be required
   by 'them' in the next line; the common
   use of a singular verb with a plural subject makes Dyce's conjecture probable
   (see collations).
216 **passions** passionate outbursts
220 **o'erflow** become flooded; but since Titus
   insists that earth, air, and water so res-

pond to one another that they become
almost indistinguishable, the literal sense
of 'o'erflow' is important: the earth seems
to liquefy. This argument might also be
used to support the Q1 'sighs doth flow'
(l. 224).
223 **coil** ado
224 **blow** The F2 correction, adopted by
   most editors, seems more logical than Q1
   'flow' (see collations) for the movement of
   sighs or wind, but see note on 'o'erflow'
   (l. 220).

For why my bowels cannot hide her woes,
But like a drunkard must I vomit them.   230
Then give me leave, for losers will have leave
To ease their stomachs with their bitter tongues.
        Enter a Messenger with two heads and a hand

MESSENGER

Worthy Andronicus, ill art thou repaid
For that good hand thou sent'st the Emperor.
Here are the heads of thy two noble sons,
And here's thy hand in scorn to thee sent back –
Thy grief their sports, thy resolution mocked,
That woe is me to think upon thy woes,
More than remembrance of my father's death.   *Exit*

MARCUS

Now let hot Etna cool in Sicily,   240
And be my heart an ever-burning hell!
These miseries are more than may be borne.
To weep with them that weep doth ease some deal,
But sorrow flouted at is double death.

LUCIUS

Ah, that this sight should make so deep a wound,
And yet detested life not shrink thereat!
That ever death should let life bear his name,
Where life hath no more interest but to breathe!
        Lavinia kisses Titus

MARCUS

Alas, poor heart, that kiss is comfortless
As frozen water to a starvèd snake.   250

TITUS

When will this fearful slumber have an end?

239 *Exit*] F; *not in* Q1   248.1 *Lavinia kisses Titus*] *not in* Q1

229 **For why** because
  bowels (considered the seat of compassion)
  her 'old possessive pron. of the 3rd person pl. = their' (Onions)
231–2 **losers . . . tongues** Proverbial (*ODEP*, p. 485; Tilley L458).
232 **stomachs** resentments (supposed to be bred in the stomach)
233 ff. Aaron later boasts (5.1.114–15) that he watched the return of the heads and hand; Maxwell suggests in a note on those lines that Aaron might peep from

behind a traverse here.
237 **their sports** i.e. the amusement of the Emperor and his entourage. See Aaron's description of the Empress's merriment (5.1.118–20).
240 **Etna** Sicilian volcano
243 **To . . . weep** Compare 'weep with them that weep' (Romans 12: 15).
  some deal somewhat
244 **flouted at** mocked
246 **shrink** slip away
247 **bear his name** i.e. be called 'life'
250 **starvèd** numbed

MARCUS

  Now farewell, flatt'ry, die Andronicus;
  Thou dost not slumber: see thy two sons' heads,
  Thy warlike hand, thy mangled daughter here;
  Thy other banished son with this dear sight
  Struck pale and bloodless, and thy brother, I,
  Even like a stony image, cold and numb.
  Ah, now no more will I control thy griefs;
  Rend off thy silver hair, thy other hand
  Gnawing with thy teeth, and be this dismal sight   260
  The closing up of our most wretched eyes.
  Now is a time to storm; why art thou still?
TITUS Ha, ha, ha!
MARCUS

  Why dost thou laugh? It fits not with this hour.
TITUS

  Why, I have not another tear to shed;
  Besides, this sorrow is an enemy,
  And would usurp upon my wat'ry eyes,
  And make them blind with tributary tears.
  Then which way shall I find Revenge's cave?
  For these two heads do seem to speak to me,   270
  And threat me I shall never come to bliss
  Till all these mischiefs be returned again
  Even in their throats that hath committed them.
  Come, let me see what task I have to do;
     ⌈*He and Lavinia rise*⌉
  You heavy people, circle me about,
  That I may turn me to each one of you,
  And swear unto my soul to right your wrongs.
     Marcus, Lucius, and Lavinia circle Titus. He pledges
     them

---

259 Rend] Q1 (Rent)   274 do;] doe, Q1; do. F3   274.1 *He . . . rise*] *not in* Q1   275 about,] Q3; about. Q1   277 wrongs.] F1; wrongs, Q1   277.1–2 *Marcus . . . them*] *not in* Q1

255 **dear** grievous
258 **control** try to restrain
268 **tributary** paid in tribute to conquering sorrow
274.1 *He . . . rise* Though it is not clear when they rise, they must do so before the business of ll. 275–7.
274–7 **do; . . . about, . . . wrongs.** The

punctuation of Q1 (see collations) is clearly wrong, making ll. 276–7 dependent on l. 278.
275 **heavy** sorrowful
277.1–2 *pledges them* A simple ritual, such as handshaking or bowing to each of them in turn, is needed.

The vow is made. Come, brother, take a head,
And in this hand the other will I bear;
And, Lavinia, thou shalt be employed in this;   280
Bear thou my hand, sweet wench, between thy teeth.
(*To Lucius*) As for thee, boy, go get thee from my sight;
Thou art an exile, and thou must not stay;
Hie to the Goths and raise an army there;
And if ye love me, as I think you do,
Let's kiss and part, for we have much to do.

> *Exeunt all but Lucius*

LUCIUS

Farewell, Andronicus, my noble father,
The woefull'st man that ever lived in Rome!
Farewell, proud Rome, till Lucius come again!
He loves his pledges dearer than his life.   290
Farewell, Lavinia, my noble sister,
O would thou wert as thou tofore hast been!
But now nor Lucius nor Lavinia lives
But in oblivion and hateful griefs.

---

280 this] HUDSON (*conj.* Lettsom); these Armes Q1; these things F   286.1 *all but Lucius*] *not in*
Q1; *Manet Lucius* F   290 loves] Q1; leaves ROWE

280 **this** The Q1 reading, 'these Armes' (see collations), has seemed wrong to almost all succeeding editors. The F correction, 'these things', makes tolerable sense but leaves the line metrically very irregular. Lettsom's conjecture, adopted by Hudson, and later by Dover Wilson, improves the metre. Hudson also dropped 'And' from the beginning of the line on the assumption that it 'crept in by mistake from the line above'. W. A. Wright (Cambridge edition) made the ingenious suggestion that the line in the manuscript copy ended at 'employed'; that someone had written 'arms' over 'teeth' in the following line as a possible alternative to a ludicrous piece of business, but failed to cross out 'teeth'; and that the Q1 compositor, taking 'Armes' for part of l. 280, filled in the gap with 'in these'. A variant of this suggestion is one made by Bolton that the line originally read as in this text, and that the compositor substituted 'these' for 'this'. The comparative lengths of the two lines make either of these sug-

gestions plausible. The manuscript might have read:

> ... be imployde in this, Armes
> ... wench betweene thy teeth:

With Dover Wilson I adopt a reading which presupposes a minimum of alteration by the compositor.

281 **Bear ... teeth** Condemned as ludicrous by some critics, this piece of business poses a serious problem for the director, and one which may even have been recognized in Shakespeare's time (see previous note). It is undoubtedly authentic, however, and no more grotesque than Lavinia's writing in the sand (4.1.76).

290 **loves** Some editors accept Rowe's emendation 'leaves', altering the punctuation to make 'till' (l. 289) the beginning of a sentence ending with 'life'. But, as Baildon points out, 'loves' is defensible as the explanation of why Lucius will surely return.

292 **tofore** formerly

If Lucius live, he will requite your wrongs,
And make proud Saturnine and his empress
Beg at the gates like Tarquin and his queen.
Now will I to the Goths and raise a power,
To be revenged on Rome and Saturnine.   *Exit Lucius*

3.2   *A banquet. Enter Titus Andronicus, Marcus, Lavinia,*
        and the Boy (Lucius' son)

TITUS

So, so, now sit, and look you eat no more
Than will preserve just so much strength in us
As will revenge these bitter woes of ours.
Marcus, unknit that sorrow-wreathen knot;
Thy niece and I, poor creatures, want our hands,
And cannot passionate our tenfold grief
With folded arms. This poor right hand of mine
Is left to tyrannize upon my breast,
Who, when my heart, all mad with misery,
Beats in this hollow prison of my flesh,   10
Then thus I thump it down.
(*To Lavinia*) Thou map of woe, that thus dost talk in signs,
When thy poor heart beats with outrageous beating,
Thou canst not strike it thus to make it still.
Wound it with sighing, girl, kill it with groans;
Or get some little knife between thy teeth,
And just against thy heart make thou a hole,

3.2] CAPELL (*subs.*); *not in* F, *which first prints the scene*   1 TITUS] *An.* F (*and so throughout this scene, but nowhere else*)   13 with outrageous] F2; *without ragious* F1   14 still.] *still?* F1 ; *still:* F3

297 **Tarquin** Tarquinius Superbus, the King of Rome who was expelled with his family after his son Sextus Tarquinius raped Lucrece; see note on 2.1.109.
3.2 The text of this scene appears first in F (see Introduction, pp. 40–3). The location is a room in Titus' house. Benches and a table, set with dishes and knives, are brought on stage for the 'banquet'.
0.1 *banquet* In this case, a light repast rather than a feast.
4 **unknit . . . knot** unfold your arms (folded arms were a sign of grief or melancholy)
5 **want** lack

6 **passionate** movingly express
8 **tyrannize upon** i.e. by beating
9 **Who** i.e. which, referring to 'hand'; but in l. 11 'I' is substituted as subject of the clause
12 **map** picture, image
15 **Wound . . . sighing** Alluding to the belief that each sigh draws a drop of blood from the heart.
16–17 **knife . . . heart** The relation of the scene to *Lucrece* is shown by the close parallel between these lines and 'against my heart | Will fix a sharp knife' (ll. 1137–8).

That all the tears that thy poor eyes let fall
May run into that sink, and soaking in,
Drown the lamenting fool in sea-salt tears.   20

MARCUS
Fie, brother, fie! Teach her not thus to lay
Such violent hands upon her tender life.

TITUS
How now! Has sorrow made thee dote already?
Why, Marcus, no man should be mad but I.
What violent hands can she lay on her life?
Ah, wherefore dost thou urge the name of hands,
To bid Aeneas tell the tale twice o'er,
How Troy was burnt and he made miserable?
O, handle not the theme, to talk of hands,
Lest we remember still that we have none.   30
Fie, fie, how franticly I square my talk,
As if we should forget we had no hands
If Marcus did not name the word of hands!
Come, let's fall to; and, gentle girl, eat this.
Here is no drink! Hark, Marcus, what she says –
I can interpret all her martyred signs –
She says she drinks no other drink but tears,
Brewed with her sorrow, mashed upon her cheeks.
Speechless complainer, I will learn thy thought;
In thy dumb action will I be as perfect   40
As begging hermits in their holy prayers.
Thou shalt not sigh, nor hold thy stumps to heaven,
Nor wink, nor nod, nor kneel, nor make a sign,
But I of these will wrest an alphabet,
And by still practice learn to know thy meaning.

---

35 drink!] drinke? F   39 complainer, I] CAPELL; complaynet, I F1; complaint, O I F2

19 **sink** receptacle
20 **fool** Often used affectionately; compare
    'my poor fool is hang'd' (*Lear*, 5.3.305).
27–8 **To . . . miserable** An allusion to the
    Aeneid, ii. 2, where Aeneas, asked by Dido
    to tell his story, says how painful it is to
    renew his grief.
30 **still** continually
31 **square** shape
35 **drink!** In relation to Titus' next lines an

exclamation seems more likely than a
question. The Q1 punctuation (see collations) may be explained by the fact that
an interrogation point was often used for
an exclamation.
38 **mashed** i.e. for brewing
40 **action** gesture
    perfect fully understanding
43 **wink** close the eyes
45 **still** constant

BOY

Good grandsire, leave these bitter deep laments;
Make my aunt merry with some pleasing tale.

MARCUS

Alas, the tender boy, in passion moved,
Doth weep to see his grandsire's heaviness.

TITUS

Peace, tender sapling! Thou art made of tears,   50
And tears will quickly melt thy life away.
Marcus strikes the dish with a knife
What dost thou strike at, Marcus, with thy knife?

MARCUS

At that that I have killed, my lord – a fly.

TITUS

Out on thee, murderer! Thou kill'st my heart;
Mine eyes are cloyed with view of tyranny;
A deed of death done on the innocent
Becomes not Titus' brother. Get thee gone;
I see thou art not for my company.

MARCUS

Alas, my lord, I have but killed a fly.

TITUS

'But'? How if that fly had a father, brother?   60
How would he hang his slender gilded wings,
And buzz lamenting doings in the air!
Poor harmless fly,
That, with his pretty buzzing melody,
Came here to make us merry! And thou hast killed him.

MARCUS

Pardon me, sir; it was a black ill-favoured fly,
Like to the Empress' Moor; therefore I killed him.

TITUS   O, O, O!

Then pardon me for reprehending thee,

---

52 thy] F2; *not in* F1   53 fly] F2; Flys F1   54 thee,] F3; the F1   55 are] F2; *not in* F1   60
father, brother] HUDSON (*conj.* Ritson); father and mother F   65 Came . . . him] *one line in*
CAPELL; *two lines, divided after* merry *in* F   66 Pardon . . . fly] *one line in* POPE; *two lines, divided
after* sir *in* F

48 **passion** sorrow   'he' in the next line.
60 **father, brother** Ritson's ingenious conjec-   62 **lamenting doings** lamentations
   ture (see collations) results in a more   66 **ill-favoured** ugly
   regular metre and fits with the pronoun

For thou hast done a charitable deed.   70
Give me thy knife; I will insult on him,
Flattering myself as if it were the Moor
Come hither purposely to poison me.
There's for thyself (*striking the fly*), and that's for
        Tamora. Ah, sirrah!
Yet I think we are not brought so low
But that between us we can kill a fly
That comes in likeness of a coal-black Moor.

MARCUS

Alas, poor man! Grief has so wrought on him,
He takes false shadows for true substances.

TITUS

Come, take away. Lavinia, go with me;   80
I'll to thy closet, and go read with thee
Sad stories chancèd in the times of old.
Come, boy, and go with me; thy sight is young,
And thou shalt read when mine begin to dazzle. *Exeunt*

4.1   *Enter Lucius' son and Lavinia running after him, and*
       the Boy flies from her with his books under his arm.
       Enter Titus and Marcus

BOY

Help, grandsire, help! My aunt Lavinia
Follows me everywhere, I know not why.
Good uncle Marcus, see how swift she comes.
Alas, sweet aunt, I know not what you mean.
        ⌈*He drops his books*⌉

MARCUS

Stand by me, Lucius; do not fear thine aunt.

TITUS

She loves thee, boy, too well to do thee harm.

---

72 myself] F2; my selfes F1   74 *striking the fly*] *not in* F   Tamora] Tamira F
    4.1] ROWE (*subs.*); *Actus Quartus* F; *not in* Q1   1 BOY] F; *Puer* Q1 (*and so throughout this scene*
and the next)   4.1 *He drops his books*] *not in* Q1

71 **insult on** exult over   80 **take away** clear the table
72 **Flattering . . . if** deceiving myself with the   81 **closet** private room
    thought that   84 **mine** i.e. my eyes
74 **sirrah** (term of address used to an in-   **dazzle** become blurred
    ferior)   4.1 The location is Titus' garden. The table
79 **shadows . . . substances** Proverbial   from the preceding scene is removed, but
    (*ODEP*, p. 110; Tilley S951).   the benches are left.

145

BOY

Ay, when my father was in Rome she did.

MARCUS

What means my niece Lavinia by these signs?

TITUS

Fear her not, Lucius; somewhat doth she mean;
See, Lucius, see how much she makes of thee;   10
Somewhither would she have thee go with her.
Ah, boy, Cornelia never with more care
Read to her sons than she hath read to thee
Sweet poetry and Tully's *Orator*.

⌈MARCUS⌉

Canst thou not guess wherefore she plies thee thus?

BOY

My lord, I know not, I, nor can I guess,
Unless some fit or frenzy do possess her;
For I have heard my grandsire say full oft,
Extremity of griefs would make men mad.
And I have read that Hecuba of Troy   20
Ran mad for sorrow; that made me to fear,
Although, my lord, I know my noble aunt
Loves me as dear as e'er my mother did,
And would not but in fury fright my youth,
Which made me down to throw my books and fly,
Causeless perhaps; but pardon me, sweet aunt,
And, madam, if my uncle Marcus go,
I will most willingly attend your ladyship.

MARCUS Lucius, I will.

⌈*Lavinia turns over the books which Lucius has let fall*⌉

12 Ah] Q3; A Q1   15 MARCUS] CAPELL; Q1 *continues to Titus*   29.1 *Lavinia . . . fall*] MALONE *after* Capell; *not in* Q1

9 **somewhat** something
12 **Cornelia** The prototypical Roman mother, honoured for the way she educated her sons, the Gracchi, who became famous tribunes.
13 **Read** gave instruction
14 **Tully's *Orator*** Marcus Tullius Cicero's treatise *Orator* or his *De oratore*.
15 **MARCUS** Since young Lucius' reference to Titus (l. 18) shows that he is addressing Marcus, Capell gave Marcus l. 15 (see collations). Some editors give him the preceding five lines as well, but these seem to follow directly from Titus' 'somewhat doth she mean', while l. 15 is similar to the question Marcus asks at l. 8.

15 **plies** importunes
20 **Hecuba** See note on 1.1.136.
24 **but in fury** except in madness
28 **attend** wait upon
29.1 ***Lavinia . . . fall*** Capell and Malone saw that the text required some such business, but it is not clear when young

TITUS

How now, Lavinia? Marcus, what means this?   30
Some book there is that she desires to see.
Which is it, girl, of these? – Open them, boy. –
But thou art deeper read and better skilled;
Come and take choice of all my library,
And so beguile thy sorrow, till the heavens
Reveal the damned contriver of this deed.
Why lifts she up her arms in sequence thus?

MARCUS

I think she means that there were more than one
Confederate in the fact; ay, more there was;
Or else to heaven she heaves them for revenge.   40

TITUS

Lucius, what book is that she tosseth so?

BOY

Grandsire, 'tis Ovid's *Metamorphoses*;
My mother gave it me.

MARCUS   For love of her that's gone,
Perhaps she culled it from among the rest.

TITUS

Soft, so busily she turns the leaves!
Help her; what would she find? Lavinia, shall I read?
This is the tragic tale of Philomel,
And treats of Tereus' treason and his rape;
And rape, I fear, was root of thy annoy.

MARCUS

See, brother, see; note how she quotes the leaves.   50

TITUS

Lavinia, wert thou thus surprised, sweet girl?
Ravished and wronged, as Philomela was,

36–7] *Between these lines* F *introduces* What booke? *as a separate line*   42 *Metamorphoses*]
Metamorphosis Q1   52 Philomela] Q1 (*Phlomela*)

Lucius drops the books nor exactly what
Lavinia does.

33 **deeper read** i.e. than a schoolboy
36–7 The F insertion of 'What booke?' between these lines (see collations) must be
an error (see Introduction, p. 40, and
note the occurrence of the words in l. 41).
39 **fact** crime

41 **tosseth** Lavinia is trying to turn the
pages.
46 **Help her** Dyce thought this might be a
stage direction, but it fits naturally into
Titus' speech.
47–8 **Philomel, . . . Tereus'** See note on
2.3.43.
49 **annoy** injury
50 **quotes** scrutinizes

Forced in the ruthless, vast, and gloomy woods?
See, see; ay, such a place there is, where we did hunt –
O, had we never, never hunted there! –
Patterned by that the poet here describes,
By nature made for murders and for rapes.

MARCUS

O, why should nature build so foul a den,
Unless the gods delight in tragedies?

TITUS

Give signs, sweet girl, for here are none but friends,   60
What Roman lord it was durst do the deed.
Or slunk not Saturnine, as Tarquin erst,
That left the camp to sin in Lucrece' bed?

MARCUS

Sit down, sweet niece; brother, sit down by me.
Apollo, Pallas, Jove, or Mercury
Inspire me, that I may this treason find!
My lord, look here; look here, Lavinia;
    He writes his name with his staff, and guides it with
    feet and mouth
This sandy plot is plain; guide, if thou canst,
This after me. I have writ my name
Without the help of any hand at all.   70
Cursed be that heart that forced us to this shift!
Write thou, good niece, and here display at last
What God will have discovered for revenge.
Heaven guide thy pen to print thy sorrows plain,
That we may know the traitors and the truth!

---

53 **ruthless . . . woods** Compare Aaron's
  description at 2.1.129.
  vast waste, desolate
56 **Patterned by** on the pattern of
  poet . . . describes The place where
  Philomela is raped is 'deep hidden in the
  ancient woods' (*Metamorphoses*, vi.
  520–1).
62 **Tarquin** See note on 2.1.109.
  erst once
65 **Apollo . . . Mercury** Titus' invocation of
  these four among the most important
  Greco-Roman deities may be explained
  by the traditional association of Apollo
  with oracles and prophecy, Pallas Athene

with wisdom, law, and order, and Jove
(or Jupiter), the supreme deity, with the
punishment of crime. Mercury was his
agent and messenger.
68 **plain** flat
69 **This . . . name** A short line, in which a
  pause after 'me' may take the place of a
  syllable (see note on 4.2.136). Some
  editors have emended by adding another
  word in the second half of the line.
71 **shift** stratagem
73 **will** i.e. wishes to
  discovered for revenge revealed to be
  avenged

> *She takes the staff in her mouth, and guides it with*
> *her stumps, and writes*

O, do ye read, my lord, what she hath writ?

⌈TITUS⌉

'*Stuprum* – Chiron – Demetrius.'

MARCUS

What, what! The lustful sons of Tamora

Performers of this heinous, bloody deed?

TITUS

Magni dominator poli,   80

Tam lentus audis scelera, tam lentus vides?

MARCUS

O, calm thee, gentle lord, although I know

There is enough written upon this earth

To stir a mutiny in the mildest thoughts,

And arm the minds of infants to exclaims.

My lord, kneel down with me; Lavinia, kneel;

And kneel, sweet boy, the Roman Hector's hope;

> *They kneel*

And swear with me, as, with the woeful fere

And father of that chaste dishonoured dame,

Lord Junius Brutus sware for Lucrece' rape,   90

That we will prosecute by good advice

Mortal revenge upon these traitorous Goths,

And see their blood, or die with this reproach.

> *They rise*

77 TITUS] MAXWELL; Q1 *continues to Marcus, repeating the speech prefix for him at l. 78*; Q3 *assigns both ll. 76 and 77 to Titus*   87 hope] Q2; hop Q1 (*type loose at end of line*; h *damaged*)   87.1 *They kneel*] *not in* Q1   93.1 *They rise*] *not in* Q1

77 **Stuprum . . . Demetrius** The Q1 attachment of this line to the preceding speech by Marcus is surely wrong, as shown by the repetition of the speech-prefix '*Marcus.*' at l. 78 (see collations). But the assignment of both ll. 76 and 77 to Titus by Q3 is unsatisfactory, since Titus nowhere addresses Marcus as 'my lord'. Maxwell's solution is the most satisfactory. *Stuprum* rape (Latin)

80–1 **Magni . . . vides** 'Ruler of the great heavens, dost thou so calmly hear crimes, so calmly look upon them?' (Latin, adapted from Seneca, *Hippolytus*, ll. 671–2, where the first half-line is '*Magne regnator deum*', 'great ruler of the gods').

86 **exclaims** outcries

87 **Roman Hector** i.e. Lucius, now the champion of Rome as Hector was of Troy

88 **fere** husband

90 **Junius Brutus** leader of the rebellion which drove the Tarquins out of Rome after the rape of Lucrece; see *Lucrece*, Argument and ll. 1807 ff. **sware** swore

91 **by good advice** after careful planning

93 **reproach** dishonour

TITUS

   'Tis sure enough, an you knew how;
   But if you hunt these bear-whelps, then beware:
   The dam will wake an if she wind ye once;
   She's with the lion deeply still in league,
   And lulls him whilst she playeth on her back;
   And when he sleeps will she do what she list.
   You are a young huntsman, Marcus; let alone;   100
   And come, I will go get a leaf of brass,
   And with a gad of steel will write these words,
   And lay it by. The angry northern wind
   Will blow these sands like Sibyl's leaves abroad,
   And where's our lesson then? Boy, what say you?

BOY

   I say, my lord, that if I were a man,
   Their mother's bedchamber should not be safe
   For these base bondmen to the yoke of Rome.

MARCUS

   Ay, that's my boy! Thy father hath full oft
   For his ungrateful country done the like.   110

BOY

   And, uncle, so will I an if I live.

TITUS

   Come, go with me into mine armoury.
   Lucius, I'll fit thee, and withal my boy
   Shall carry from me to the Empress' sons
   Presents that I intend to send them both.
   Come, come; thou'lt do my message, wilt thou not?

BOY

   Ay, with my dagger in their bosoms, grandsire.

TITUS

   No, boy, not so; I'll teach thee another course.

95–6 beware: . . . once;] beware, . . . once, Q1

96 **wind** scent
97 **still** always
99 **list** likes
100 **let alone** i.e. let it alone
101 **leaf** sheet (for engraving)
102 **gad** sharp point
104 **Sibyl's leaves** leaves on which the Cumaean Sibyl wrote her prophecies, and which were sometimes blown away

before they could be read
113 **fit thee** furnish you with what you need
    withal moreover
113–4 **my boy | Shall** Titus' use of the third person in addressing young Lucius has unnecessarily disturbed some editors. It has long been a common practice in speaking to children.

Lavinia, come; Marcus, look to my house;
Lucius and I'll go brave it at the court;   120
Ay, marry, will we, sir, and we'll be waited on.

Exeunt Titus, Lavinia, and Boy

MARCUS

O, heavens, can you hear a good man groan,
And not relent, or not compassion him?
Marcus, attend him in his ecstasy,
That hath more scars of sorrow in his heart
Than foemen's marks upon his battered shield,
But yet so just that he will not revenge.
Revenge the heavens for old Andronicus!   *Exit*

4.2   *Enter Aaron, Chiron, and Demetrius at one door; and*
         at the other door young Lucius and another with a
         bundle of weapons, and verses writ upon them

CHIRON

Demetrius, here's the son of Lucius;
He hath some message to deliver us.

AARON

Ay, some mad message from his mad grandfather.

BOY

My lords, with all the humbleness I may,
I greet your honours from Andronicus –
(*Aside*) And pray the Roman gods confound you both.

DEMETRIUS

Gramercy, lovely Lucius; what's the news?

BOY (*aside*)

That you are both deciphered, that's the news,
For villains marked with rape. – May it please you,

121.1 *Titus, Lavinia, and Boy*] *not in* Q1
   4.2] POPE (*subs.*); *not in* Q1

120 **brave it** swagger, put on a good show
   (compare 'court it', 2.1.92)
121 **marry** indeed (originally an oath by the
   Virgin Mary)
   waited on heeded
123 **compassion** i.e. have compassion for
124 **ecstasy** fit of madness
128 **Revenge the heavens** may the heavens
   take revenge
4.2 The location is in the Emperor's palace;

the benches from the preceding scene are
needed (see l. 132).
0.2 *another* Presumably an attendant, who,
   after presenting the weapons to Chiron
   and Demetrius at ll. 14–15, leaves with
   the Boy.
6 **confound** destroy
7 **Gramercy** thanks
8 **deciphered** detected

My grandsire, well advised, hath sent by me   10
The goodliest weapons of his armoury
To gratify your honourable youth,
The hope of Rome, for so he bid me say;
And so I do, and with his gifts present
Your lordships, that, whenever you have need,
You may be armèd and appointed well;
And so I leave you both – (*aside*) like bloody villains.

Exit ⌈*with attendant*⌉

DEMETRIUS

What's here? A scroll, and written round about,
Let's see:
'*Integer vitae, scelerisque purus,*   20
Non eget Mauri iaculis, nec arcu.'

CHIRON

O, 'tis a verse in Horace; I know it well;
I read it in the grammar long ago.

AARON

Ay, just; a verse in Horace – right, you have it.
(*Aside*) Now, what a thing it is to be an ass!
Here's no sound jest! The old man hath found their guilt,
And sends them weapons wrapped about with lines
That wound, beyond their feeling, to the quick.

---

15 that] POPE; *not in* Q1   17.1 with attendant] CAPELL (*subs.*); *not in* Q1   20–1 *Integer . . . arcu*]
so printed by THEOBALD; *one line in* Q1   24 AARON] *Moore* Q1

10 **well advised** upon reflection; possibly, as
    Dover Wilson says, 'contradicting Aaron,
    l. 3'.
12 **gratify** show gratitude to, please
15 **that** Pope's emendation (see collations)
    not only improves the metre; it is almost
    essential for the sense.
16 **appointed** equipped
17.1 **with attendant** I accept Capell's conjec-
    ture that the 'other' who enters with
    young Lucius is an attendant, and that he
    goes off here (see collations and note on
    0.2).
20–1 **Integer . . . arcu** 'The man of upright
    life and free from crime does not need the
    javelins or bow of the Moor' (Latin, from
    Horace, *Odes*, I. xxii. 1–2, one of the best-
    known Latin poems). J. W. Binns com-
    ments: 'modern editions of Horace read

    Mauris iaculis . . . Shakespeare, however,
    no doubt knew the lines as quoted in
    Lily's *Brevissima Institutio* (London,
    1570), . . . [sig.] H6ᵛ, and there the read-
    ing is *Mauri*, which should therefore be
    retained. Whichever reading is adopted
    . . . the meaning is much the same'
    (*Shakespeare Survey* 35 (Cambridge,
    1982), 119–28; p. 123).
23 **grammar** Presumably William Lily's
    standard Latin grammar, where the
    poem is quoted twice (see preceding
    note).
24 **just** precisely
26 **no sound** (ironical; he means it is a good
    jest)
28 **beyond . . . feeling** i.e. although they
    (Chiron and Demetrius) do not feel the
    injury

But were our witty Empress well afoot,
She would applaud Andronicus' conceit; 30
But let her rest in her unrest awhile. –
And now, young lords, was't not a happy star
Led us to Rome, strangers, and more than so,
Captives, to be advancèd to this height?
It did me good before the palace gate
To brave the tribune in his brother's hearing.

DEMETRIUS
But me more good to see so great a lord
Basely insinuate and send us gifts.

AARON
Had he not reason, Lord Demetrius?
Did you not use his daughter very friendly? 40

DEMETRIUS
I would we had a thousand Roman dames
At such a bay, by turn to serve our lust.

CHIRON
A charitable wish, and full of love!

AARON
Here lacks but your mother for to say amen.

CHIRON
And that would she for twenty thousand more.

DEMETRIUS
Come, let us go and pray to all the gods
For our belovèd mother in her pains.

AARON ⌈*aside*⌉
Pray to the devils; the gods have given us over.
      Trumpets sound

DEMETRIUS
Why do the Emperor's trumpets flourish thus?

CHIRON
Belike for joy the Emperor hath a son. 50

29 **witty** quick-witted
afoot up and about (instead of in childbed; see ll. 31, 47)
30 **conceit** idea, device
36 **brave** taunt, defy (referring, presumably,
to something that happened shortly
before their entrance)
38 **insinuate** curry favour
42 **At...bay** so brought to bay (as in a hunt)

45 **more** i.e. more Roman dames
47 **pains** labour pains
48 *aside* Aaron may speak directly to Chiron
and Demetrius, but more likely, as Johnson thought, aside; as in some of his earlier speeches, he seems to be mocking the
Empress' sons.
50 **Belike** very likely

153

DEMETRIUS

Soft, who comes here?

Enter Nurse with a blackamoor child

NURSE   God morrow, lords.

O, tell me, did you see Aaron the Moor?

AARON

Well, more or less, or ne'er a whit at all,

Here Aaron is, and what with Aaron now?

NURSE

O, gentle Aaron, we are all undone.

Now help, or woe betide thee evermore!

AARON

Why, what a caterwauling dost thou keep!

What dost thou wrap and fumble in thy arms?

NURSE

O, that which I would hide from heaven's eye,

Our Empress' shame and stately Rome's disgrace;   60

She is delivered, lords, she is delivered.

AARON

To whom?

NURSE   I mean she is brought abed.

AARON

Well, God give her good rest! What hath he sent her?

NURSE   A devil.

AARON

Why, then she is the devil's dam; a joyful issue.

NURSE

A joyless, dismal, black, and sorrowful issue.

Here is the babe, as loathsome as a toad

Amongst the fair-faced breeders of our clime;

---

51 God . . . lords] *separate line in* F; *with l. 52 in* Q1   God] Q1; Good Q3   68 fair-faced] WILSON
(*following OED*); fairefast Q1; fairest Q3

51 **God morrow** The Q1 reading is justifiable
as short for 'God give you good morrow',
which was 'variously corrupted' (*OED*,
'good morrow'); compare 'God ye god
morrow', (Chapman, *May Day*, ed. Parrott, 2.1.225); some editors adopt the Q3
alteration to 'Good morrow' (see collations).

53 **more** Aaron's pun on 'Moor' is characteristic of his sardonic humour.

62 **abed** i.e. childbed; she has given birth

65 **issue** outcome

66 **issue** offspring

67 **loathsome as a toad** Proverbial (Tilley,
T361).

68 **fair-faced** The *OED* is probably right in so
interpreting Q1 'fairefast', though it
records no other instance of this spelling;
compare 'bare-faste' (*Hamlet*, Q2,
4.5.165); Q3 'fairest' makes less good
sense (see collations).

The Empress sends it thee, thy stamp, thy seal,
And bids thee christen it with thy dagger's point.   70

AARON
Zounds, ye whore! Is black so base a hue?
(*To the baby*)
Sweet blowse, you are a beauteous blossom, sure.

DEMETRIUS
Villain, what hast thou done?

AARON
That which thou canst not undo.

CHIRON
Thou hast undone our mother.

AARON
Villain, I have done thy mother.

DEMETRIUS
And therein, hellish dog, thou hast undone her.
Woe to her chance, and damned her loathèd choice!
Accursed the offspring of so foul a fiend!

CHIRON It shall not live.   80

AARON It shall not die.

NURSE
Aaron, it must; the mother wills it so.

AARON
What, must it, nurse? Then let no man but I
Do execution on my flesh and blood.

DEMETRIUS
I'll broach the tadpole on my rapier's point.
Nurse, give it me; my sword shall soon dispatch it.

AARON (*taking the child and drawing his sword*)
Sooner this sword shall plough thy bowels up.
Stay, murderous villains; will you kill your brother?

---

87 *taking . . . sword*] *not in* Q1

71 **Zounds** by God's (Christ's) wounds; one
of the strongest oaths (F. A. Shirley,
*Swearing and Perjury in Shakespeare's
Plays* (London and Boston, 1979), p. 22).
72 **blowse** Normally a red-faced wench; in
applying it ironically to his baby Aaron
continues his reaction against the nurse's
contempt for blackness.
73-6 The scene contains an unusually large

number of short lines such as these alter-
nating trimeters and tetrameters; compare also ll. 62, 64, 80, 81.
76 **done** copulated with
78 **chance** luck
78-9 **damned . . . Accursed** i.e. damned be
. . . accursed be
85 **broach** impale

Now, by the burning tapers of the sky,
That shone so brightly when this boy was got,   90
He dies upon my scimitar's sharp point
That touches this, my first-born son and heir.
I tell you, younglings, not Enceladus,
With all his threat'ning band of Typhon's brood,
Nor great Alcides, nor the god of war
Shall seize this prey out of his father's hands.
What, what, ye sanguine, shallow-hearted boys,
Ye white-limed walls, ye alehouse painted signs!
Coal-black is better than another hue,
In that it scorns to bear another hue;   100
For all the water in the ocean
Can never turn the swan's black legs to white,
Although she lave them hourly in the flood.
Tell the Empress from me, I am of age
To keep mine own, excuse it how she can.

DEMETRIUS

Wilt thou betray thy noble mistress thus?

AARON

My mistress is my mistress, this myself,
The vigour and the picture of my youth:
This before all the world do I prefer;
This maugre all the world will I keep safe,   110
Or some of you shall smoke for it in Rome.

DEMETRIUS

By this our mother is forever shamed.

---

90 **got** begotten
91 **scimitar's** Aaron is given an appropriate weapon (see Fig. 5, p. 48).
93 **Enceladus** One of the giants who waged war on the Olympian gods.
94 **Typhon** A gigantic monster and the father of monsters; he also warred with the gods.
95 **Alcides** Hercules
97 **sanguine** red-faced (as opposed to black)
shallow-hearted cowardly
98 **white-limed** whitewashed; may allude to the 'whited sepulchres' of Matthew 23:27, meaning 'hypocrites'. Dover Wilson cites *Piers Plowman* (C), xvii. 267, where hypocrisy is compared to 'a wal whit-lymed' (ed. Skeat, Oxford, 1886).
alehouse . . . signs i.e. crude represen-
tations of men
99–100 **Coal-black . . . hue** That black will take no other hue is proverbial (*ODEP*, p. 65; Tilley B436).
101–2 **For . . . white** Compare 'To wash an Ethiop (blackamoor, Moor) white' (*ODEP*, p. 868; Tilley E186).
101 **ocean** (trisyllabic here and elsewhere when the metre requires it)
103 **lave** wash
107 **this** i.e. the baby
108 **vigour** Probably 'figure', of which it was a variant in Middle English; otherwise 'vitality, active force'.
110 **maugre** in spite of
111 **smoke** suffer (like one burned at the stake)

CHIRON

Rome will despise her for this foul escape.

NURSE

The Emperor in his rage will doom her death.

CHIRON

I blush to think upon this ignomy.

AARON

Why, there's the privilege your beauty bears.
Fie, treacherous hue, that will betray with blushing
The close enacts and counsels of thy heart!
Here's a young lad framed of another leer;
Look how the black slave smiles upon the father,   120
As who should say, 'Old lad, I am thine own.'
He is your brother, lords, sensibly fed
Of that self blood that first gave life to you,
And from that womb where you imprisoned were
He is enfranchisèd and come to light.
Nay, he is your brother by the surer side,
Although my seal be stampèd in his face.

NURSE

Aaron, what shall I say unto the Empress?

DEMETRIUS

Advise thee, Aaron, what is to be done,
And we will all subscribe to thy advice.   130
Save thou the child, so we may all be safe.

AARON

Then sit we down, and let us all consult.
My son and I will have the wind of you;
Keep there; now talk at pleasure of your safety.

DEMETRIUS (*to the Nurse*)

How many women saw this child of his?

---

124 that] Q3; your Q1

---

113 **escape** escapade
115 **ignomy** ignominy
118 **close enacts** secret ordinances
119 **leer** complexion
122–3 **sensibly fed | Of** made capable of sensation by
123 **self** same
124 **that** Q1 'your' is possible, but seems likely to be a printer's error (see col-

lations); if 'that' was written 'y^t' it could easily have been mistaken for 'y^r'.
126 **surer side** i.e. the mother's side; proverbial (*ODEP*, p. 546; Tilley M1205).
130 **subscribe** agree
133 **have . . . you** sit at a safe distance to watch you (as a hunter keeps downwind to watch his prey)

AARON

Why, so, brave lords! When we join in league,
I am a lamb, but if you brave the Moor,
The chafèd boar, the mountain lioness,
The ocean swells not so as Aaron storms.
(*To the Nurse*) But say again, how many saw the
    child?   140

NURSE

Cornelia, the midwife, and myself,
And no one else but the delivered Empress.

AARON

The Empress, the midwife, and yourself.
Two may keep counsel when the third's away;
Go to the Empress, tell her this I said.
    He kills her
Weeke, weeke! So cries a pig preparèd to the spit.

DEMETRIUS

What mean'st thou, Aaron? Wherefore didst thou
    this?

AARON

O Lord, sir, 'tis a deed of policy.
Shall she live to betray this guilt of ours?
A long-tongued babbling gossip? No, lords, no.   150
And now be it known to you my full intent.
Not far, one Muliteus my countryman
His wife but yesternight was brought to bed;
His child is like to her, fair as you are.
Go pack with him, and give the mother gold,

---

152 Muliteus] Q1 ; Muley lives, STEEVENS *conj.*

---

136 **join** The metrical irregularity of the line
leads Maxwell to suspect that the true
reading should be 'are joined', the original 'ioind' having been misread as 'ioine'
and 'are' omitted. It is quite possible,
however, that the Q1 reading is correct,
a pause after 'lords!' taking the place of
one syllable.

138 **chafèd** enraged

144 **Two . . . away** Proverbial; compare
'Three (two) may keep counsel if two
(one) be away' (*ODEP*, p. 417; Tilley
T257).

148 **policy** prudent calculation; but see also
note on 2.1.105.

152–3 **one . . . wife** i.e. the wife of one
Muliteus, my countryman. The well-
known Moorish name 'Muly' lends
credence to Steevens's ingenious conjecture: 'one *Muley* lives, my countryman.
His wife' (see collations), adopted by Maxwell. The Q1 reading makes sense, however, and, as Maxwell admits, a classi-
cized name such as 'Muliteus' is not out
of place in this play.

155 **pack** conspire

And tell them both the circumstance of all,
And how by this their child shall be advanced,
And be receivèd for the Emperor's heir,
And substituted in the place of mine,
To calm this tempest whirling in the court;   160
And let the Emperor dandle him for his own.
Hark ye, lords; (*pointing to the Nurse*) you see I have
    given her physic,
And you must needs bestow her funeral;
The fields are near, and you are gallant grooms.
This done, see that you take no longer days,
But send the midwife presently to me.
The midwife and the nurse well made away,
Then let the ladies tattle what they please.

CHIRON
Aaron, I see thou wilt not trust the air
With secrets.

DEMETRIUS   For this care of Tamora,   170
Herself and hers are highly bound to thee.
                    Exeunt Chiron and Demetrius carrying off
                    the Nurse's body

AARON
Now to the Goths, as swift as swallow flies,
There to dispose this treasure in mine arms,
And secretly to greet the Empress' friends.
Come on, you thick-lipped slave, I'll bear you hence;
For it is you that puts us to our shifts.
I'll make you feed on berries and on roots,
And feed on curds and whey, and suck the goat,
And cabin in a cave, and bring you up
To be a warrior, and command a camp.   *Exit*   180

---

162 *pointing to the Nurse*] *not in* Q1   169–70 Aaron . . . secrets] *divided by* THEOBALD; *one line in* Q1   171.1–2 *Chiron . . . body*] *not in* Q1   178 feed] Q1; feast HANMER

156 **circumstance of all** all the details
162 **physic** medicine
163 **bestow** provide
164 **grooms** fellows
165 **days** time
176 **that . . . shifts** who oblige us to devise

stratagems
177–8 **feed . . . feed** The unusual repetition led Hanmer to the emendation 'feast' in l. 178 (see collations).
179 **cabin** lodge

4.3   *Enter Titus, old Marcus, his son Publius, young Lucius,*
        and other gentlemen (Sempronius, Caius) with bows,
        and Titus bears the arrows with letters on the ends
        of them

TITUS

Come, Marcus, come; kinsmen, this is the way.
Sir boy, let me see your archery;
Look ye draw home enough, and 'tis there straight.
Terras Astraea reliquit; be you remembered, Marcus,
She's gone, she's fled. Sirs, take you to your tools.
You, cousins, shall go sound the ocean,
And cast your nets;
Happily you may catch her in the sea,
Yet there's as little justice as at land.
No; Publius and Sempronius, you must do it;   10
'Tis you must dig with mattock and with spade,
And pierce the inmost centre of the earth.
Then when you come to Pluto's region,
I pray you deliver him this petition;
Tell him it is for justice and for aid,
And that it comes from old Andronicus,
Shaken with sorrows in ungrateful Rome.
Ah, Rome! Well, well, I made thee miserable
What time I threw the people's suffrages
On him that thus doth tyrannize o'er me.   20
Go, get you gone, and pray be careful all,
And leave you not a man-of-war unsearched;

4.3] CAPELL *(subs.)*; *not in* Q1   0.1 *his son Publius*] *not in* Q1   0.2 *Sempronius, Caius*] *not in* Q1
7–8 And . . . sea] *as here* MAXWELL; *one line in* Q1; *ll. 4–8 rearranged by* CAPELL, *ending with*
'reliquit', 'fled', 'shall', 'nets', 'sea'

4.3 The location is a public place near the
     palace; the benches from the preceding
     scenes have been removed.
1–24 **Come . . . justice** The Q1 punctuation
     of this speech is unusually light, consist-
     ing entirely of commas except for a colon
     after 'land' (l. 9) and full stops after
     'Rome' (l. 17), 'me' (l. 20), and 'justice'
     (l. 24). Editors vary greatly in their
     distribution of semicolons, colons, and
     full stops.
3 **home** to the full extent
4–8 Since there is no way to make regular
     blank verse of these lines (see collations),
     it seems best to rearrange them as little as

possible. I follow Maxwell in making only
one change, dividing the longest line into
ll. 7–8.

4 *Terras . . . reliquit* 'Astraea (goddess of
   justice) has left the earth' (Latin, from
   Ovid, *Metamorphoses*, i. 150); the depar-
   ture of Astraea, part of Ovid's description
   of the Age of Iron, precedes his account of
   the attack on Olympus by the giants.
   be you remembered remember
8 **Happily** perhaps
9 **there's** i.e. there (in the sea) there is
13 **Pluto** god of the underworld
19 **What time** when

This wicked Emperor may have shipped her hence,
And, kinsmen, then we may go pipe for justice.
MARCUS
O Publius, is not this a heavy case,
To see thy noble uncle thus distract?
PUBLIUS
Therefore, my lords, it highly us concerns
By day and night t'attend him carefully,
And feed his humour kindly as we may,
Till time beget some careful remedy.   30
MARCUS
Kinsmen, his sorrows are past remedy.
But ⌈   ⌉
Join with the Goths, and with revengeful war
Take wreak on Rome for this ingratitude,
And vengeance on the traitor Saturnine.
TITUS
Publius, how now? How now, my masters?
What, have you met with her?
PUBLIUS
No, my good lord, but Pluto sends you word
If you will have Revenge from hell, you shall;
Marry, for Justice, she is so employed,   40
He thinks, with Jove in heaven, or somewhere else,
So that perforce you must needs stay a time.
TITUS
He doth me wrong to feed me with delays.
I'll dive into the burning lake below,
And pull her out of Acheron by the heels.
Marcus, we are but shrubs, no cedars we,
No big-boned men framed of the Cyclops' size,

32 But] *catchword in* Q1

24 **pipe** whistle; i.e. look in vain
25 **heavy case** sad situation
26 **distract** distraught, mad
29 **feed his humour** cater to his whims
30 **careful** showing care or concern
32 **But** . . . In Q1 this word appears as the catchword at the foot of one page, although the first word on the following page is 'Join' (l. 33), suggesting that one or more lines may have been omitted.

34 **wreak** revenge
37 **her** i.e. Justice
44 **burning lake** probably Phlegethon, the burning river of Hades
45 **Acheron** another river in Hades, which it represents here by synecdoche
46 **shrubs, no cedars** The opposition was proverbial (Tilley C208).
47 **Cyclops** one-eyed giants (as in the *Odyssey*, ix)

But metal, Marcus, steel to the very back,
Yet wrung with wrongs more than our backs can bear;
And sith there's no justice in earth nor hell,   50
We will solicit heaven and move the gods
To send down justice for to wreak our wrongs.
Come, to this gear. You are a good archer, Marcus.
      He gives them the arrows
'*Ad Jovem*', that's for you; here, '*Ad Apollinem*';
'*Ad Martem*', that's for myself;
Here, boy, 'To Pallas'; here 'To Mercury';
'To Saturn', Caius, not to Saturnine;
You were as good to shoot against the wind.
To it, boy! Marcus, loose when I bid.
Of my word, I have written to effect;   60
There's not a god left unsolicited.

MARCUS

Kinsmen, shoot all your shafts into the court;
We will afflict the Emperor in his pride.

TITUS

Now, masters, draw. O, well said, Lucius!
Good boy, in Virgo's lap; give it Pallas.

MARCUS

My lord, I aim a mile beyond the moon;
Your letter is with Jupiter by this.

TITUS

Ha, ha! Publius, Publius, what hast thou done?
See, see, thou hast shot off one of Taurus' horns.

57 Saturn,] CAPELL; *Saturnine*, to Q1   67, 79, 83 Jupiter] *Iubiter* Q1

48 **steel . . . back** Proverbial (*ODEP*, p. 773; Tilley S842).
50 **sith** since
53 **to this gear** about this business
54–5 '*Ad Jovem*' . . . '*Ad Apollinem*' . . . '*Ad Martem*' To Jove . . . To Apollo . . . To Mars (Latin); see note on 4.1.65. The god of war is added to the earlier list, and later Saturn is added; see note on 2.3.31.
58 **were . . . to** might as well (as appeal to Saturninus)
59 **loose** let fly
60 **Of my word** on my word, truly
64 **well said** well done
65 **Virgo** the constellation of the Virgin (associated with Astraea)

66 **aim . . . moon** 'He casts beyond the moon' was a proverbial phrase meaning 'indulge in wild conjecture' (*ODEP*, p. 106; Tilley M1114); Marcus intends Titus to take his words literally.
67 **Jupiter** The Q1 spelling 'Jubiter' (corresponding to a common pronunciation) here and in ll. 79 and 83 may derive from its intentional use in l. 84 to represent the Clown's misunderstanding (see Cercignani, p. 312).
69 **thou hast** The metre requires the pronunciation 'thou'st' (see Cercignani, p. 291).
69, 71 **Taurus, Aries** constellations of the Bull and the Ram

MARCUS

    This was the sport, my lord: when Publius shot,   70
    The Bull, being galled, gave Aries such a knock
    That down fell both the Ram's horns in the court,
    And who should find them but the Empress' villain?
    She laughed, and told the Moor he should not choose
    But give them to his master for a present.

TITUS

    Why there it goes; God give his lordship joy!
        Enter the Clown with a basket and two pigeons in it
    News, news from heaven! Marcus, the post is come.
    Sirrah, what tidings? Have you any letters?
    Shall I have justice? What says Jupiter?

CLOWN Ho, the gibbet-maker? He says that he hath taken   80
    them down again, for the man must not be hanged till the
    next week.

TITUS But what says Jupiter, I ask thee?

CLOWN Alas, sir, I know not Jubiter; I never drank with him
    in all my life.

TITUS Why, villain, art thou not the carrier?

CLOWN Ay, of my pigeons, sir; nothing else.

TITUS Why, didst thou not come from heaven?

CLOWN From heaven? Alas, sir, I never came there. God
    forbid I should be so bold to press to heaven in my young   90
    days. Why, I am going with my pigeons to the tribunal
    plebs, to take up a matter of brawl betwixt my uncle and
    one of the Emperal's men.

MARCUS (*to Titus*) Why, sir, that is as fit as can be to serve
    for your oration; and let him deliver the pigeons to the
    Emperor from you.

---

77 News . . . come.] *so* ROWE 1714; *two lines divided after* heauen, *and given to Clowne* Q1 ; *two lines, similarly divided, with repeated prefix 'Titus'* Q2   78 Sirrah] Q2 ; *Titus.* Sirra Q1   84–5 Alas . . . life] *prose in* CAPELL; *verse, divided after 'Iubiter,'* Q1

72 **horns** (leading to another joke about cuckoldry)
    in the court i.e. into the Emperor's palace
73 **villain** servant (but with a play on the current meaning)
76.1 *Clown* The word meant both a rustic and the actor who played low-comic parts.
80 **gibbet-maker** The Clown's effort to make sense of 'Jupiter,' which he hears as

    'Jubiter' (see l. 84 and note on l. 67).
81 **them** i.e. the gallows
    must not be is not to be
86 **carrier** postman
91–2 **tribunal plebs** mispronunciation of 'tribunus plebis', tribune of the people
92 **take up** arrange a friendly settlement of
93 **Emperal** the Clown's version of 'Emperor'
95 **oration** petition

TITUS Tell me, can you deliver an oration to the Emperor
   with a grace?
CLOWN Nay, truly sir, I could never say grace in all my life.
TITUS

  Sirrah, come hither; make no more ado,   100
  But give your pigeons to the Emperor.
  By me thou shalt have justice at his hands.
  Hold, hold; meanwhile, here's money for thy charges.
  Give me pen and ink.
     Writes
  Sirrah, hast thou a knife? Come, let me see it.
     Takes knife and gives it to Marcus
  Here, Marcus, fold it in the oration;
  For thou hast made it like an humble suppliant.
  And when thou hast given it to the Emperor,
  Knock at my door, and tell me what he says.
CLOWN God be with you, sir; I will.   *Exit*   110
TITUS

  Come, Marcus, let us go. Publius, follow me.   *Exeunt*

4.4   *Enter Emperor and Empress and her two sons,*
    Chiron and Demetrius, and attendants; the Emperor
    brings the arrows in his hand that Titus shot at him
SATURNINUS

  Why, lords, what wrongs are these! Was ever seen
  An emperor in Rome thus overborne,
  Troubled, confronted thus, and, for the extent
  Of egall justice, used in such contempt?

104–5 ink. . . . Sirrah] This edition; inke. | Sirra, can you with a grace deliuer vp a Supplication?
| *Clowne.* I sir. | *Titus.* Then here is a Supplication for you, and when you | come to him, at the
first approch you must kneele, then | kisse his foote, then deliuer vp your pidgeons, and then
| looke for your reward. Ile bee at hand sir, see you doe it | brauelie. | *Clowne.* I warrant you sir,
let me alone. | *Titus.* Sirra Q1   104.1 *Writes*] *not in* Q1   105.1 *Takes . . . Marcus*] *not in* Q1
    4.4] CAPELL (*subs.*); *not in* Q1   0.2 *Chiron . . . attendants*] *not in* Q1

98 **with a grace** gracefully
104–5 **ink . . . Sirrah** The Q1 lines omitted
  in this edition were probably intended
  to be cancelled when a substitute
  passage was written (see collations and
  Appendix E).
107 **For . . . suppliant** A puzzling line: does
  'it' refer to the knife or to the oration?
  None of the explanations offered (e.g. in

such editions as Wilson, Maxwell, or
Riverside) is entirely satisfactory; the
puzzle may be due to incomplete revision
(see Appendix E).
4.4 The location is in the palace with a
  throne for Saturninus.
2 **overborne** oppressed
3 **extent** exercise
4 **egall** equal (from the French '*égal*')

My lords, you know, as know the mightful gods,
However these disturbers of our peace
Buzz in the people's ears, there nought hath passed
But even with law against the wilful sons
Of old Andronicus. And what an if
His sorrows have so overwhelmed his wits?   10
Shall we be thus afflicted in his wreaks,
His fits, his frenzy, and his bitterness?
And now he writes to heaven for his redress.
See, here's to Jove, and this to Mercury,
This to Apollo, this to the god of war –
Sweet scrolls to fly about the streets of Rome!
What's this but libelling against the senate,
And blazoning our unjustice everywhere?
A goodly humour, is it not, my lords –
As who would say, in Rome no justice were?   20
But if I live, his feignèd ecstasies
Shall be no shelter to these outrages;
But he and his shall know that justice lives
In Saturninus' health, whom, if he sleep,
He'll so awake as he in fury shall
Cut off the proud'st conspirator that lives.

TAMORA

My gracious lord, my lovely Saturnine,
Lord of my life, commander of my thoughts,
Calm thee, and bear the faults of Titus' age,
Th'effects of sorrow for his valiant sons,   30
Whose loss hath pierced him deep and scarred his heart;
And rather comfort his distressèd plight
Than prosecute the meanest or the best
For these contempts. (*Aside*) Why, thus it shall become

5 as know] CAMBRIDGE; *not in* Q1   34 *Aside*] F (*placed after l. 35*); *not in* Q1

5 **as know** This conjectural addition by the
   Cambridge editors (see collations) makes
   sense of the line and brings it to normal
   length; it is highly plausible, since the
   repetition of 'know' could easily lead the
   printer to skip two words.
8 **even** in accord
11 **wreaks** acts of vengeance
18 **blazoning** proclaiming
19 **humour** whim
24 **whom** i.e. Saturninus

25 **he'll so awake** Titus will so arouse (by his
   'outrages')
   as he i.e. Saturninus. Another interpretation of these lines is that Saturninus will
   waken a sleeping justice, and Rowe accordingly changed 'he' to 'she' in ll. 24
   and 25. If 'he' is correct it is unlikely that
   justice is meant (note the references to
   justice as a woman in the preceding
   scene).

High-witted Tamora to gloze with all;
But, Titus, I have touched thee to the quick;
Thy life-blood out, if Aaron now be wise,
Then is all safe, the anchor in the port.
        Enter Clown

How now, good fellow? Wouldst thou speak with us?
CLOWN Yea, forsooth, an your mistress-ship be Emperial.   40
TAMORA Empress I am, but yonder sits the Emperor.
CLOWN 'Tis he. God and Saint Stephen give you godden. I
    have brought you a letter and a couple of pigeons here.
        Saturninus reads the letter
SATURNINUS Go, take him away and hang him presently.
CLOWN How much money must I have?
TAMORA Come, sirrah, you must be hanged.
CLOWN Hanged, by' Lady! Then have I brought up a neck
    to a fair end.   *Exit guarded*
SATURNINUS

Despiteful and intolerable wrongs!
Shall I endure this monstrous villainy?   50
I know from whence this same device proceeds.
May this be borne? – As if his traitorous sons,
That died by law for murder of our brother,
Have by my means been butchered wrongfully?
Go, drag the villain hither by the hair.
Nor age nor honour shall shape privilege;
For this proud mock I'll be thy slaughterman,
Sly frantic wretch, that holpst to make me great,
In hope thyself should govern Rome and me.
        Enter Messenger, Aemilius
SATURNINUS

What news with thee, Aemilius?   60
AEMILIUS

Arm, my lords! Rome never had more cause:

43.1 *Saturninus] He* Q1   48 *guarded] not in* Q1   59.1 *Messenger] Nutius (for 'Nuntius')* Q1

35 **High-witted** clever
   gloze use fair words
37 **Thy . . . out** i.e. once you are dead
40 **Emperial** Apparently the Clown's
   feminine form for 'Emperal' (4.3.93).
42 **godden** good evening
47 **by' Lady** by Our Lady
56 **shape privilege** afford special treatment

57 **slaughterman** executioner
58 **holpst** helped
59.1 *Messenger* The use of the Latin '*nuntius*'
   for 'messenger' in the early editions (see
   collations) derived from Roman drama,
   but, as Maxwell points out, had also been
   appropriated in texts of medieval drama.

The Goths have gathered head, and with a power
Of high-resolvèd men, bent to the spoil,
They hither march amain, under conduct
Of Lucius, son to old Andronicus,
Who threats, in course of this revenge, to do
As much as ever Coriolanus did.

SATURNINUS

Is warlike Lucius general of the Goths?
These tidings nip me, and I hang the head
As flowers with frost, or grass beat down with storms.   70
Ay, now begins our sorrows to approach;
'Tis he the common people love so much;
Myself hath often heard them say,
When I have walkèd like a private man,
That Lucius' banishment was wrongfully,
And they have wished that Lucius were their emperor.

TAMORA

Why should you fear? Is not your city strong?

SATURNINUS

Ay, but the citizens favour Lucius,
And will revolt from me to succour him.

TAMORA

King, be thy thoughts imperious like thy name.   80
Is the sun dimmed, that gnats do fly in it?
The eagle suffers little birds to sing,
And is not careful what they mean thereby,
Knowing that with the shadow of his wings
He can at pleasure stint their melody;
Even so mayest thou the giddy men of Rome.
Then cheer thy spirit; for know, thou Emperor,
I will enchant the old Andronicus
With words more sweet and yet more dangerous
Than baits to fish, or honey-stalks to sheep,   90

---

68 SATURNINUS] *King* QI (*and so ll. 78, 93, 103*)   85 melody;] melody. QI   86 Rome.] Rome, QI

62 **gathered head** raised an army
power armed force
63 **bent to the spoil** intent on plunder
64 **amain** at full speed
conduct leadership
67 **Coriolanus** The hero of Shakespeare's last
tragedy; Roman general who was
banished from the city, and returned

leading an army of Rome's enemies.
75 **wrongfully** i.e. wrongfully done
83 **is not careful** does not care
85 **stint** stop
90 **honey-stalks** clover; '"Honey-suckle"
was anciently a name for red clover, and
is still in Warwickshire' (Onions). Too
much clover is harmful to sheep.

When as the one is wounded with the bait,
The other rotted with delicious feed.
SATURNINUS
But he will not entreat his son for us.
TAMORA
If Tamora entreat him, then he will;
For I can smooth and fill his agèd ears
With golden promises, that were his heart
Almost impregnable, his old ears deaf,
Yet should both ear and heart obey my tongue.
(*To Aemilius*) Go thou before to be our ambassador;
Say that the Emperor requests a parley   100
Of warlike Lucius, and appoint the meeting
Even at his father's house, the old Andronicus.
SATURNINUS
Aemilius, do this message honourably,
And if he stand in hostage for his safety,
Bid him demand what pledge will please him best.
AEMILIUS
Your bidding shall I do effectually.   *Exit*
TAMORA
Now will I to that old Andronicus,
And temper him with all the art I have,
To pluck proud Lucius from the warlike Goths.
And now, sweet Emperor, be blithe again,   110
And bury all thy fear in my devices.
SATURNINUS
Then go incessantly, and plead to him.   *Exeunt*

92 feed] Q3; seede Q1 (feede)   97 ears] Q1 (yeares); eares F   99 before to be] Q1; before, be
CAPELL   104 in] Q1; on F4   112 incessantly] CAPELL; sucessantly Q1; successantly Q2

92 **rotted** 'Of sheep: Affected by the rot'
(*OED*). The 'rot' is a disease of the liver.
95 **smooth** flatter
97 **ears** See note on 2.3.160.
99 **before to be** Capell's omission of 'to' is
tempting and may be right, but the added
syllable does not constitute a great irregularity; see Cercignani, p. 291.
104 **stand in** insist on (*OED*, 72e); although
this passage is the only one cited for this
meaning, there are many examples of a

closely related meaning, 'to persevere or
persist in' (72b); it therefore seems unnecessary to accept the F4 emendation
'stand on' (see collations).
108 **temper** work on
112 **incessantly** immediately. Since Q1
'sucessantly', however spelt (see collations), is an otherwise unrecorded word,
Capell's conjecture is plausible; *incessam-
ment* in French is used in the same sense.

5.1 ⌈*Flourish.*⌉ *Enter Lucius with an army of Goths with drums and soldiers*

LUCIUS

Approvèd warriors and my faithful friends,
I have receivèd letters from great Rome
Which signifies what hate they bear their emperor,
And how desirous of our sight they are.
Therefore, great lords, be as your titles witness,
Imperious, and impatient of your wrongs;
And wherein Rome hath done you any scath,
Let him make treble satisfaction.

A GOTH

Brave slip, sprung from the great Andronicus,
Whose name was once our terror, now our comfort,   10
Whose high exploits and honourable deeds
Ingrateful Rome requites with foul contempt,
Be bold in us; we'll follow where thou lead'st,
Like stinging bees in hottest summer's day
Led by their master to the flowered fields,
And be advengèd on cursèd Tamora.

⌈ALL THE GOTHS⌉

And as he saith, so say we all with him.

LUCIUS

I humbly thank him, and I thank you all.
But who comes here, led by a lusty Goth?
   Enter a Goth, leading of Aaron with his child in his arms

5.1] ROWE (*subs.*); *Actus Quintus* F; *not in* QI   0.1 *Flourish*] F; *not in* QI   0.2 *soldiers*] QI;
Colours CAPELL   9 A GOTH] *Goth* QI (*and so ll. 121, 152, 162*)   sprung] QI (*sprong*); sprung
Q2   17 ALL THE GOTHS] *Omn.* (*for 'Omnes'*) F2; QI *continues to Goth; The other Goths* WILSON

5.1 The location is near Rome. There may be
   a property tree (see l. 47).
1 **Approvèd** tested
2 **letters** i.e. a letter. The plural was
   frequently used in this sense.
7 **scath** injury
9 **slip** scion
   sprung QI 'sprong' (see collations) is a
   variant like those discussed by Cercignani, p. 130.
10 **Whose** refers to Lucius
13 **bold** confident
15 **master** It was thought that the hive was
   ruled by a king bee.

16 **advengèd** a Latinate form of 'avenged'
   cursèd Tamora Shakespeare does not explain why the Goths have turned against
   her. Broude points out that Goths
   were often favourably portrayed in
   Renaissance England, and that in
   Shakespeare's play the only villainous
   Goths are the Empress and her sons (pp.
   28–32).
17 ALL THE GOTHS Although the F2 reading
   (see collations) is only a guess, it is almost
   certainly correct; the line cannot belong
   to the speaker of the preceding lines.

SECOND GOTH

    Renownèd Lucius, from our troops I strayed   20
    To gaze upon a ruinous monastery,
    And as I earnestly did fix mine eye
    Upon the wasted building, suddenly
    I heard a child cry underneath a wall.
    I made unto the noise, when soon I heard
    The crying babe controlled with this discourse:
    'Peace, tawny slave, half me and half thy dame!
    Did not thy hue bewray whose brat thou art,
    Had nature lent thee but thy mother's look,
    Villain, thou mightst have been an emperor.   30
    But where the bull and cow are both milk-white,
    They never do beget a coal-black calf.
    Peace, villain, peace!' – even thus he rates the babe –
    'For I must bear thee to a trusty Goth,
    Who, when he knows thou art the Empress' babe,
    Will hold thee dearly for thy mother's sake.'
    With this, my weapon drawn, I rushed upon him,
    Surprised him suddenly, and brought him hither,
    To use as you think needful of the man.

LUCIUS

    O worthy Goth! This is the incarnate devil   40
    That robbed Andronicus of his good hand;
    This is the pearl that pleased your Empress' eye;
    And here's the base fruit of her burning lust.
    Say, wall-eyed slave, whither wouldst thou convey
    This growing image of thy fiendlike face?

20 SECOND GOTH] CAPELL; *Goth* Q1

20 **SECOND GOTH** Q1 uses the prefix '*Goth*' for
all speeches by individual Goths (see
collations). Since it is obvious that the
speaker of these lines does not speak
ll. 9–16, it is useful to distinguish him as
'Second Goth', but it is impossible to be
sure whether one of these two or yet
another Goth should speak ll. 121,
152–3, 162, and 5.3.3. For these
speeches I accept the indeterminate 'A
Goth'. The assignment of these speeches
in performance will depend in part, as no
doubt it did in Shakespeare's time, on the
size of the company.

22 **earnestly** attentively
23 **wasted** ruined
26 **controlled** calmed
27 **tawny** black (see 4.2.71)
    slave (said playfully, as is 'villain' below)
    dame mother
28 **bewray** reveal
    brat child (not necessarily derogative)
39 **use . . . of** deal with
42 **pearl . . . eye** 'A black man is a pearl in a
fair woman's eye' (*ODEP*, p. 64; Tilley
M79).
44 **wall-eyed** with fiercely glaring eyes

Why dost not speak? What, deaf? Not a word?
A halter, soldiers; hang him on this tree,
And by his side his fruit of bastardy.

AARON

Touch not the boy; he is of royal blood.

LUCIUS

Too like the sire for ever being good.   50
First hang the child, that he may see it sprawl –
A sight to vex the father's soul withal.
Get me a ladder.

     Goths bring a ladder, which Aaron is made to climb

AARON   Lucius, save the child,
And bear it from me to the Empress.
If thou do this, I'll show thee wondrous things,
That highly may advantage thee to hear.
If thou wilt not, befall what may befall,
I'll speak no more but 'Vengeance rot you all!'

LUCIUS

Say on, and if it please me which thou speak'st,
Thy child shall live, and I will see it nourished.   60

AARON

And if it please thee? Why, assure thee, Lucius,
'Twill vex thy soul to hear what I shall speak;
For I must talk of murders, rapes, and massacres,
Acts of black night, abominable deeds,
Complots of mischief, treason, villainies,
Ruthful to hear, yet piteously performed,

---

53 Get . . . ladder] *assigned to Lucius by* POPE 1728 (*conj.* Theobald); *beginning of Aaron's speech in* Q1   53 Goths . . . climb] This edition; *Ladder brought*: Aaron *led up it* CAPELL; *not in* Q1
58 'Vengeance . . . all!'] CAMBRIDGE; *without inverted commas in* Q1

---

51 **sprawl** twitch in the death agony
53 **Get . . . ladder** The early texts, which have no stage direction here, begin Aaron's next speech with these words (see collations), but Pope was undoubtedly right in assigning them to Lucius, who has just ordered a halter to be brought. Aaron has no reason to want a ladder.
58 **'Vengeance . . . all!'** Although Q1 does not so indicate (see collations), this curse is not what Aaron now pronounces, but what he threatens to pronounce if his child is killed.

59, 61 **and** In l. 59 'and' seems to be a connective, though when Aaron repeats it in l. 61 it is part of the phrase 'and if', normally spelt 'an if' in this edition. As Maxwell says, the repetition shows 'the absence of any sense in sixteenth-century English that two different words are in question'.
60 **nourished** nursed, cared for
64 **abominable** See note on 2.3.74.
66 **Ruthful** lamentable
    piteously so as to arouse pity

And this shall all be buried in my death,
Unless thou swear to me my child shall live.
LUCIUS
Tell on thy mind; I say thy child shall live.
AARON
Swear that he shall, and then I will begin.   70
LUCIUS
Who should I swear by? Thou believest no god;
That granted, how canst thou believe an oath?
AARON
What if I do not? – As indeed I do not,
Yet, for I know thou art religious,
And hast a thing within thee callèd conscience,
With twenty popish tricks and ceremonies,
Which I have seen thee careful to observe,
Therefore I urge thy oath; for that I know
An idiot holds his bauble for a god,
And keeps the oath which by that god he swears,   80
To that I'll urge him: therefore thou shalt vow
By that same god, what god soe'er it be,
That thou adorest and hast in reverence,
To save my boy, to nourish and bring him up,
Or else I will discover nought to thee.
LUCIUS
Even by my god I swear to thee I will.
AARON
First know thou, I begot him on the Empress.
LUCIUS
O most insatiate and luxurious woman!
AARON
Tut, Lucius, this was but a deed of charity
To that which thou shalt hear of me anon: 90
'Twas her two sons that murdered Bassianus;
They cut thy sister's tongue and ravished her,
And cut her hands and trimmed her as thou sawest.
LUCIUS
O detestable villain! Call'st thou that trimming?

76 **popish** A characteristic anachronism;   head) carried by a court fool.
Aaron adopts the standard Protestant   88 **luxurious** lecherous
ridicule of Roman Catholic ritual.   90 **To** i.e. compared to
79 **bauble** The stick (often with a carved

AARON

Why, she was washed and cut and trimmed,

And 'twas trim sport for them which had the doing of it.

LUCIUS

O barbarous, beastly villains like thyself!

AARON

Indeed, I was their tutor to instruct them.

That codding spirit had they from their mother,

As sure a card as ever won the set;   100

That bloody mind I think they learned of me,

As true a dog as ever fought at head.

Well, let my deeds be witness of my worth:

I trained thy brethren to that guileful hole

Where the dead corpse of Bassianus lay;

I wrote the letter that thy father found,

And hid the gold within that letter mentioned,

Confederate with the Queen and her two sons;

And what not done, that thou hast cause to rue,

Wherein I had no stroke of mischief in it?   110

I played the cheater for thy father's hand,

And when I had it, drew myself apart,

And almost broke my heart with extreme laughter.

I pried me through the crevice of a wall,

When, for his hand, he had his two sons' heads,

Beheld his tears, and laughed so heartily

That both mine eyes were rainy like to his;

And when I told the Empress of this sport,

She sounded almost at my pleasing tale,

And for my tidings gave me twenty kisses.   120

95–6 **Why . . . it** To add the first two words of l. 96 to the preceding line, as editors since Capell have done in order to produce two pentameters, is to put a false metrical emphasis on ''twas' and thus obscure the speech rhythm.

96 **trim** fine

99 **codding** (the only recorded occurrence of the word) probably a pun on 'cod' in the sense of 'testicle' and the slang sense of 'hoax' (though the latter is not recorded before the nineteenth century), hence lustful and joking; there may also be a play on 'card' in l. 100.

100 **sure . . . card** Proverbial (*ODEP*,

p. 789; Tilley C74).

100 **set** game

102 **at head** The best bulldogs attacked the bull's head.

104 **trained** lured

111 **cheater** '(a) cheat, swindler; (b) escheater, an officer who looked after the king's escheats (estates forfeited to the crown) and thus would have plenty of opportunity for fraudulent activity' (Kittredge).

114 **pried me** spied

119 **sounded** swooned. The archaic variant spelling is retained here for the sake of the metre.

A GOTH

What, canst thou say all this and never blush?

AARON

Ay, like a black dog, as the saying is.

LUCIUS

Art thou not sorry for these heinous deeds?

AARON

Ay, that I had not done a thousand more.
Even now I curse the day – and yet I think
Few come within the compass of my curse –
Wherein I did not some notorious ill:
As kill a man, or else devise his death;
Ravish a maid, or plot the way to do it;
Accuse some innocent, and forswear myself;   130
Set deadly enmity between two friends;
Make poor men's cattle break their necks;
Set fire on barns and haystacks in the night,
And bid the owners quench them with their tears.
Oft have I digged up dead men from their graves,
And set them upright at their dear friends' door,
Even when their sorrows almost was forgot,
And on their skins, as on the bark of trees,
Have with my knife carvèd in Roman letters,
'Let not your sorrow die, though I am dead.'   140
But I have done a thousand dreadful things
As willingly as one would kill a fly,
And nothing grieves me heartily indeed,
But that I cannot do ten thousand more.

133 haystacks] Q1 (haystalks); haystakes Q2; haystacks Q3   141 But] Q1; Tut Q2

121 A GOTH This speech prefix and the next three are centred in Q1; see note on 1.1.1.

122 like . . . dog 'To blush like a black dog' was proverbial irony (*ODEP*, p. 71; Tilley D507).

128–40 As . . . dead The striking resemblance between this cheerful catalogue of horrors and the boasts of Marlowe's Barabas in *The Jew of Malta* (probably 1589–90), 2.3.176–202, has often been noted.

132 Make . . . necks A four-foot line, which some editors have sought to regularize

with added words such as 'fall and' (Hudson).

133 haystacks Maxwell retains the Q1 spelling 'haystalks' (see collations) on the ground that it is a dialectal variant, but it is not recorded before 1750; the 'l' in Q1 is easily explained as a foul-case error.

141 But The Q2 reading, 'Tut' (see collations), is attractive, because characteristic of Aaron (see l. 89 above), and some editors adopt it, but there are no grounds for rejecting the Q1 reading. The word appears as 'Tut' in the Peacham MS.

LUCIUS (*to a Goth*)
  Bring down the devil, for he must not die
  So sweet a death as hanging presently.
      Aaron is brought down
AARON
  If there be devils, would I were a devil,
  To live and burn in everlasting fire,
  So I might have your company in hell,
  But to torment you with my bitter tongue.   150
LUCIUS
  Sirs, stop his mouth, and let him speak no more.
      Aaron is gagged.
      Enter Aemilius
A GOTH
  My lord, there is a messenger from Rome
  Desires to be admitted to your presence.
LUCIUS Let him come near.
  Welcome, Aemilius; what's the news from Rome?
AEMILIUS
  Lord Lucius, and you princes of the Goths,
  The Roman Emperor greets you all by me,
  And, for he understands you are in arms,
  He craves a parley at your father's house,
  Willing you to demand your hostages,   160
  And they shall be immediately delivered.
A GOTH What says our general?
LUCIUS
  Aemilius, let the Emperor give his pledges
  Unto my father and my uncle Marcus,
  And we will come. March away.   ⌈*Flourish.*⌉ *Exeunt*

5.2 *Enter Tamora disguised as Revenge* ⌈*in a chariot*⌉, *and her*
      two sons, Chiron as Rape, and Demetrius as Murder

TAMORA
  Thus, in this strange and sad habiliment

146.1 *Aaron . . . down*] *not in* Q1   151.1 *Aaron is gagged*] *not in* Q1   165 *Flourish. Exeunt*] F;
not in Q1; *Exeunt* Q3
  5.2] ROWE (*subs.*); *not in* Q1   0.1–2 *Enter . . . Murder*] This edition; *Enter Tamora and her two
sons disguised* Q1

5.2 The location is a court in Titus' house in Rome. The Elizabethan staging is debatable.

I will encounter with Andronicus,
And say I am Revenge, sent from below
To join with him and right his heinous wrongs.
Knock at his study, where they say he keeps,
To ruminate strange plots of dire revenge;
Tell him Revenge is come to join with him,
And work confusion on his enemies.

> *They knock, and Titus opens his study door ⌈above⌉*

TITUS

Who doth molest my contemplation?
Is it your trick to make me ope the door,   10
That so my sad decrees may fly away,
And all my study be to no effect?
You are deceived, for what I mean to do
See here in bloody lines I have set down;
And what is written shall be executed.

TAMORA

Titus, I am come to talk with thee.

TITUS

No, not a word; how can I grace my talk,

8.1 *above*] *not in* Q1

Richard Hosley (*Shakespeare Survey 10* (Cambridge, 1957), p. 86, n. 4) and Maxwell (note on 5.2.69 in third edition of *Titus*, 1961) doubt the use of the upper stage in this scene or the next. A temporary structure providing a raised and enclosed space at the back of the stage is conceivable but considerably more cumbersome than the tomb for Act 1. It is clear, in any case, that Titus in this scene must first appear above the other characters, since Tamora twice (ll. 33, 43) asks him to 'come down'. Despite certain problems which I discuss as they arise, the use of the upper stage seems to me the simplest solution.

0.1–3 *disguised as Revenge . . . Rape, and . . . Murder* See ll. 3, 45; the references to Revenge's 'chariot' or 'wagon' (ll. 47, 48, 51, 54) suggest that Tamora is drawn on stage like Titus in 1.1. This spectacular effect would be especially appropriate to the masque-like quality of this episode. Since her sons remain with Titus when she leaves, some attendants would have

to be provided to draw the chariot.
1 **sad habiliment** sombre costume

5 **study** i.e. study door
  keeps stays
8 **confusion** destruction
8.1 **They . . . above** Unless there is a temporary structure to which they climb, they must knock at one of the entrance doors. If the upper stage is used, Titus may be in a curtained section of it, such as was probably used occasionally as a music room (*Revels History of Drama in English*, volume III: 1576–1613 (New York and London, 1975), p. 173). By drawing back the curtain he may be thought to be opening his door. In his hands he has the papers to which he refers (l. 14). The absence of an actual door for him to open is an objection to this way of staging the scene, but much business on the Elizabethan stage was unrealistic by modern standards.
11 **sad decrees** serious ordinances

Wanting a hand to give it action?

Thou hast the odds of me; therefore no more.

TAMORA

If thou didst know me, thou wouldst talk with me.   20

TITUS

I am not mad; I know thee well enough:

Witness this wretched stump, witness these crimson
     lines,

Witness these trenches made by grief and care,

Witness the tiring day and heavy night,

Witness all sorrow that I know thee well

For our proud Empress, mighty Tamora.

Is not thy coming for my other hand?

TAMORA

Know, thou sad man, I am not Tamora;

She is thy enemy, and I thy friend.

I am Revenge, sent from th'infernal kingdom   30

To ease the gnawing vulture of thy mind

By working wreakful vengeance on thy foes.

Come down and welcome me to this world's light;

Confer with me of murder and of death.

There's not a hollow cave or lurking place,

No vast obscurity or misty vale,

---

18 it action] F; that accord Q1; it that accord POPE   28 Know, thou] CAPELL; Know thou Q1;
Know thou, F4

---

18 **Wanting** lacking

to . . . action to accompany my talk with appropriate gestures. The rejected Q1 reading 'to give that accord' (see collations) is understandable if 'that' refers to 'my talk,' but it is somewhat awkward and metrically defective. The F reading, adopted here, makes excellent sense, since 'action' as a rhetorical term meant 'delivery,' and included gesture as well as intonation. As F probably consulted a prompt copy, this may have been the wording used in performance. B. L. Joseph shows the great importance attached to gesture in seventeenth-century oratory (*Elizabethan Acting* (Oxford, 1951), pp. 34–59), and reproduces diagrams of the correct use of both hands. Though mistakenly supposing that Titus has lost his *right* hand, Joseph shows that

the question in ll. 17–18 is a natural one (pp. 53, 59). In Thomas Middleton's *The Ant and the Nightingale* (1604) this scene is recalled by a mutilated soldier who speaks of 'my lamentable action of one arm, like old Titus Andronicus' (*Works*, ed. A. H. Bullen (1885–6), viii. 94).

19 **odds of** advantage over; i.e. two hands to one

22 **crimson lines** (see l. 14)

31 **gnawing vulture** An allusion to Prometheus, part of whose punishment was to have a vulture feed on his liver while he was bound to a rock (see note on 2.1.17).

32 **wreakful** revengeful

36 **obscurity** i.e. dark or dismal place. The lines recall earlier descriptions of the place where Lavinia was raped, such as 4.1.53.

Where bloody murder or detested rape
Can couch for fear, but I will find them out,
And in their ears tell them my dreadful name,
Revenge, which makes the foul offender quake.   40
TITUS

Art thou Revenge? And art thou sent to me
To be a torment to mine enemies?
TAMORA

I am; therefore come down and welcome me.
TITUS

Do me some service ere I come to thee.
Lo, by thy side where Rape and Murder stands,
Now give some surance that thou art Revenge:
Stab them, or tear them on thy chariot wheels,
And then I'll come and be thy wagoner,
And whirl along with thee about the globe,
Provide thee two proper palfreys, black as jet,   50
To hale thy vengeful wagon swift away,
And find out murderers in their guilty caves;
And when thy car is loaden with their heads,
I will dismount, and by thy wagon wheel
Trot like a servile footman all day long,
Even from Hyperion's rising in the east
Until his very downfall in the sea;
And day by day I'll do this heavy task,
So thou destroy Rapine and Murder there.
TAMORA

These are my ministers, and come with me.   60

---

49 Globe,] This edition (*conj.* Walker); Globes. Q1; globe. CAPELL *conj.*   52 murderers] CAPELL;
murder Q1   caves] F2; cares Q1   56 Hyperion's] F2 (*Hiperions*); *Epeons* Q1; *Eptons* F1

38 **couch** lie hidden
46 **surance** (Shakespeare's only use of this
   form of the word) assurance, in the sense
   of 'pledge' or 'guarantee'
49 **globe** Although 'globes' as in Q1 (see
   collations) is possible in the sense of
   'planets' or 'stars', the rest of the passage
   shows that travel around the earth is
   meant.
50 **thee two** Rowe omitted 'thee' to mend the
   metre, but the insistent repetition in the
   speech of 'thou', 'thee', and 'thy' suggests
   that the Q1 reading is correct.

50 **proper** handsome
51 **hale** pull
52 **murderers . . . caves** See collations; this
   passage in Q1 contains an unusual number of what appear to be printer's errors.
53 **car** chariot
56 **Hyperion's** the sun-god's; Q1 '*Epeons*'
   (see collations) was probably due to a
   misreading of the manuscript, where, by
   scribal convention, 'p' stood for 'per-',
   giving the phonetic spelling 'Epereons'
   (see J. G. McManaway, *Shakespeare Survey 3* (Cambridge, 1950), p. 44).

TITUS

Are they thy ministers? What are they called?

TAMORA

Rape and Murder, therefore callèd so

'Cause they take vengeance of such kind of men.

TITUS

Good Lord, how like the Empress' sons they are,

And you the Empress! But we worldly men

Have miserable, mad, mistaking eyes.

O sweet Revenge, now do I come to thee,

And if one arm's embracement will content thee,

I will embrace thee in it by and by.   *Exit ⌈above⌉*

TAMORA

This closing with him fits his lunacy.   70

Whate'er I forge to feed his brain-sick humours

Do you uphold and maintain in your speeches,

For now he firmly takes me for Revenge,

And, being credulous in this mad thought,

I'll make him send for Lucius his son;

And whilst I at a banquet hold him sure,

I'll find some cunning practice out of hand

To scatter and disperse the giddy Goths,

Or at the least make them his enemies.

See, here he comes, and I must ply my theme.   80

    Enter Titus below

---

61 Are they] F2; Are them Q1   65 worldly] Q2; wordlie Q1   69 *Exit above*] *not in* Q1   71
humours] Q1; fits Q2   80.1 *Enter . . . below*] *not in* Q1

61 **they** Q1 'them' (see collations) is almost
    certainly a mistake, though the ac-
    cusative case is occasionally used as a
    nominative in Elizabethan English.
    What . . . called? Following Titus'
    previous speech, the question is
    thoroughly improbable, even though
    Titus is feigning madness. Maxwell sug-
    gests plausibly that ll. 44–59 were added
    after the rest of the dialogue was written.
    If so, this is another instance of Shake-
    speare's failure to tidy up his final draft
    (see notes on 1.1.35, 69.6, 96–149,
    341–90).
64–5 **Good . . . Empress** The repeated
    evidence that Titus recognizes his
    enemies contributes to the theatrical ef-

fectiveness of this scene. Tamora appears
blinded by confidence in her renowned
cleverness.
65 **worldly** of this world (but not with the
    modern implication of 'materialistic')
69 *above* See headnote on staging.
70 **closing** agreeing
71 **forge** invent
    humours Maxwell observes that the Q2
    reading 'fits' (see collations) was probably
    due to the illegibility of Q1 at this place on
    leaf I4ʳ; the word 'shalt' on the other side
    was apparently also illegible, and was
    replaced by 'maist' (see l. 106, collations).
77 **practice** scheme
    out of hand on the spur of the moment

TITUS

    Long have I been forlorn, and all for thee.
    Welcome, dread Fury, to my woeful house;
    Rapine and Murder, you are welcome too.
    How like the Empress and her sons you are!
    Well are you fitted, had you but a Moor;
    Could not all hell afford you such a devil?
    For well I wot the Empress never wags
    But in her company there is a Moor;
    And, would you represent our Queen aright,
    It were convenient you had such a devil.   90
    But welcome as you are; what shall we do?

TAMORA

    What wouldst thou have us do, Andronicus?

DEMETRIUS

    Show me a murderer, I'll deal with him.

CHIRON

    Show me a villain that hath done a rape,
    And I am sent to be revenged on him.

TAMORA

    Show me a thousand that hath done thee wrong,
    And I will be revengèd on them all.

TITUS (*to Demetrius*)

    Look round about the wicked streets of Rome,
    And when thou find'st a man that's like thyself,
    Good Murder, stab him; he's a murderer.   100
    (*To Chiron*) Go thou with him, and when it is thy hap
    To find another that is like to thee,
    Good Rapine, stab him; he is a ravisher.
    (*To Tamora*) Go thou with them, and in the Emperor's
        court
    There is a queen attended by a Moor;
    Well shalt thou know her by thine own proportion,
    For up and down she doth resemble thee;
    I pray thee, do on them some violent death;
    They have been violent to me and mine.

106 shalt] Q1; maist Q2

85 **Well . . . fitted** i.e. you are well furnished   90 **convenient** fitting
    to resemble the Empress   107 **up and down** altogether
87 **wags** moves about

TAMORA
　Well hast thou lessoned us; this shall we do.   110
　But would it please thee, good Andronicus,
　To send for Lucius, thy thrice-valiant son,
　Who leads towards Rome a band of warlike Goths,
　And bid him come and banquet at thy house,
　When he is here, even at thy solemn feast,
　I will bring in the Empress and her sons,
　The Emperor himself, and all thy foes,
　And at thy mercy shall they stoop and kneel,
　And on them shalt thou ease thy angry heart.
　What says Andronicus to this device?   120
TITUS (*calling*)
　Marcus, my brother, 'tis sad Titus calls.
　　　Enter Marcus
　Go, gentle Marcus, to thy nephew Lucius;
　Thou shalt inquire him out among the Goths.
　Bid him repair to me and bring with him
　Some of the chiefest princes of the Goths;
　Bid him encamp his soldiers where they are.
　Tell him the Emperor and the Empress too
　Feast at my house, and he shall feast with them.
　This do thou for my love, and so let him,
　As he regards his agèd father's life.   130
MARCUS
　This will I do, and soon return again.   *Exit*
TAMORA
　Now will I hence about thy business,
　And take my ministers along with me.
TITUS
　Nay, nay, let Rape and Murder stay with me,
　Or else I'll call my brother back again,
　And cleave to no revenge but Lucius.
TAMORA (*aside to her sons*)
　What say you, boys? Will you abide with him,
　Whiles I go tell my lord the Emperor

121 *calling*] *not in* Q1   121.1 *Enter Marcus*] *placed here by* THEOBALD; *after l. 120 in* Q1
131 *Exit*] *not in* Q1

115 **solemn** ceremonious   124 **repair** come

How I have governed our determined jest?
Yield to his humour, smooth and speak him fair,   140
And tarry with him till I turn again.

TITUS (*aside*)

I knew them all, though they supposed me mad,
And will o'erreach them in their own devices,
A pair of cursèd hell-hounds and their dame.

DEMETRIUS

Madam, depart at pleasure; leave us here.

TAMORA

Farewell, Andronicus; Revenge now goes
To lay a complot to betray thy foes.

TITUS

I know thou dost; and, sweet Revenge, farewell.

                                        Exit Tamora

CHIRON

Tell us, old man, how shall we be employed?

TITUS

Tut, I have work enough for you to do.   150
Publius, come hither, Caius and Valentine.

     Enter Publius, Caius, and Valentine

PUBLIUS What is your will?

TITUS Know you these two?

PUBLIUS

The Empress' sons, I take them, Chiron, Demetrius.

TITUS

Fie, Publius, fie! Thou art too much deceived;
The one is Murder, and Rape is the other's name;
And therefore bind them, gentle Publius;
Caius and Valentine, lay hands on them.
Oft have you heard me wish for such an hour,

148.1 *Exit Tamora*] *not in* Q1   151.1 *Enter . . . Valentine*] *not in* Q1   154 *Chiron, Demetrius*]
Q1; Chiron and Demetrius THEOBALD

139 **governed . . . jest** managed the jest we
    planned
140 **smooth . . . fair** flatter and humour him
141 **turn** return
154 **take them** i.e. take them to be
    Chiron, Demetrius Theobald's emen-
    dation, 'Chiron and Demetrius' (see col-
    lations) has the advantage of sounding

more natural, but to accept it one must
either assume that the dialogue drops
briefly into prose or make an overlong
verse line even longer. It seems preferable
to retain the Q1 reading; as spoken, this
long line, following two short lines, does
not sound very irregular.

And now I find it; therefore bind them sure,   160
And stop their mouths if they begin to cry.   *Exit*

CHIRON
   Villains, forbear; we are the Empress' sons.

PUBLIUS
   And therefore do we what we are commanded.
   Stop close their mouths; let them not speak a word.
   Is he sure bound? Look that you bind them fast.
         Enter Titus Andronicus with a knife, and Lavinia with
         a basin

TITUS
   Come, come, Lavinia; look, thy foes are bound.
   Sirs, stop their mouths; let them not speak to me,
   But let them hear what fearful words I utter.
   O villains Chiron and Demetrius,
   Here stands the spring whom you have stained with mud,   170
   This goodly summer with your winter mixed.
   You killed her husband, and for that vile fault
   Two of her brothers were condemned to death,
   My hand cut off, and made a merry jest;
   Both her sweet hands, her tongue, and that more dear
   Than hands or tongue, her spotless chastity,
   Inhuman traitors, you constrained and forced.
   What would you say if I should let you speak?
   Villains, for shame you could not beg for grace.
   Hark, wretches, how I mean to martyr you: 180
   This one hand yet is left to cut your throats,
   Whiles that Lavinia 'tween her stumps doth hold
   The basin that receives your guilty blood.
   You know your mother means to feast with me,
   And calls herself Revenge, and thinks me mad.
   Hark, villains, I will grind your bones to dust,
   And with your blood and it I'll make a paste,
   And of the paste a coffin I will rear,

---

161 *Exit*] not in Q1

160 **sure** securely
161 **cry** i.e. cry out
163 **therefore** for that very reason
170 **spring . . . mud** Compare 'Mud not the
       fountain that gave drink to thee' (*Lucrece*,

l. 577), spoken by Lucrece to Tarquin
(noted by Parrott, p. 35).
188 **coffin** A standard Elizabethan term for a
       pie-crust.

And make two pasties of your shameful heads,
And bid that strumpet, your unhallowed dam,   190
Like to the earth swallow her own increase.
This is the feast that I have bid her to,
And this the banquet she shall surfeit on,
For worse than Philomel you used my daughter,
And worse than Procne I will be revenged.
And now prepare your throats; Lavinia, come,
Receive the blood, and when that they are dead,
Let me go grind their bones to powder small,
And with this hateful liquor temper it,
And in that paste let their vile heads be baked.   200
Come, come, be every one officious
To make this banquet, which I wish may prove
More stern and bloody than the Centaurs' feast.
        He cuts their throats
So now bring them in, for I'll play the cook,
And see them ready against their mother comes.

                                              Exeunt

5.3   *Enter Lucius, Marcus, and the Goths with Aaron
          prisoner and his child in the arms of an attendant*
LUCIUS

Uncle Marcus, since 'tis my father's mind
That I repair to Rome, I am content.

5.3] CAPELL (*subs.*); *not in* Q1   0.1–2 *with . . . attendant*] *not in* Q1

---

189 **pasties** pies. The gruesome details of
Titus' culinary plans are not so remote
from Elizabethan cookery as might be
supposed. There are many recipes for
baking calves' heads in pastry 'coffins'.

191 **Like . . . increase** swallow her offspring
('increase') as the earth assimilates its
dead children when they are buried

194–5 **Philomel . . . Procne** See note on
2.3.43 and Introduction, pp. 27–8.

199 **temper** moisten

201 **officious** busy

203 **Centaurs' feast** The wedding feast of
Hippodamia and Pirithous, which ended
in a bloody battle between the Lapiths
and the Centaurs, vividly described in
Ovid's *Metamorphoses*, xii. 210 ff.

203.1 *He . . . throats* Various sorts of ex-

travagance in spectacle were apparently
as welcome to an Elizabethan audience as
rhetorical extravagance. Since modern
taste in both spectacle and rhetoric is notably different, some directors cut this
gruesome and grotesque piece of business, as Peter Brook did in his famous
1955 production. There the victims were
dragged off stage to be killed, but in John
Barton's 1981 production they died on
stage.

205 **against . . . comes** in expectation of their
mother's arrival

5.3 This is one of the scenes in Elizabethan
drama in which the imagined location
changes while characters are on stage.
Most of the scene apparently takes place
in a court in Titus' house (from which, at

184

A GOTH

And ours with thine, befall what fortune will.

LUCIUS

Good uncle, take you in this barbarous Moor,
This ravenous tiger, this accursèd devil;
Let him receive no sust'nance, fetter him,
Till he be brought unto the Empress' face
For testimony of her foul proceedings.
And see the ambush of our friends be strong;
I fear the Emperor means no good to us.   10

AARON

Some devil whisper curses in my ear,
And prompt me that my tongue may utter forth
The venomous malice of my swelling heart.

LUCIUS

Away, inhuman dog, unhallowed slave!
Sirs, help our uncle to convey him in;
        ⌜*Flourish within*⌝
The trumpets show the Emperor is at hand.
                              Exeunt Goths with Aaron

        Sound trumpets. Enter Emperor and Empress with
        Aemilius, Tribunes, and others

SATURNINUS

What, hath the firmament more suns than one?

3 A GOTH] *Goth* QI   15.1 *Flourish within*] This edition; *Flourish* F; *not in* QI   16.1 *Exeunt*
. . . *Aaron*] *not in* QI   16.3 *Aemilius*] *not in* QI   17 SATURNINUS] *King* QI (*and so ll. 25, 30, 39,*
40, 47, 52, 58)

l. 141, people 'go into' the house). In the
opening lines, however, Lucius speaks to
Marcus as if they were on their way to
Rome from their meeting-place outside
the city. By the time of Lucius' second
speech they have arrived at the house,
but have not yet had a chance to find out
how many of their friends are there.
When Saturninus and Tamora enter, the
location is a part of the house (such as a
court) where the banquet can be served.
The Elizabethan staging is again debatable. Although Hosley and Maxwell (see
headnote to 5.2 and Maxwell's note on
5.3.66) doubt the use of the upper stage,
it again provides the simplest solution.
The offer of Marcus and Lucius to hurl
themselves down (ll. 131–5) and
Aemilius' request that Marcus bring
Lucius to the waiting crowd require both

Andronici to be removed from the others
and above them. Again a temporary
structure is conceivable.

3 **ours** As Maxwell points out, the reply
does not exactly fit the preceding speech,
though the general sense is clear: the
Goths are of the same mind as Lucius.
4 **in** i.e. into Titus' house
15 **Sirs . . . in** It is clear from what follows
that Marcus remains on stage, turning
Aaron over to the Goths.
15.1 **Flourish within** The Folio direction at
this point (see collations) probably in-
dicates an off-stage 'flourish', to which
Lucius refers in his next line. As the Emperor and Empress enter the trumpets
sound again.
17 **What . . . one** Kittredge thinks that
'Lucius has assumed the manner of an

LUCIUS

What boots it thee to call thyself a sun?

MARCUS

Rome's emperor and nephew, break the parle;

These quarrels must be quietly debated.   20

The feast is ready which the care-full Titus

Hath ordained to an honourable end,

For peace, for love, for league, and good to Rome.

Please you, therefore, draw nigh and take your places.

SATURNINUS Marcus, we will.

> *A table brought in. The company sit down.*
> *Trumpets sounding, enter Titus like a cook, placing the*
> *dishes, and Lavinia with a veil over her face,*
> ⌈*young Lucius, and others*⌉

TITUS

Welcome, my lord; welcome, dread Queen;

Welcome, ye warlike Goths; welcome, Lucius;

And welcome, all. Although the cheer be poor,

'Twill fill your stomachs; please you eat of it.

SATURNINUS

Why art thou thus attired, Andronicus?   30

TITUS

Because I would be sure to have all well

To entertain your highness and your Empress.

TAMORA

We are beholding to you, good Andronicus.

TITUS

An if your highness knew my heart, you were.

---

25 will.] Q1; will. *Hoboyes* F   25.1 *A table . . . in*] F; *not in* Q1   *The company sit down*] *not in* Q1
25.2 *Trumpets sounding*] Q1; *Sound trumpets* Q2   25.3 *dishes*] Q1; *meate on the table* Q2   25.4
young . . . others] MALONE; *not in* Q1   28 all.] F (all:); all Q1; all, Q2

emperor', but his reply shows that Saturninus' words are to be taken as naïve self-
praise.
18 **boots it thee** good does it do you
19 **break the parle** interrupt the discourse,
i.e. stop quarrelling; or perhaps, 'begin
the parley' (Johnson)
21 **care-full** sorrowful
25.2 *Trumpets sounding* F calls for
'hoboyes' instead of trumpets as the banquet begins – an alternative accompaniment (see collations). This stage direction

is the first of several passages where Q2
varies notably from Q1. These differences
have been explained by the hypothesis
that the last three leaves of the copy of
Q1 used by the printer of Q2 were
damaged (see Introduction, p. 39).
25.4 *young . . . others* The early editions
provide no entry for young Lucius (see
collations), but it is logical for him and
some supporters of the Andronici to enter
with Titus.
28 **cheer** hospitality, i.e. food

My lord the Emperor, resolve me this:
Was it well done of rash Virginius
To slay his daughter with his own right hand,
Because she was enforced, stained, and deflowered?

SATURNINUS

It was, Andronicus.

TITUS   Your reason, mighty lord?

SATURNINUS

Because the girl should not survive her shame,   40
And by her presence still renew his sorrows.

TITUS

A reason mighty, strong, and effectual;
A pattern, precedent, and lively warrant
For me, most wretched, to perform the like.
Die, die, Lavinia, and thy shame with thee,
And with thy shame thy father's sorrow die.
    He kills her

SATURNINUS

What hast thou done, unnatural and unkind?

TITUS

Killed her for whom my tears have made me blind.
I am as woeful as Virginius was,
And have a thousand times more cause than he   50
To do this outrage, and it now is done.

SATURNINUS

What, was she ravished? Tell who did the deed.

TITUS

Will't please you eat? Will't please your highness feed?

TAMORA

Why hast thou slain thine only daughter thus?

46.1 *He kills her*] F; *not in* Q1

35 **resolve** answer
36–8 **Virginius ... deflowered** Livy tells how
the Roman centurion Virginius killed his
daughter to *prevent* her from being raped
by Appius Claudius. As Nørgaard points
out, however (pp. 139–40), another version of the story was current in Shakespeare's time. In *The Pilgrimage of Princes*
(1573), for instance, Lodowick Lloyd
writes: 'Then Appius Claudius ... against
all right and reason willingly and wilfully

ravished Virginia, the daughter of Virginius, which after that her own father
slew her in the open sight of Rome' (fol.
79ᵛ). Nørgaard traces the origins of this
version back to Orosius.
40 **Because** probably 'in order that'; Maxwell notes that the word is often used in
this sense in Elizabethan English (see
OED, 'because', B2).
47 **unkind** (a) unnatural (b) cruel
48 **tears ... blind** Compare 2.4.52, 3.1.268.

187

TITUS

Not I; 'twas Chiron and Demetrius.
They ravished her and cut away her tongue,
And they, 'twas they that did her all this wrong.

SATURNINUS

Go fetch them hither to us presently.

TITUS

Why there they are, both bakèd in this pie,
Whereof their mother daintily hath fed,   60
Eating the flesh that she herself hath bred.
'Tis true, 'tis true; witness my knife's sharp point.
        He stabs the Empress

SATURNINUS

Die, frantic wretch, for this accursèd deed.
        He kills Titus

LUCIUS

Can the son's eye behold his father bleed?
There's meed for meed, death for a deadly deed.
        He kills Saturninus. ⌈*A great tumult, during which
        Marcus and Lucius go to the upper stage*⌉

MARCUS

You sad-faced men, people and sons of Rome,
By uproars severed, as a flight of fowl
Scattered by winds and high tempestuous gusts,
O, let me teach you how to knit again
This scattered corn into one mutual sheaf,   70

---

59 this] Q1; that Q2   63 SATURNINUS] *Emperour* Q1   63.1 *He . . . Titus*] *not in* Q1   65.1 *He
. . . Saturninus*] *not in* Q1   *A great tumult*] CAPELL; *not in* Q1   65.1–2 *during . . . stage*] This
edition; *the* Andronici, *and their Friends, gain the Steps of* Titus' House: Tumult ceases CAPELL;
Exeunt Lucius, Marcus, Aemilius, and others and enter above RIVERSIDE (*after* Globe); *not in* Q1

---

59 **this** The second passage of Q2 variant
readings (see collations and note on l.
25.2).

65 **meed for meed** measure for measure

65.1–2 *A . . . stage* Since Marcus and Lucius
offer to hurl themselves down at l. 131,
they probably go to their elevated
position immediately after Lucius kills
Saturninus. It has been objected that
there is no dialogue to occupy the time
they would need to reach the upper
stage; for the very next words are to be
spoken by Marcus. It is easy to imagine
business that would fill this short time,
however. In Peter Brook's production, for

example, Saturninus staggered half-way
across the stage before collapsing; and no
doubt the friends of the Andronici move
into position to ward off any attack by
followers of Saturninus. Capell's direction, 'A great tumult', seems justified.
Some editors send Aemilius, young
Lucius, and others up with Marcus and
Lucius, but Aemilius' speech at l. 136
shows that he is at some distance from
Marcus and Lucius; there is no need for
anyone to go up with them.

70 **corn** grain
mutual sheaf one whose parts are related

These broken limbs again into one body;
Lest Rome herself be bane unto herself,
And she whom mighty kingdoms curtsy to,
Like a forlorn and desperate castaway,
Do shameful execution on herself.
But if my frosty signs and chaps of age,
Grave witnesses of true experience,
Cannot induce you to attend my words,
(*To Lucius*)
Speak, Rome's dear friend, as erst our ancestor,
When with his solemn tongue he did discourse   80
To lovesick Dido's sad attending ear
The story of that baleful burning night
When subtle Greeks surprised King Priam's Troy.
Tell us what Sinon hath bewitched our ears,
Or who hath brought the fatal engine in
That gives our Troy, our Rome, the civil wound.
My heart is not compact of flint nor steel,
Nor can I utter all our bitter grief,
But floods of tears will drown my oratory
And break my utt'rance, even in the time   90
When it should move ye to attend me most,
And force you to commiseration.

71 body;] CAPELL (*subs.*); body. Q1   72 Lest] CAPELL; *Romane Lord.* Let Q1; *Goth.* Let F   92 And
. . . to] Q1; Lending your kind Q2

71–2 **body;** | **Lest** Q1 ends Marcus' speech with 'body', and assigns the next lines, beginning with 'Let', to '*Romane Lord*' (see collations). How this happened is difficult to explain, but I believe all the lines given to this anonymous character belong to Marcus, as Capell thought. Not only is it strange to give this long and important speech to an unknown Roman, but the references to 'my frosty signs and chaps of age', which are exactly right for Marcus, are otherwise pointless. Furthermore, the grammatical construction in which they occur – 'But if . . . Cannot induce you to attend my words' – seems to be directly related to Marcus' plea – 'O, let me teach you . . .'. As for 'Lest', Capell's emendation makes much better sense of the passage. There is no reason for Marcus or anyone else to ask, however ironically, that Rome 'do

shameful execution on herself'.
72 **bane** poison
76 **frosty . . . chaps** white hairs and cracked skin
78 **attend** pay attention to
79 **erst** once
    our ancestor i.e. Aeneas, who tells Dido the story of the fall of Troy in Book II of the *Aeneid*. This reference makes it particularly hard to explain the F ascription of this speech to '*Goth*' (see l. 72, collations).
84 **Sinon** the traitor who induced the Trojans to admit the wooden horse (*the fatal engine*, l. 85)
86 **civil wound** injury received in a civil war
87 **compact** composed
92–6 **And . . . Demetrius** The third passage of Q2 variant readings (see collations and note on l. 25.2).

Here's Rome's young captain; let him tell the tale,
While I stand by and weep to hear him speak.
LUCIUS
Then, gracious auditory, be it known to you
That Chiron and the damned Demetrius
Were they that murderèd our Emperor's brother,
And they it were that ravishèd our sister.
For their fell faults our brothers were beheaded,
Our father's tears despised, and basely cozened   100
Of that true hand that fought Rome's quarrel out,
And sent her enemies unto the grave.
Lastly myself unkindly banishèd,
The gates shut on me, and turned weeping out,
To beg relief among Rome's enemies,
Who drowned their enmity in my true tears,
And oped their arms to embrace me as a friend.
I am the turned-forth, be it known to you,
That have preserved her welfare in my blood,
And from her bosom took the enemy's point,
Sheathing the steel in my advent'rous body.   110
Alas, you know I am no vaunter, I;
My scars can witness, dumb although they are,
That my report is just and full of truth.
But soft, methinks I do digress too much,
Citing my worthless praise. O, pardon me,
For when no friends are by, men praise themselves.
MARCUS
Now is my turn to speak. Behold the child:
        Points to Aaron's baby
Of this was Tamora deliverèd,
The issue of an irreligious Moor,   120

---

93 Here's . . . young] Q1; Here is a Q2   94 While . . . by] Q1; Your harts will throb Q2   95 gracious] Q1; noble Q2   96 Chiron . . . damned] Q1; cursed *Chiron* and Q2   118.1 *Points . . . baby] not in* Q1

95 **Then . . . you** Presumably spoken as a pentameter by contracting 'audit'ry' and 'be't' (see Cercignani, pp. 277, 289).
98 **they it were** In this construction the verb sometimes agreed with the complement (see *OED*, 'it', B2).
99 **fell** cruel

100 **and basely** i.e. and he was basely **cozened** cheated
101 **fought . . . out** fought to a finish
117 **when . . . themselves** Compare the proverbial 'He dwells far from neighbours (has ill neighbours) that is fain to praise himself' (*ODEP*, p. 560; Tilley N117).

Chief architect and plotter of these woes.
The villain is alive in Titus' house,
And as he is to witness this is true,
Now judge what cause had Titus to revenge
These wrongs unspeakable, past patience,
Or more than any living man could bear.
Now have you heard the truth; what say you, Romans?
Have we done aught amiss? Show us wherein,
And from the place where you behold us pleading
The poor remainder of Andronici   130
Will hand in hand all headlong hurl ourselves,
And on the ragged stones beat forth our souls,
And make a mutual closure of our house.
Speak, Romans, speak, and if you say we shall,
Lo, hand in hand, Lucius and I will fall.

AEMILIUS
Come, come, thou reverend man of Rome,
And bring our emperor gently in thy hand,
Lucius, our emperor; for well I know
The common voice do cry it shall be so.

⌈ROMANS⌉
Lucius, all hail, Rome's royal emperor!   140

MARCUS (*to attendants*)
Go, go into old Titus' sorrowful house
And hither hale that misbelieving Moor
To be adjudged some direful slaught'ring death
As punishment for his most wicked life.
        Exeunt attendants. ⌈*Marcus and Lucius come down*⌉

124 cause] F4; course Q1   124–6 revenge... bear.] F; reuenge.... beare, Q1   129 pleading]
Q1; now Q2   131 hurl ourselves] Q1; cast vs downe Q2   132 souls] Q1; braines Q2   136
Come] Q1; Come, Marcus come MAXWELL *conj.*   140 ROMANS] CAPELL (*Rom.*); *Marcus*
Q1   143 adjudged] Q3; adiudge Q1   144.1 *Exeunt attendants*] *not in* Q1   *Marcus ... down*]
This edition; *Lucius, and the rest, come down; with them, young* Lucius. CAPELL; *not in* Q1

121 **architect** See the discussion of this word in the Introduction, p. 15.
125 **patience** endurance
129–32 **pleading . . . souls** The fourth passage of Q2 variant readings (see collations and note on l. 25.2).
132 **ragged** rough
133 **mutual closure** common end
136 **Come . . . Rome** A short line; Maxwell's conjecture, 'Come, Marcus, come' (see collations) is made plausible by the

analogies of 3.1.143 and 4.3.1.
140, 145 **ROMANS** Both lines are given to Marcus in Q1 (see collations), presumably because the manuscript was unclear, but the lines are obviously intended to confirm Aemilius' statement about 'the common voice'. Since a demonstration of support may last for several minutes, it allows time for Marcus and Lucius to come down to the main stage.

⌈ROMANS⌉

    Lucius, all hail, Rome's gracious governor!
LUCIUS

    Thanks, gentle Romans. May I govern so,
    To heal Rome's harms and wipe away her woe!
    But, gentle people, give me aim a while,
    For nature puts me to a heavy task.
    Stand all aloof, but, uncle, draw you near   150
    To shed obsequious tears upon this trunk.
    O, take this warm kiss on thy pale cold lips,
            He kisses Titus
    These sorrowful drops upon thy bloodstained face,
    The last true duties of thy noble son.
MARCUS (*kissing Titus*)

    Tear for tear and loving kiss for kiss
    Thy brother Marcus tenders on thy lips.
    O, were the sum of these that I should pay
    Countless and infinite, yet would I pay them.
LUCIUS (*to his son*)

    Come hither, boy, come, come, and learn of us
    To melt in showers; thy grandsire loved thee well;   160
    Many a time he danced thee on his knee,
    Sung thee asleep, his loving breast thy pillow;
    Many a story hath he told to thee,
    And bid thee bear his pretty tales in mind,
    And talk of them when he was dead and gone.
MARCUS

    How many thousand times hath these poor lips,
    When they were living, warmed themselves on thine!
    O now, sweet boy, give them their latest kiss;
    Bid him farewell; commit him to the grave;

---

145 ROMANS] CAPELL (*Rom.*); Q1 *continues to Marcus*   152.1 *He . . . Titus*] *not in* Q1   153
bloodstained] F3 (*subs.*); bloodslaine Q1   155 *kissing Titus*] *not in* Q1   163 story] Q1; matter
Q2   164–8 And . . . kiss;] Q1; Meete and agreeing with thine infancie, | In that respect then,
like a louing child. | Shed yet some small drops from thy tender spring, | Because kind nature
doth require it so, | Friends should associate friends in griefe and woe. Q2

---

148 **aim**   encouragement   (literally,
   guidance)
149 **puts me to** sets me
151 **obsequious** dutiful (without the modern
   sense of 'servile'); especially (by associa-

tion with 'obsequies') dutiful in performing funeral rites
163–8 **story . . . kiss** The fifth passage of Q2
   variant readings (see collations and note
   on l. 25.2).

Do them that kindness, and take leave of them.   170

BOY

O, grandsire, grandsire, ev'n with all my heart
Would I were dead, so you did live again!
O Lord, I cannot speak to him for weeping;
My tears will choke me if I ope my mouth.

    Enter attendants with Aaron

⌈AEMILIUS⌉

You sad Andronici, have done with woes.
Give sentence on this execrable wretch
That hath been breeder of these dire events.

LUCIUS

Set him breast-deep in earth and famish him;
There let him stand and rave and cry for food.
If anyone relieves or pities him,   180
For the offence he dies; this is our doom.
Some stay to see him fastened in the earth.

AARON

Ah, why should wrath be mute and fury dumb?
I am no baby, I, that with base prayers
I should repent the evils I have done;
Ten thousand worse than ever yet I did
Would I perform, if I might have my will.
If one good deed in all my life I did,
I do repent it from my very soul.

LUCIUS

Some loving friends convey the Emperor hence,   190
And give him burial in his father's grave.

---

170 them . . . them] Q1 ; him . . . him, F   171 BOY] *Puer* Q1   174.1 *Enter . . . Aaron*] not in Q1
175 AEMILIUS] GLOBE (*conj.* Dyce); *Romane* Q1 ; *Romans* F   191 father's] ROWE; fathers Q1 ;
fathers' KITTREDGE (*following anon. conj.*)

---

170 **them** the lips (l. 166). The F reading,
'him' (see collations), follows l. 169 more
naturally, but this is an 'improvement'
rather than the correction of an error.
Maxwell suggests that l. 169 may have
been an afterthought; without it l. 170
presents no problem.

175 AEMILIUS Q1 gives these lines to
'*Romane*' (see collations), but the speech,
like ll. 72–94, is not likely to have been
assigned to an unknown character.
Dyce's conjecture that Aemilius should

be the speaker is a good one, since he
earlier (l. 136) spoke to the Andronici on
behalf of the Roman people.

191 **father's** The Q1 spelling (see collations)
does not show whether this refers to
Saturninus' father or to his ancestors
(fathers). In favour of the singular form is
its recall of Saturninus' opening speech,
'I am his first-born son . . .'. In the theatre,
of course, it would be impossible to distinguish between the two.

My father and Lavinia shall forthwith
Be closèd in our household's monument.
As for that ravenous tiger, Tamora,
No funeral rite, nor man in mourning weed,   195
No mournful bell shall ring her burial;
But throw her forth to beasts and birds to prey;
Her life was beastly and devoid of pity,
And being dead, let birds on her take pity.   *Exeunt*

Finis the Tragedy of Titus Andronicus

195 rite] Q1 (right)   199 dead . . . pity] Q1 ; so, shall haue like want of pitty | See iustice done on *Aron* that damn'd Moore, | By whom our heauie haps had their beginning : | Than afterwards to order well the state, | That like euents may nere it ruinate. Q2

197 **to prey** i.e. to prey upon
199–199.1 **And . . . *Andronicus*** In this final passage of variant readings the printer of Q2 not only altered the final line of the play but added four more (see collations). There may have been a substantial tear, which made it impossible to tell how many lines were missing.

THE PROSE HISTORY OF TITUS ANDRONICUS

THE complete text of the chapbook printed by Cluer Dicey at some time between 1736 and 1764 (see Introduction, p. 28) is given below. Punctuation and spelling have been modernized as in the text of the play. Departures from the control text, except for the correction of the most obvious typographical errors, are recorded.

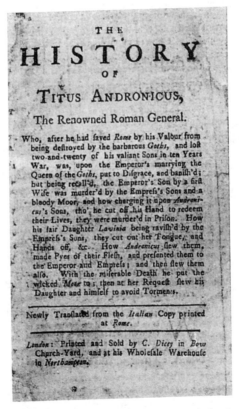

THE

HISTORY

OF

TITUS ANDRONICUS,

The Renowned Roman General.

Who, after he had saved *Rome* by his Valour from being destroyed by the barbarous *Goths*, and lost two-and-twenty of his valiant Sons in ten Years War, was, upon the Emperor's marrying the Queen of the *Goths*, put to Disgrace, and banish'd; but being recall'd, the Emperor's Son by a first Wife was murder'd by the Empress's Sons and a bloody Moor; and how charging it upon *Andronicus*'s Sons, tho' he cut off his Hand to redeem their Lives, they were murder'd in Prison. How his fair Daughter *Lavinia* being ravish'd by the Empress's Sons, they cut out her Tongue, and Hands off, &c. How *Andronicus* slew them, made Pyes of their Flesh, and presented them to the Emperor and Empress; and then slew them also. With the miserable Death he put the wicked *Moor* to; then at her Request slew his Daughter and himself to avoid Torments.

Newly Translated from the *Italian* Copy printed at *Rome*.

London: Printed and Sold by C. *Dicey* in *Bow* Church-Yard, and at his Wholesale Warehouse in *Northampton*.

Fig. 9. The title-page of the chapbook *Titus Andronicus*

THE
TRAGICAL HISTORY
OF
TITUS ANDRONICUS, &C.

CHAP. I

How Rome *being besieged by the barbarous* Goths, *and being at the point to yield through famine, it was unexpectedly rescued by* Andronicus, *with the utter defeat of the enemy, for which he was received in triumph.*

WHEN the Roman Empire was grown to its height, and the greatest part of the world was subjected to its imperial throne, in the time of Theodosius, a barbarous northern people out of Swedeland, Denmark, and Gothland came into Italy in such numbers under the leading of Tottilius, their King, that they overran it with fire and sword, plundering churches, ripping up women with child, and deflowering virgins in so horrid and barbarous a manner that the people fled before them like flocks of sheep.

To oppose this destroying torrent of the Goths, a barbarous people, strangers to Christianity, the Emperor raised a mighty army in Greece, Italy, France, Spain, Germany, and England, and gave battle under the passage of the Alpine mountains, but was overthrown with the loss of threescore thousand of his men, and flying to Rome, was besieged in it by a numerous host of these barbarians, who pressed so hard to beat down the walls and enter with a miserable slaughter of the citizens that such as could get over the River Tiber fled in a fearful manner to a distant country. The siege lasting ten months, such a famine arose that no unclean thing was left uneaten; dogs, cats, horses, rats, and mice were curious dainties. Thousands died in the streets of hunger, and most of those that were alive looked more like glass than living creatures; so that, being brought to the last extremity, the vulgar sort came about the Emperor's palace, and with piteous cries implored him either to find some means to get them food to stay their fleeting lives or make the best terms he could, and open the gates to the enemy.

This greatly perplexed him; the former he could not do, and the latter he knew would not only uncrown him, if he escaped with his life, but be the ruin of the Roman Empire; yet in the greatest of this extremity he unexpectedly found relief.

Titus Andronicus, a Roman senator, and a true lover of his country, hearing in Graecia, where he was governor of the province of Achaia, what straits Rome and his sovereign were brought into by the barbarous nations, got together friends, and sold whatever he had of value to hire soldiers; so that with his small army he secretly marched away, and falling upon the mighty army of the enemy (when they were drowned, as it were, in security, wine, and sleep, resolved to make a general storm the next day, in which they had undoubtedly carried the city), he and his sons, entering their camp, and followed by the rest, made such a slaughter that the cry and confusion were exceeding great. Some changed sleep into death, others vomited wine and blood mixed together through the wounds they received; some lost heads at once, others[1] arms. Tottilius, in this confusion being awakened, had his first care to convey away his queen and two sons, who were newly come to the camp, and then laboured to rally his flying men; but being desperately charged by Andronicus, he was thrown from his horse and much wounded, many lives being lost in remounting him; whereupon, seeing the slaughter so great by the pale beams of the moon, and not knowing the number of his adversaries, having caused the retreat to be sounded, he fled in great confusion, and left the rich spoils of his camp, the wealth of many plundered nations, to Andronicus and his soldiers; who, being expert in war, would not meddle with them that night, but stood to their arms till the morning.

CHAP. II

How in ten years' war, with the loss of two-and-twenty of his valiant sons, he won many famous battles, slew Tottilius, *King of the* Goths, *and did many other brave exploits, &c.*

The watch upon the walls of Rome, having heard a confused cry and the clashing of arms, were greatly astonished, but could not think what it should mean; for the camps of the barbarous Goths extended in a large circuit about the famous city; however the captains of the guards advertised the Emperor of it, who sent out scouts, but they, fearful of approaching too near the enemy in the night, could get certain intelligence only that they heard the groans and cries, as they thought, of dying men. However, the shades of night being dispelled, and the glorious sun casting forth a cheerful light, the porters of the gate, espying three men coming towards it, and soon after being come up, knocked with great earnestness, they took the courage to demand what they were and what they required.

'I am,' said one of them, 'Andronicus, your friend, and desire admittance to speak with the Emperor, since the news I bring will no doubt be pleasing to him.'

Upon this, lifting up his helmet, they knew him with joy, knowing him to be a very worthy patriot, thinking he came to do them good, as he had often done in their great distress, when the Huns and Vandals invaded the empire some years before, and were beaten out by him.

The Emperor no sooner heard he was come, but he ran from his palace to meet him, and would not suffer him to kneel, but embraced him tenderly

---

[1] others] other

as a brother, saying, 'Welcome, Andronicus, in this, the time of our greatest misery. It was thy counsel I wanted, to know how to free us from this barbarous enemy, against whose force the city cannot long hold out.'

'May it please your majesty,' replied Andronicus, 'let those fears be banished. The work is done to you unknown; I and my twenty-five sons and what friends and soldiers I could get have this night fallen into their quarters, cut off fifty thousand of them, and their scattered remains with their king are fled.'

At this the Emperor was astonished, and scarce could believe it, though he very well knew the integrity of Andronicus, till his own captains came and told him the siege was raised, with a miserable slaughter, but by whom they knew not, unless the enemy had fallen out among themselves, and the troops they could yet see in view were but inconsiderable. Now these were those that belonged to Andronicus, who, as soon as it was day, were in pursuit of the enemy under the command of his five-and-twenty sons.

This surprising news was no sooner spread in the city but the joy of the people was exceeding great; and when they knew who was their deliverer they went in procession and sung his praises. After that he rode in a triumphant chariot through the city, crowned with an oaken garland, the people shouting, trumpets sounding, and all other expressions and demonstrations of joy that a grateful people could afford their deliverer, in which he behaved himself so humble that he gained the love of all.

This was no sooner over but he desired the Emperor to join what forces he could with those that he had brought, and speedily pursue the enemy before he could gather new strength, that he might beat him out of Italy and his other countries, where he yet held strong garrisons. This was embraced as good counsel, and the senators, by the Emperor's mandate, assembled with joy, who chose with one consent Andronicus their general. He was not slow in mustering his forces, nor in the speedy pursuit. He found they had passed the Alps, and that their army was increased by new supplies; yet he gave them battle, and, charging through the thickest of their squadrons hand to hand, slew Tottilius and beat down his standard; whereupon the Goths fled, and the slaughter continued for many miles, covering all the lanes and roads with the bodies of the dead; and in the pursuit he took the Queen of the Goths captive, and brought her to Rome; for which signal victory he had a second triumph, and was styled the deliverer of his country. But his joy was a little eclipsed by the loss of five of his sons, who died courageously fighting in battle.

CHAP. III

How the Emperor, *weary of so tedious a war, contrary to the mind and persuasions of* Andronicus, *married the Queen of the* Goths, *and concluded a peace; how she tyrannized, and her sons slew the Prince that was betrothed to Andronicus' daughter, and hid him in the forest.*

The Goths having found the pleasantness of these fruitful countries, resolved not so to give them over, but, encouraged by Tottilius' two sons, Alaricus and Abonus, sent for fresh forces, and made a desolation in the Roman provinces, continuing a ten-years' war, wherein the valiant Andronicus, captain-general of the empire, gained many victories over them with great effusion of blood on either side. But those barbarous people still increasing in their numbers, the Emperor desiring peace, it was agreed to, in consideration he should marry Attava, Queen of the Goths, and in case he should die without issue, her sons might succeed in the empire. Andronicus opposed this very much, as did many others,[1] knowing, through the Emperor's weakness, that she, being an imperious woman and of a haughty spirit, would govern him as she pleased, and enslave the noble empire to strangers. However, it was carried on with a high hand, and great preparations were made for the royal nuptials, though with very little rejoicing among the people; for what they expected soon followed.

The Queen of the Goths, being made Empress, soon began to show her disposition according to the cruelty of her nation and temper, persuading the easy Emperor to place the Goths in the places of his most trusty friends, and having, above all, vowed revenge on Andronicus, who most opposed her proceedings, she procured him to be banished; but the people, whose deliverer he had been in their greatest extremity, calling to mind that and his many other good services, rose unanimously in arms, and went clamouring to the palace, threatening to fire it and revenge so base an indignity on the Queen if the decree which had been passed against all reason was not speedily revoked. This put her and the Emperor into such a fear[2] that their request was[3] granted; and now she plotted by more private ways to bring the effects of revenge and implacable hatred about more secretly.

She had a Moor as revengeful as herself, whom she trusted in many great affairs, and was usually privy to her secrets, so far that from private dalliances she grew pregnant, and brought forth a blackamoor child. This grieved the Emperor extremely, but she allayed his anger by telling him it was conceived by the force of imagination, and brought many suborned women and physicians to testify the like had often happened. This made the Emperor send the Moor into banishment, upon pain of death never to return to Rome; but her lust, and confidence she had put in him as the main engine to bring about her devilish designs, made her plot to have that

---

[1] others,] other;,
[2] fear] Fears
[3] was] *catchword, but omitted on following page*

decree revoked; when, having got the Emperor into a pleasant humour, she feigned herself sick, telling him withal she had seen a vision which commanded her to call back the innocent Moor from banishment or she should never recover of that sickness. The kind, good-natured Emperor, who could not resist her tears and entreaties, with some difficulty consented to it, provided he should be commanded to keep always out of her sight, lest the like mischance might happen as had been before. This she seemingly consented to, and he was immediately sent for, and the former familiarities continued between them though more privately.

Andronicus, besides his sons, had a very fair and beautiful daughter named Lavinia, brought up in all singular virtues, humble, courteous, and modest, insomuch that the Emperor's only son by a former wife fell extremely in love with her, seeking her favour by all virtuous and honourable ways, insomuch that, after a long courtship, with her father and the Emperor's consent she was betrothed to him.

The Queen of the Goths, hearing this, was much enraged, because from such a marriage might spring princes that might frustrate her ambitious designs, which was to make her sons emperors jointly. Wherefore she laboured all she could to frustrate it by declaring what a disgrace it would be to the Emperor to marry his son to the daughter of a subject, who might have a queen with a kingdom to her dowry. But, finding the Prince constant, she resolved to take him out of the way; so it was plotted between her, the Moor, and her two sons that they should invite him to hunt in the great forest on the banks of the River Tiber, and there murder him. This was effected by shooting him through the back with a poisoned arrow which came out at his breast, of which wound he fell from his horse and immediately died. Then they digged a very deep pit in a pathway and threw him in, covering it lightly with boughs, and sprinkling earth on it; and so, returning, reported they had lost the Prince in the forest, and though they had sought and called everywhere, they could not find him.

CHAP. IV

How the wicked Moor, who had laid with the Empress, and got into her favour above all others, betrayed Andronicus' *three sons, and charged the Prince's murder on them, for which they were cast into a dungeon and, after their father had cut off his hand to save them, were beheaded.*

The fair Lavinia no sooner heard the Prince was missing but she fell into great sorrow and lamentation, her heart misgiving her of some treachery, and thereupon she entreated her brothers to go in search of him, which they did with all speed; but being dogged by the Moor and the Queen of Goths' two sons, they unluckily coming in the way where the pit was digged, they fell both in upon the dead body and could not, by reason of the great depth, get out. Their cruel enemies no sooner saw this but they hasted to the court and sent the guards in search of the murdered Prince, who found Andronicus' two sons with the dead body, which they drew up and carried prisoners to the court, where the Moor and the other two falsely swore against them that they had often heard them threaten revenge on the Prince, because he had put them to the foil in a tournament at jousting. This, and the circumstances of their being found, with the vehement aggravation, was a sufficient ground to the Emperor to believe, who loved his son entirely, and was much grieved for his death, and though they denied it with all the protestations imaginable, and pleaded their innocence, demanded the combat against their accusers, which by the law of arms they ought to have been allowed, they were immediately loaden with irons and cast into a deep dungeon among noisome creatures, as frogs, toads, serpents, and the like, where, notwithstanding all the intercessions that were made, they continued eating the filth that they found in that place.

At last the Queen, designing to work her revenge on Andronicus, sent the Moor in the Emperor's name to tell him, if he designed to save his sons from the misery and death that would ensue, he should cut off his right hand and send it to court. This the good-natured father scrupled not to do; no, nor had it been his life to ransom them, he would have freely parted with it; whereupon, laying his hand on a block, he gave the wicked Moor his sword, who immediately struck it off, and inwardly laughed at the villainy. Then, departing with it, he told him his sons should be sent to him in a few hours; but whilst he was rejoicing with the hopes of their delivery a hearse came to his door with guards, which made his aged heart to tremble. The first thing they presented him was his hand, which they said would not be accepted; and the next was his three sons beheaded. At this woeful sight, overcome with grief, he fainted away on the dead bodies; and when he recovered again, he tore his hoary hair, which age and his lying in winter camps for the defence of his country had made as white as snow, pouring out floods of tears; but found no pity from the hardened villains, who left him with scoffs in the midst of his woeful lamentations with his sorrowful daughter. Yet this was not all, for soon after, another to be deplored affliction followed, as shall in the next chapter be shown.

CHAP. V

How the two lustful sons of the Empress, with the assistance of the Moor, in a barbarous manner ravished Lavinia, Andronicus' *beautiful daughter, and cut out her tongue and cut off her hands to prevent discovery; yet she did it by writing in the dust with a wand, &c.*

The fair and beautiful Lavinia for the loss of her lover[1] and brothers, so basely murdered by treachery, tore her golden hair, shed floods of tears, and with her nails offered violence to that lovely face kings had adored and beheld with admiration. She shunned all company, retiring to woods and groves to utter her piteous complaints and cries to the senseless trees, when one day, being watched thither by the Moor, he gave notice of it to the Queen's two sons, who, like the wicked Elders and chaste Susanna, had a long time burned in lust, yet knew her virtues were proof against all temptations, and therefore it could not be obtained but by violence; so, thinking this an opportunity to serve their turns, immediately repaired to the grove, and setting the Moor to watch on the outborders, soon found her pensive and sorrowful, yet comely and beautiful in tears, when unawares, before she saw them, like two ravenous tigers, they seized the trembling lady, who struggled all she could and cried out piteously for help; and seeing what their wicked intentions bent at, she offered them her throat, desiring they would bereave her of her life, but not of her honour; however, in a villainous manner, staking her down by the hair of her head, and binding her hands behind her, they turned up her nakedness, and forced their way into her closet of chastity, taking it by turns, the elder beginning first, and the younger seconding him as they had before agreed on; and having tired themselves in satiating their beastly appetites, they began to consider how they should come off when such a villainy was discovered; whereupon, calling the Moor to them, they asked his advice, who wickedly counselled them to make all sure, seeing they had gone thus far, by cutting out her tongue to hinder her telling tales, and her hands off to prevent her writing a discovery. This the cruel wretches did whilst she in vain entreated 'em to take away her life, since they had bereaved her of her honour, which was dearer to her. And in this woeful condition they left the lady, who had expired for the loss of blood, had not her uncle Marcus happened accidentally, soon after, to come in search of her, who, at the woeful sight overcome with sorrow, could hardly keep life in himself; yet, recovering his spirits, he bound up her wounds and conveyed her home.

Poor Andronicus' grief for this sad disaster was so great that no pen can write or words express. Much ado they had to restrain him from doing violence upon himself; he cursed the day he was born to see such miseries fall on himself and family, intreating her to tell him, if she could any ways do it by signs, who had so villainously abused her. At last the poor lady, with a flood of tears gushing from her eyes, taking a wand between her stumps, wrote these lines:

> The lustful sons of the proud Empress
> Are doers of this hatefull wickedness.

[1] lover] Lovers

Hereupon he vowed revenge at the hazard of his own and all their lives, comforting his daughter with this when nothing else would do.

CHAP. VI

How Andronicus, feigning himself mad, found means to entrap the Empress' two sons in a forest, where, binding them to a tree, he cut their throats, made pies of their flesh, and served them up to the Emperor and Empress, then slew them, set the Moor quick in the ground, and then killed his daughter and himself.

Andronicus, upon these calamities, feigned himself distracted, and went raving about the city, shooting his arrows towards heaven as in defiance, calling to hell for vengeance, which mainly pleased the Empress and her sons, who thought themselves now secure; and though his friends required justice of the Emperor against the ravishers; yet they could have no redress, he rather threatening them if they insisted on it; so that, finding they were in a bad case, and that in all probability their lives would be the next, they conspired together to prevent that mischief and revenge themselves. Lying in ambush in the forest when the two sons went a-hunting, they surprised them, and binding them to a tree, pitifully crying out for mercy, though they would give none to others, Andronicus cut their throats whilst Lavinia, by his command, held a bowl between her stumps to receive the blood. Then conveying the bodies home to his own house privately, he cut the flesh into fit pieces and ground the bones to powder, and made of them two mighty pasties, and invited the Emperor and Empress to dinner, who thinking to make sport with his frantic humour, came; but when they had eat of the pasties he told them what it was; and thereupon giving the watchword to his friends, they immediately issued out, slew the Emperor's guards, and lastly the Emperor and his cruel wife after they had sufficiently upbraided them with the wicked deeds they had done. Then seizing on the wicked Moor, the fearful villain fell on his knees, promising to discover all; but when he had told how he had killed the Prince, betrayed the three sons of Andronicus by false accusation, and counselled the abuse to the fair Lavinia, they scarce knew what torments sufficient to devise for him; but at last, digging a hole, they set him in the ground to the middle alive, smeared him over with honey, and so, between the stinging of bees and wasps and starving, he miserably ended his wretched days. After this, to prevent the torments he expected when these things came to be known, at his daughter's request he killed her; and so, rejoicing he had revenged himself on his enemies to the full, fell on his own sword and died.

THE BALLAD OF TITUS ANDRONICUS

THE text of 'Titus Andronicus' Complaint' is given from the earliest surviving version, in Richard Johnson's *The Golden Garland of Princely Pleasures and Delicate Delights*, printed in 1620 (see Introduction, p. 4). Spelling and punctuation have been modernized. A few typographical errors have been silently corrected.

Titus Andronicus' Complaint

To the Tune of Fortune[1]

You noble minds and famous martial wights,
That in defence of native country fights,
Give ear to me that ten years fought for Rome,
Yet reaped disgrace when I returnèd home.

In Rome I lived in fame full threescore years,
By name belovèd dear of all his peers,
Full five-and-twenty valiant sons I had,
Whose forward virtues made their father glad.

For when Rome's foes their warlike forces felt,
Against them still my sons and I were sent;
Against the Goths full ten years' weary war
We spent, receiving many a bloody scar.

Just two-and-twenty of my sons were slain,
Before we did return to Rome again;
Of five-and-twenty sons I brought but three
Alive the stately towers of Rome to see.

When wars were done I conquest home did bring,
And did present my prisoners to the King;
The Queen of Goth, her sons, and eke a Moor,
Which did much murder, like was ne'er before.

[1] **Fortune** i.e. 'Fortune, my foe', a well-known song. 'In Shakespeare's day it was a tune used to march men to the gallows' (Peter J. Seng, *The Vocal Songs in the Plays of Shakespeare* (Cambridge, Mass., 1967), p. 261).

The Emperor did make this Queen his wife,
Which bred in Rome debate and deadly strife;
The Moor with her two sons did grow so proud
That none like them in Rome was then allowed.

The Moor so pleased the new-made Empress' eye
That she consented with him secretly
For to abuse her husband's marriage bed,
And so in time a blackamoor she bred.

Then she, whose thoughts to murder were inclined,
Consented with the Moor with bloody mind
Against myself, my kin, and all my friends
In cruel sort to bring them to their ends.

So when in age I thought to live in peace,
Both woe and grief began then to increase;
Amongst my sons I had one daughter bright,
Which joyed and pleasèd best my age's sight.

My dear Lavinia was betrothed as then
To Caesar's son, a young and noble man,
Who in a hunting by the Emperor's wife
And her two sons bereavèd were of life.

He, being slain, was cast in cruel wise
Into a dismal den from light of skies;
The cruel Moor did come that way as then
With my two sons, who fell into that den.

The Moor then fetched the Emperor with speed,
For to accuse them of that murderous deed;
And then my sons within the den were found;
In wrongful prison they were cast and bound.

But now behold what wounded most my mind,
The Emperor's two sons of tiger's kind
My daughter ravishèd without remorse,
And took away her honour quite perforce.

When they had tasted of so sweet a flower
Fearing their sweet should shortly turn to sour,
They cut her tongue, whereby she could not tell
How that dishonour unto her befell.

Then both her hands they falsely cut off quite,
Whereby their wickedness she could not write,
Nor with her needle on her sampler sew
The bloody workers of her direful woe.

My brother Marcus found her in a wood,
Staining the grassy ground with purple blood
That trickled from her stumps and handless arms.
No tongue at all she had to tell her harms.

But when I saw her in that woeful case,
With tears of blood I wet my agèd face;
For my Lavinia I lamented more
Than for my two-and-twenty sons before.

Whenas I saw she could not write nor speak,
With grief my agèd heart began to break;
We spread a heap of sand upon the ground,
Whereby those bloody tyrants out we found.

For with a staff, without the help of hand,
She writ these words upon that plot of sand:
'The lustful sons of the proud Empress
Are doers of this hateful wickedness.'

I tare the milk-white hairs from off my head,
I cursed the hour wherein I first was bred;
I wished the hand that fought for country's fame
In cradle's rock had first been stroken lame.

The Moor, delighting still in villainy,
Did say, to set my sons from prison free,
I should unto the King my right hand give,
And then my two imprisoned sons should live.

The Moor I caused to strike it off with speed,
Whereat I grievèd not to see it bleed,
But for my sons would willingly impart
And for their ransom send my bleeding heart.

But as my life did linger thus in pain,
They sent to me my bloodless hand again,
And therewithal the heads of my two sons,
Which filled my dying heart with fresher moans.

Then past relief, I up and down did go,
And with my tears writ in the dust my woe;
I shot my arrows towards heaven high,
And for revenge to hell did sometimes cry.

The Empress then, thinking I was mad,
Like furies she and both her sons were clad,
She named Revenge, and Rape and Murder they,
To undermine and know what I would say.

I fed their foolish veins a certain space,
Until my friends and I did find a place,
Where both her sons unto a post were bound,
Where just revenge in cruel sort was found.

I cut their throats, my daughter held the pan
Betwixt the stumps, wherein their blood then ran;
And then I ground their bones to powder small,
And made a paste for pies straight therewithal.

Then with their flesh I made two mighty pies,
And at a banquet served in stately wise
Before the Empress set this loathsome meat,
So of her sons' own flesh she well did eat.

Myself bereaved my daughter then of life;
The Empress then I slew with bloody knife,
And stabbed the Emperor immediately,
And then myself, even so did Titus die.

Then this revenge against their Moor was found:
Alive they set him half into the ground,
Whereas he stood until such time he starved;
And so God send all murderers may be served.

THE CRIMES AGAINST THE ANDRONICI

THE following summaries of the three accounts of the crimes against the Andronici, from prose history, play, and ballad, highlight the plot elements considered in discussions of the relationship between the three versions (see Introduction, pp. 29–33).

I. PROSE HISTORY

The Queen is incensed at Lavinia's betrothal to the Emperor's son; with her sons and the Moor she arranges his murder during a hunt; the body is hidden in a pit covered with boughs.

Lavinia sends her brothers into the woods; they are 'dogged' by the Moor and the Queen's sons; the young Andronici 'unluckily' fall in the pit; they are imprisoned.

The Queen tricks Titus into letting the Moor cut off his hand, then sends him the bodies of his beheaded sons; Titus tears his hair.

Lavinia mourns in the woods; Aaron notifies the Queen's lustful sons, who rape her and, on the Moor's advice, also mutilate her; Marcus finds her and takes her to Titus, who threatens to do violence to himself; Lavinia writes the names, and he vows revenge, feigns madness, and shoots arrows in the air (see pp. 200–3).

2. PLAY

The Empress's sons tell Aaron of their lust for Lavinia; he recommends rape during the next day's hunt (2.1).

Aaron hides gold; after the murder of Bassianus the body is thrown in a pit covered with briers, and Lavinia is dragged away; Quintus and Martius, led by Aaron, fall in the pit and are taken off to prison (2.3).

Lavinia is discovered by Marcus (2.4).

Titus pleads for his sons; sees Lavinia, led by Marcus; threatens to cut off his hands; Aaron brings the deceptive offer from the Emperor and cuts off Titus' hand; Titus gets the heads of his sons and vows revenge (3.1).

Lavinia writes the names (4.1). Titus and his kinsmen shoot arrows in the air (4.3).

3. BALLAD

After the betrothal of Lavinia to 'Caesar's son' the Queen and her sons murder him during a hunt; the body is thrown in a 'darksome den'.

The Moor brings Titus' sons, who fall in and are imprisoned.

The Queen's sons rape and mutilate Lavinia.

Marcus finds her and takes her to Titus, who mourns; Lavinia writes the names; Titus tears his hair.

The Moor brings the deceptive message and cuts off Titus' hand; Titus gets the heads of his sons, weeps, shoots arrows in the air, and vows revenge.

MARCO MINCOFF'S STATEMENTS ON SOURCES

MARCO MINCOFF's theory that the play was the source of both the history and the ballad was published in 'The Source of "Titus Andronicus"', *Notes and Queries*, 216 (1971), 131–4 (see Introduction, pp. 29–31).

1. Mincoff: 'And if we take the events of the ballad, there is not one that cannot derive from the play . . .' (p. 131).

In both the prose history and ballad Lavinia marries a son of the Emperor after the Empress has had a child by the Moor.

In the play Lavinia marries the Emperor's brother before Aaron's child is born, though she and Bassianus taunt the Empress with the accusation that her affair with Aaron has smirched her honour and made the Emperor 'noted long' (2.3.72–86).

2. Mincoff: 'In the history the queen alone has been captured at the beginning of the wars, and there is no triumphal conclusion to them' (p. 131).

It is true that there is no single triumphal conclusion, but two triumphs are mentioned in the prose history: '. . . when [the people] knew who was their deliverer . . . he rode in a triumphant chariot through the city'; '. . . in the pursuit he took the Queen of the Goths captive, and brought her to Rome; for which signal victory he had a second triumph' (p. 198).

3. Mincoff: '. . . there is not one single point beyond what is contained in the ballad that clearly connects Shakespeare's play with the history' (p. 132).

One connecting link is the description in the prose history of hiding the body of Lavinia's betrothed in a deep pit, 'covering it lightly with boughs' (p. 200). In the play the 'pit' or 'hole' is 'covered with rude-growing briers' (2.3.199), but the detail is omitted in the ballad (p. 205).

THE FALSE START IN 4.3

REPRODUCED below is the passage in Q1 corresponding to 4.3.97–109 of this edition; line numbers based on this edition have been added to facilitate reference.

Titus. Tell mee, can you deliuer an Oration to the Em-	97
perour with a grace.	98
Clowne. Nay truelie sir, I could neuer say grace in all	99
my life.	99a
Titus. Sirra come hither, make no more adoo,	100
But giue your pidgeons to the Emperour,	101
By mee thou shalt haue iustice at his hands,	102
Hold, hold, meane while here's money for thy charges,	103
Giue me pen and inke.	104
Sirra, can you with a grace deliuer vp a Supplication?	104a
Clowne. I sir.	104b
Titus. Then here is a Supplication for you, and when you	104c
come to him, at the first approch you must kneele, then	104d
kisse his foote, then deliuer vp your pidgeons, and then	104e
looke for your reward. Ile bee at hand sir, see you doe it	104f
brauelie.	104g
Clowne. I warrant you sir, let me alone.	104h
Titus. Sirra hast thou a knife? Come let me see it.	105
Here *Marcus*, fold it in the Oration,	106
For thou hast made it like an humble Suppliant.	107
And when thou hast giuen it to the Emperour,	108
Knocke at my doore, and tell me what he saies.	109

Fig. 10. Q1, sig. H2

The repetition of Titus' question and some slight inconsistencies make it virtually certain that Shakespeare had second thoughts about this dialogue. Dover Wilson thinks that ll. 100–4b were intended as substitutes for ll. 94–9a: Maxwell finds that ll. 97–9a could most easily be dispensed with. While it is probably impossible to be completely sure which lines should have been cancelled, my omission of ll. 104a–h is based on the following reasoning: first it should be noted that the dialogue shifts from verse into prose at the Clown's first speech (l. 80), and back into verse at l. 100. The scene also ends in verse, but with Titus' question at l. 104a, which is almost a repetition of his earlier question (ll. 97–8), prose re-appears briefly (through l. 104h). In this second prose passage, which again concerns Titus' message to the Emperor, it is referred to as a 'supplication', whereas, both earlier and later, it is called an 'oration'. In Titus' directions for delivering the supplication he says he will be 'at hand' (l. 104f), whereas later, giving directions for the oration, he tells the Clown to 'Knock at my door, and tell me what he says' (l. 109). Thus, if the prose lines (104a–h) are omitted, the repeated material is eliminated as well as the inconsistencies in terminology and in the proposed presentation. The dialogue, after one passage of prose (ll. 80–99), reverts to verse for the remainder of the scene. It is possible that the puzzling words, 'For thou hast made it like an humble suppliant' (l. 107), are also due to insertions or marginal corrections that the printer could not read. Though the exact sense now seems irretrievable, I suspect that the Clown was to be the 'humble suppliant', as in the second prose passage he was to kneel and kiss the Emperor's foot.

COPYRIGHT

THE entrances of *Titus Andronicus* in the Stationers' Register bear directly on the question of whether the prose history in the eighteenth-century chapbook existed at the time when Shakespeare wrote his play. They provide, unfortunately, only the bases for hypotheses rather than a clear answer to the question. The first entrance, on 6 February 1594, is John Danter's of 'a booke intituled a Noble Roman Historye of Tytus Andronicus', followed immediately by 'Entred also vnto him . . . the ballad thereof'.[1] J. Q. Adams suggests in his reprint of Q1 (p. 9) that the first entrance refers to the prose history, but since Danter published the play in 1594, it seems almost certain that it refers to the play. It is quite possible that it refers to both; for, as Greg says, 'it would be in keeping with Danter's character to make one entrance serve for two separate publications' (*Bibliography*, vol. i, p. xxv). Copyright to *Titus Andronicus* apparently passed (with no entrance in the Stationers' Register) to Thomas Millington and Edward White, for whom Danter printed Q1, or to White alone, for in 1600 White published Q2, and on 19 April 1602 Millington assigned 'A booke called Titus and Andronicus' to Thomas Pavier (Greg, *Bibliography*, i. 18). The fact that White again published the play in 1611 may mean, as Leo Kirschbaum[2] says, that Millington and White shared the copyright, that Millington sold White his half of the right to publish it in 1600, and that Pavier followed suit in 1611. Alternatively, according to Greg, 'All real copyright in the play lapsed on Danter's death' (*Folio*, p. 62), in which case the 1602 entrance by Pavier is a sham, as are the two succeeding entrances, unless they refer to something other than the play.

Titus Andronicus does not appear again in the Stationers' Register until 1626, though it was published for the fourth time in the Folio of 1623. What right to it had the syndicate which issued that volume? E. K. Chambers, who considers the rights of Millington, and later Pavier, to be genuine, thinks that the syndicate must have come to terms with Pavier and perhaps also with White's heirs (since White died in 1613) (*Shakespeare*, i. 140). Kirschbaum assumes that Pavier, a close associate of the Folio printers, William and Isaac Jaggard, had at least a half-share in the copyright (p. 374), but Greg supposes that 'the copy was derelict save for Pavier's very dubious claim' (*Folio*, p. 62).

---

[1] W. W. Greg, *A Bibliography of the English Printed Drama to the Restoration*, vol. i (London, 1939), p. 10. In succeeding quotations from Greg's transcription of entrances some scribal contractions have been expanded.

[2] *Shakespeare and the Stationers* (Columbus, Ohio, 1955), p. 374.

There are difficulties about assuming that the 1602 entrance in the Stationers' Register did or did not give Pavier a legitimate claim to the play. If it did, it is curious that he and Jaggard did not include it in the abortive 1619 collection now referred to as the 'Pavier Quartos' (see Greg, *Folio*, pp. 11–16). But if his claim could easily be disregarded, it is equally curious that on 4 August 1626 his widow assigned 'Tytus & Andronicus' to Edward Brewster and Robert Bird (Greg, *Bibliography*, i. 35). On 8 November 1630 Bird assigned it to Richard Cotes (Greg, *Bibliography*, i. 38), and it was transferred in 1674 to John Martin and Henry Herringman (*ibid.*, i. 73). Martin's widow later (21 August 1683) disposed of his half of the right to Robert Scott (*ibid.*, i. 76). These entrances suggest that stationers were still willing to pay for the copyright to *Titus Andronicus*, which they took to be valid.

J. Q. Adams's assumption that the 1594 entrance by Danter, as well as the subsequent transfers, applied to the prose history provides another way of interpreting the record of copyright, and offers a solution to the problem of Pavier's right. Greg, as we have seen, thinks the 1594 entrance may have been used to cover both play and prose history, and he goes on to say that 'the various subsequent transfers of the copy appear to be unrelated to the several later editions of the play' (*Bibliography*, p. xxv). It is possible, then, that White took over copyright to the play after Danter's death, and Millington to the prose history, transferring it to Pavier in 1602. In that case it might be the copyright to the prose history which continued to be transferred to other publishers. In every case *Titus Andronicus* appears in a list containing both plays and prose histories. The 1602 list is very brief: 'A booke called Thomas of Reading, The first and Second parte of henry the vj^t ij books, A booke called Titus and Andronicus'.[1] While 'book' is applied to both dramatic and non-dramatic works, it may be significant that the formula 'a book called' is here applied to the prose history of *Thomas of Reading* and to *Titus Andronicus*, but not to the Henry VI plays. In the long 1626 list the few items which are certainly plays are, with the exception of *The Spanish Tragedy*, clearly so designated. These are: 'The history of Henry the fift, and the play of the same, The spanish tragedie, M^r. Paviers right in Shakesperes plaies or any of them . . . Sr Iohn old castle a play.' Certain other items, which might at first seem to be plays, such as 'The Case is Altered', 'Historye of Hamblett', or 'History of do^r Faustus', are in fact prose histories. *Thomas of Reading* recurs in this list. The entrance of *Henry V* is puzzling in two respects. The wording suggests that there was a narrative as well as a play, though Greg doubts that there was,[2] and also

---

[1] Greg, *Bibliography*, i. 18; Greg's list, which is selective, does not include the first item, which is taken from E. Arber, *A Transcript of the Registers of the Company of Stationers of London, 1554–1640*, Text, 4 vols. (London, 1875–7), ii. 644; Arber's conventions of italicization and capitalization have been ignored.

[2] *Bibliography*, i. 270; see also Kirschbaum, pp. 266–72.

it is strange to enter the play separately, in view of the entrance covering Pavier's right 'in Shakesperes plaies'. The complicated history of rights to this play and to its predecessor, *The Famous Victories of Henry V*, may explain the separate entrance. The absence of any such explanation for *Titus Andronicus* and the failure to designate it as a play strengthen the possibility that the reference is to the prose history.

The nine items in the 1630 list include five which are certainly plays and two which are certainly prose histories; *Titus Andronicus* might be in either category and so might 'Henrye the fift', since 'Agincourt' appears as a separate item. In the 1674 list all nine items from the 1630 list join the Shakespeare plays first printed in F1, and are repeated in the 1683 list under the heading 'Shakespeare'. This might seem to prove that the *Titus Andronicus* in all these lists is the play, were it not for the inclusion of other non-Shakespearian items such as the prose histories of *Hamlet* and of *Euryalus and Lucretia*. A similar confusion may have led to the placing of the prose history of *Titus Andronicus* with the Shakespeare plays.

The evidence is not conclusive, but it leaves open the possibility that Danter, Millington, Pavier, and several others successively owned the right to a prose history of Titus Andronicus, and that at least one published edition survived into the eighteenth century to attract the attention of Cluer Dicey. A catalogue of histories published by Dicey and Richard Marshall lists many works originally published in the sixteenth and seventeenth centuries, including *Thomas of Reading*,[1] which is in the 1602 and 1626 entrances with *Titus Andronicus*. About the continuous existence and popularity of the ballad, which Dicey printed with the prose history, there is ample evidence: several entrances in the Stationers' Register refer to it and several printed versions have survived. It is reasonable to suppose that the prose history enjoyed a comparable popularity, and its popularity might even account for its failure to survive. It may have been read out of existence as was, for instance, the first edition of Thomas Deloney's *The Gentle Craft* (1597?); until 1904 Q1 of *Titus Andronicus* seemed to have suffered the same fate.

---

[1] See Adams, p. 8; the list is printed in C. Gerring, *Notes on Printers and Booksellers* (1900), pp. 110–14.

POSSIBLE ALLOCATION OF ROLES AMONG TWENTY-SEVEN ACTORS

THE chart presents a possible doubling scheme showing that *Titus Andronicus* would have required a company of at least twenty-seven actors (see Introduction, pp. 43–4). The actors are listed in the first column in order of appearance. The twelve extras who speak only an occasional line are designated by an asterisk. The first scene is presented in two columns since the extras who leave before line 60 can reappear in the triumphal procession at line 69.

KEY

AAR	Aaron	MAR	Marcus
AEM	Aemilius	MART	Martius
ALA	Alarbus	MES	Messenger
ATT	Attendant	MUT	Mutius
BAS	Bassianus	NUR	Nurse
BFOL	Bassianus' Follower	OTH	Other
BSOL	Bassianus' Soldier	PUB	Publius
CAI	Caius	QUI	Quintus
CAP	Captain	SAT	Saturninus
CHI	Chiron	SEM	Sempronius
CLO	Clown	SEN	Senator
COF	Coffin-bearer	SFOL	Saturninus' Follower
DEM	Demetrius	SOL	Soldier
1 GOT	1 Goth	SSOL	Saturninus' Soldier
2 GOT	2 Goth	TAM	Tamora
GOT	Goth	TI	Titus
JUD	Judge	TRI	Tribune
LAV	Lavinia	VAL	Valentine
LUC	Lucius	YLUC	Young Lucius

Actor	1.1	1.1	2.1	2.2	2.3	2.4	3.1	3.2	4.1	4.2	4.3	4.4	5.1	5.2	5.3
1*	TRI						TRI								TRI
2*	TRI						TRI								TRI
3*	SEN	OTH					SEN								OTH
4*	SEN	OTH					SEN								OTH
5	SAT			SAT	SAT							SAT	IGOT		SAT
6	BAS			BAS	BAS								GOT		IGOT
7*	SSOL	SOL		ATT	ATT					ATT		ATT	GOT	VAL	GOT
8*	SSOL	SOL		ATT	ATT							ATT	GOT		GOT
9*	SFOL	OTH					OTH				SEM			CAI	GOT
10*	SFOL	ALA					OTH						GOT		OTH
11*	BSOL	SOL			ATT		JUD				CAI		GOT		OTH
12*	BSOL	SOL			ATT		JUD						GOT		OTH
13*	BFOL	COF											GOT		GOT
14*	BFOL	COF											GOT		GOT
15	MAR			MAR		MAR	MAR	MAR	MAR		CLO	CLO			MAR
16	CAP														
17	MART			MART	MART		MART			NUR	PUB	AEM	AEM	PUB	AEM
18	MUT						MES								OTH
19	QUI			QUI	QUI		QUI						2GOT		2GOT
20	LUC			LUC	LUC		LUC						LUC		LUC
21	TI			TI	TI		TI	TI	TI		TI			TI	TI
22	TAM			TAM	TAM									TAM	TAM
23	CHI		CHI	CHI	CHI	CHI				CHI		CHI		CHI	
24	DEM		DEM	DEM	DEM	DEM				DEM		DEM		DEM	
25	AAR		AAR		AAR		AAR			AAR			AAR		AAR
26	LAV				LAV	LAV	LAV	LAV	LAV					LAV	LAV
27		OTH						YLUC	YLUC	YLUC	YLUC				YLUC

217

INDEX

THIS is a guide to words defined in the Commentary and to a selection of names and topics in the Introduction and Commentary. Biblical and proverbial allusions are grouped together. Comments on the text and staging and citations from other Shakespeare texts are not listed.

American Literature

British and Irish Literature

Children's Literature

Classics and Ancient Literature

Colonial Literature

Eastern Literature

European Literature

History

Medieval Literature

Oxford English Drama

Poetry

Philosophy

Politics

Religion

The Oxford Shakespeare

A complete list of Oxford Paperbacks, including Oxford World's Classics, OPUS, Past Masters, Oxford Authors, Oxford Shakespeare, Oxford Drama, and Oxford Paperback Reference, is available in the UK from the Academic Division Publicity Department, Oxford University Press, Great Clarendon Street, Oxford OX2 6DP.

In the USA, complete lists are available from the Paperbacks Marketing Manager, Oxford University Press, 198 Madison Avenue, New York, NY 10016.

Oxford Paperbacks are available from all good bookshops. In case of difficulty, customers in the UK can order direct from Oxford University Press Bookshop, Freepost, 116 High Street, Oxford OX1 4BR, enclosing full payment. Please add 10 per cent of published price for postage and packing.